JEAN CONIL'S
CUISINE FRAÎCHEUR

JEAN CONIL'S
CUISINE FRAÎCHEUR

by Jean Conil

with Roy Perrott

Foreword by Anne Willan

AURUM PRESS

Copyright © Jean Conil and Roy Perrott 1987

Edited by Norma MacMillan

Published by Aurum Press Limited,
33 Museum Street, London WC1A 1LD

ISBN 0 948149 58 2

Photographs (except those listed below) by Chris Pearsall;
styling by Christopher Conil; china by Courtier Co. Ltd.
Plates IV (above), XII (below) by Paul Turner; Plates IV (below),
VII (below) by courtesy of the Fresh Fruit and Vegetable
Information Bureau; Plate X (above) by courtesy of Kentish
Garden; Plate X (below) by courtesy of Liotro.

Illustrations by Liza Adamczewski

Typeset by Bookworm Typesetting, Manchester
Colour plates printed by Belmont Press Ltd
Printed and bound in Great Britain by The Bath Press, Avon

◆ CONTENTS ◆

ACKNOWLEDGEMENTS

The author, editor and publishers would like to express their gratitude to the following for their help, advice and support in the supplying of food and information:

Joe Beagan, Fresh Fruit and Vegetable Information Bureau; British Chicken Producers; Brenhurst Vitaquell, margarine; Armanda Courtney, British Trout Association; Elderman, Tabasco products and information on Sweetex; Flora Project for Heart Disease Prevention; Gwynn Hart and Associates, Uncle Ben's Rice; Mrs Pat Sherren, New Zealand Kiwi Fruits; Mrs Penny Smith, Renshaw Ltd; Tesco Supermarket, Neasden.

FOREWORD

Long before I met him, Jean Conil was a personal friend. His book *Gastronomic Tour of France* sat beside *Quaglino* and *Tante Marie* on my mother's bookshelf near the fire. On chilly evenings I browsed with him through the French provinces in vicarious enjoyment of 'les bonnes choses'. How could one resist a visit to the Côte d'Or with its coq au Chambertin and stuffed snails of superb quality? The Provençal soupe au pistou and squid in red wine can almost be tasted on the page.

We live in an era when a great deal of attention is paid to the infant prodigies of the international culinary scene. In contrast, chefs who have made it the hard way by steadfast application of their skills, rather than by tempestuous brilliance, tend to be neglected. Jean was writing about French cooking more than thirty-five years ago. His training goes back to the thirties, to the world of Escoffier and Boulestin. London featured large in the careers of these two masters, as it has for Jean Conil, and for once in the annals of Anglo-French kitchen rivalry the British are one up. Indeed it is thanks to the likes of Jean Conil staying in Britain that the contest has become slightly more even-sided. Witness the first flowering of *Le Caprice* in London's darker days after World War II.

When finally I met Jean in his book-lined office three years ago, he pressed upon me a cup of powerful café filtre, then plied me with questions about my own career. Had I explored the possibilities of cooking on television? Had I heard the latest 'Nouvelle' news from France? Did the students at La Varenne cooking school use the microwave? What did I think of new ingredients liked smoked duck breast and raspberry vinegar?

Jean Conil has another quality I associate with true culinary distinction – he is never at a loss for a new idea. The tradition of inventiveness in cooking goes back at least three centuries in France when *la cuisine nouvelle* was a Court craze. Cuisine Fraîcheur is but the latest variation on a theme that, Bocuse notwithstanding, has ancient roots.

ANNE WILLAN

Notes on measurements

Quantities are given in metric and imperial measures. Exact conversions from imperial to metric rarely give useful working quantities, so in this book the metric measures have been rounded up or down to a more convenient unit. For example, 1 ounce = 28.5 grams, but this is rounded down to 1oz = 25g.

Follow *only one set of measures* in a recipe; metric and imperial measures are not interchangeable.

◆ INTRODUCTION ◆

This book presents a revolutionary new cuisine for healthy living. It is semi-vegetarian in nature, using a high proportion of raw ingredients in appetising combination with lightly cooked foods. Its main ingredients include all kinds of vegetables and fruits, both home-grown and tropical, together with poultry and other white meats, eggs, fish and seafood, supplemented by nuts and cheeses. All red meat is excluded.

The need for such a well-constructed new dietary plan has long been recognised by leading western nutritionists. Though a wider public has become more aware through press reports that it is harmful to consume too much animal fat, refined sugars or highly processed foods and that their intake of fibre should be increased, this awareness has not led to significant change in most people's eating habits beyond the unexciting morning bran or an unvarying salad.

Much of the reason for this limited improvement has been the absence of expert guidance on how to put these dietary changes into practice in the kitchen. Many people may also have assumed that a high-fibre diet could only be a matter of unpalatable discipline rather than enjoyment.

With Cuisine Fraîcheur, Jean Conil – a master-chef of international repute as well as a trained nutritionist – removes this obstacle and offers every home-cook the means to produce a really healthy and delectable cuisine. Composing several hundred different ingredients into approximately 200 different recipes, he demonstrates how dishes retaining all their finest natural flavours and goodness can be produced quite easily for every meal of the day and all year round. As the book's colour photographs show, the dishes are a treat to the eye as well as the palate.

It is believed to be the first cookery book that fully implements the latest advice of the nutritionists while offering a range of recipes capable of meeting the needs of vegetarian and non-vegetarian alike at the highest standards of preparation.

How far is this radical change in eating habits really needed? Many people who show an intelligent concern about their food and who nowadays avoid indulgence in confectionery, fatty meats or 'junk food' tend to feel they are doing enough to maintain their best level of fitness.

That this could be a fallacy has been shown very clearly by several recent expert reports on the average western diet published in Britain and the United States. In 1977, a Senate Committee began to sound the alarm by declaring, in the McGovern Report, that 'too much fat, too much sugar or salt, can be and are linked directly to heart disease, cancer, obesity and stroke among other killer diseases [and have] great and very harmful effects on our health.'

Much the same point was emphatically made by three separate enquiries into the British diet in the 1980s. The reports of the National Advisory Committee on Nutritional Education (NACNE) and the Committee on Medical Aspects of Food Policy (COMA), both government-sponsored, spelled out the changes the public needed to make:

1. Eat less fat. Cut down the total by 25 per cent and, in place of animal fats, use polyunsaturated fats such as sunflower and other vegetable oils and margarines. The amount of these is not specified, but other experts suggest that even these 'healthier fats' should not form more than 10 per cent of total calorie intake. Suggested total fat intake is 30 per cent of total calorie intake.

2. Eat less sugar. Cut down by 50 per cent.

3. Eat less salt. Cut to 5 grams daily (about 1 teaspoonful).

4. Eat more fibre. Increase intake by 50 per cent to 30 grams daily, in the form of whole food, cereals, vegetables and fruit.

Driving home much the same message, the Booker Health Report of 1986, arising from a long study of the British diet by University of London food scientists, showed that people were seriously lacking in a wide range of essential nutrients, minerals and vitamins through incorrect feeding. One of the most striking deficiencies revealed was that 98 per cent of women and 90 per cent of men had an inadequate intake of folate, a mineral largely derived from leafy, green vegetables and easily lost through cooking. Lack of folate is connected with bone disease.

Summing up the government reports, the *Sunday Times* said: 'The food we eat in Britain and other western countries – red meat, cheese, butter, jam, milk and eggs – is the single major cause of the diseases we suffer and die from.'

There is now overwhelming evidence world-wide that only a diet high in plant foods with their nutrients intact (that is, mostly eaten raw) can ensure optimum health, prolong the life-span and, provided other rules are followed, lead to that state of positive well-being enjoyed by a tiny minority of western adults.

Application of this knowledge has only gradually been reaching the kitchen. Jean Conil, with an instinct for healthy food derived from his rural French upbringing, was one of the few London restaurateurs to present a variety of salads on his menus in the 1960s, and even rarer in serving marinated raw fish like the Japanese (whose high consumption of raw food, incidentally, helps to give them the lowest rate of heart disease of any industrial nation).

The arrival of Nouvelle Cuisine stirred a degree of interest in healthier eating with its avoidance of heavy sauces and greater use of uncooked ingredients. Though a useful step forward, it fell a long way short of the radical movement for change that nutritionists were calling for. Its over-emphasis on artistic presentation at the expense of content, with minute vegetable portions seen more as decoration than as vital nutrients, confined its use to high-class restaurants, with little practical guidance for the average household.

Cuisine Fraîcheur is the natural and logical successor to Nouvelle Cuisine, with the important difference that it aims to transform the diet of a much wider public and to be more radical in its improvements. It teaches a new attitude to food and its preparation. It is a cuisine that at last fully matches the advice of world nutritionists while creating for all seasons an array of dishes that are appetising, economical and within the scope of the average home-cook.

The introductions to each chapter describe the principles and methods that Jean Conil recommends for cooking and serving healthy food. For example, in many cases, pastry is replaced by fruit and vegetable containers, or very low-fat home-made phyllo pastry is used. Delightful sauces are made with fruit juice and low-fat yogurt. Poultry and fish may be lightly cooked or emerge with striking new flavours from a marinade. Drinks are made from fresh fruits liquidised with their skin; these are an excellent means of adding fibre to the diet, particularly for older people who may find crunchy fruits difficult to chew. The many appetising desserts primarily use the natural sweetness of fruit, and occasionally a little honey, rather than refined sugar.

The author also recommends minimal cooking as one of the corner-stones of his cuisine, convinced that over-cooking is one of the major causes of dietary deficiencies. Cooked in smaller portions, white meat and fish can be lightly poached or just marinated and, as with vegetables, thus keep their best possible content of essential minerals, vitamins and enzymes.

As the technique of combining raw and cooked food will be relatively new to most readers, Jean Conil offers guidance on what ingredients make the best partnerships, and the herbs and spices that further enhance them. And despite what has been said about Nouvelle Cuisine's zeal about artistic effect, the author is a firm believer in presenting dishes well – he sweeps away the myth that a healthy diet should look like a form of medicine. Cuisine Fraîcheur, and the Love Apple Diet based on it, are about the deep pleasures and satisfaction to be had in serving truly wholesome food; and bringing it to table looking its best is an important statement of pride in this.

This cuisine is timely in more than its health-consciousness. Jean Conil estimates that there are now some 500 more varieties of fruit, vegetables and herbs in the shops and supermarkets than there were ten years ago, but only a fraction of them are used in most homes because of uncertainty about their preparation and possibilities. They include new salad ingredients and many tropical fruits and vegetables, ideal for this Cuisine. The recipe notes in this book include advice on choosing these products at the shop in their best condition, tips on culinary uses and information about their dietary merits.

While not every individual dish may contain the recommended proportion of fibre (such a requirement would unduly narrow the recipes' variety), the reader can readily adjust this content upwards over the day in several ways: by adding more raw garnish to a particular dish; by a supplement of fresh fruit or crudités between meals; or by arranging the right, high-fibre level in drinks and meals taken over a period. To help the reader in this choice, the author has devised the Love Apple Diet.

How is this book best used? Jean Conil naturally believes that Cuisine Fraîcheur and its principles need to be adopted wholeheartedly on the lines indicated in the Love Apple Diet if they are to become the basis of a healthier and happier way of life. However, the author also recognises that some may want to try it gradually, using the diet menus on one or two days a week or sampling drinks or dishes at random. The recipes cover the full repertoire of meal-courses; for the occasional user trying out the Cuisine there are ideas for a variety of occasions and any such sampling will be a step in the right direction.

The Love Apple Diet
The Love Apple Diet consists of a selection of dishes from Cuisine Fraîcheur, from which a day's menus can be composed. It is presented on page 216. The menus are balanced to

provide the right combination of fibre, protein and other elements. Over the day they provide three parts of raw food to one part of cooked food, thus amply fulfilling the nutritionists' view of the healthiest diet imaginable within the state of present knowledge.

The suggested menus can, of course, be modified. Vegetarians need to make adjustments to the Love Apple Diet to ensure adequate protein intake (see page 218 for further information).

The 'love apple' of the title is an old romantic name for the tomato. It also refers back to the use of the word 'apple' in early times as a metaphor for all fruits generally – hence it is a diet that helps you to look after your health in a loving and caring way.

It is not a 'gimmick' diet that relies upon some supposedly magical ingredient, such as pineapple or bananas. It aims to be a diet for all-round good health rather than essentially for slimming, yet it may, in practice, work better for the overweight than those strict regimes relying upon low intake. All the recipes watch their calories very carefully and a day's menus from the diet chart will produce a calorie-count of between 2000 and 2500, quite enough to sustain the average adult. So long as other obvious rules are followed, such as the need for exercise and the moderation or avoidance of alcohol, then the user will gradually find and maintain a normal weight.

Jean Conil believes that this oblique approach to weight problems is the only one likely to succeed for most people over the long term. Mealtimes are meant to be enjoyable, an unchangeable part of everyone's psychology. Where this pleasureable element is missing (and who ever met a happy 'slimmer' of the traditional type?), as in low-intake or single-ingredient diets or those using uninspiring supplements out of a packet, conflicts are quickly set up in the dieter. Deficiencies of essential nutrients can occur; hunger and monotony add their pressures and the stage is set for a return to the chocolate box.

The Love Apple Diet has none of these shortcomings. The fresh fruit and crudités allowed and encouraged between meals further ensure that hunger should never be a problem. It is complete, appetising, highly varied and relies upon enjoyment rather than discipline to ensure that good health and correct weight are maintained naturally. Jean Conil believes that those who give the Love Apple Diet a fair trial will not return to the harmful dietary habits of the past.

LES BOISSONS NOURISSANTES
NOURISHING DRINKS

While fruit and vegetable juices are nowadays entirely familiar, many people are unaware of the rich variety of combinations that can be made and how they can add sparkle and very healthy properties to the everyday diet.

There are several advantages in taking a good proportion of your Cuisine Fraîcheur diet in liquid form. It will go a long way to supplying, in a very palatable way, the 1.2 litres (2 pints) of liquid the body needs each day to function properly. The drinks are quick and easy to make. And, as the recipes in the following pages show, they can cover a wide and intriguing range of flavours, textures and nutritional properties.

These drinks are unashamedly meant to be enjoyable. They look attractive in the glass and are delicious on the palate. The recipes are grouped under various headings: early morning drinks, fibrous fruit drinks that assist in a high-fibre diet, light and refreshing fruit cups, combined vegetable and fruit juice drinks, milk beverages, including various fruity shakes made with fresh or soya milk and nutty milk drinks, tisanes or herbal infusions, and relaxing bedtime beverages.

A reminder may be useful about the way in which these juices benefit health, apart from their content of vitamins and minerals. Many fruits, such as papaya, pineapple, figs, watermelon and kiwi fruit, are rich in enzymes. These enzymes start the process of breaking down protein which eventually will be turned into amino acids by other enzymes in the body, and finally reach the blood stream as nutrients. If protein is not broken down properly, it is wasted.

Coffee, tea and cocoa have not been included here because they contain caffeine, a harmful stimulant. There is also a strong medical prejudice in Britain against taking tea with any meat meal because it is thought that the tannin in the tea 'tans' the protein of the meat, making it indigestible.

As will be seen, the drinks serve a range of dietary needs. Vegans, for example, who avoid animal milks, can find a pleasant substitute in liquidised beverages made with nuts, or combinations of soya milk, fruit and nuts, all with a good protein content. In the fruit drinks, and especially in the tisanes, there are agreeable alternatives to tea, coffee and alcohol, which this diet rules out. For the reader habituated to an aperitif before a meal, why not continue the custom but in healthier form – that is with a sparkling fruit cup or cocktail, free of alcohol? One gets a similar 'bite' to the palate without the toxins. Even straight and unblended fruit juices can be given new zest with fresh herbs like lemon balm or a slice of a different citrus fruit.

Fresh fruit, vegetables and herbs are highly desirable in making these drinks. Even the more exotic fruits are nowadays found in supermarkets in due season. If you have to shop in smaller towns then a special order placed with your greengrocer for mangoes, fresh pineapple or other less usual items should produce results, especially if you can arrange with like-minded friends to order a rather larger quantity.

However, some flexibility is necessary, and wherever possible I have made some rarer ingredients optional or suggested an alternative. So long as a reasonable effort is made to carry out the Fraîcheur philosophy – and if you will compare a glass of freshly squeezed orange juice with one from a carton at least your palate will know that it was well worth the trouble – then some resort to convenience foods and drinks is acceptable to supply a missing ingredient. If you are unable to get the fresh article sometimes, then packaged or concentrated fruit and vegetable juice may be used.

Getting some herbs in fresh form may be a little more problematical. But once you have tasted what excellent drinks they make, either on their own, or lending aroma to a fruit drink, you may well be persuaded into the pleasant task of starting a small herbarium, either in the garden or a window-box. Seeds are readily available at seedmen's or herbalists.

Just when to take these drinks has a good deal to do with personal choice. The recipe section opens with suggestions for early morning drinks, which most people would prefer to be a fruit juice combination, at least in warmer months. The mid-morning and afternoon drink could also be a fruit juice or tisane. Tisanes are excellent at bedtime. The concluding section on Bedtime Drinks also includes some hot and milky combinations for those who find them soothing.

Mechanical Tools

To extract pure juice you need the following: (1) an ordinary stainless lemon juice presser; (2) a fruit crusher which is available separately or as part of a food processor; (3) an electric blender-liquidiser to get the pulp well ground and mixed with the liquid; (4) a fruit extractor which will not crush the seeds or pips, which are bitter in some fruits such as grapes. A proper grape presser could be useful for large quantities of juice for parties. This is obtainable at shops selling brewing and wine-making products. Also desirable are strainers and a nylon sieve for filtering juices and perhaps a pestle and mortar for pounding fruit and nuts.

◆ EARLY MORNING DRINKS ◆

Most of us need a thirst-quencher on waking and what better form could this take than a tangy fruit drink? For simple and refreshing flavour, it is hard to beat a glass of fresh lemon juice diluted with hot water to taste. For variety, and in warmer weather, the citrus and other fruits lend themselves to interesting permutations. Here are some examples of these morning wakeners.

Citronnade au miel ◆ Lemon juice with honey

1 teaspoon honey
150ml/5fl oz hot water
juice of 1 lemon
juice of ½ orange

Dissolve the honey in the water and blend in the two fruit juices. Drink in a cup or in a glass first thing in the morning. **Serves 2.**

Grenadine ◆ Pomegranate drink

juice of 1 pomegranate, or 1 tablespoon grenadine syrup
150ml/5fl oz fresh orange juice
2 ice cubes

Mix the ingredients together. Drink in the summertime first thing in the morning or during the night if you wake up. **Serves 2.**

Pamplemoussette ◆ Grapefruit drink

150ml/5fl oz fresh grapefruit juice
1 teaspoon blackcurrant cordial
2 ice cubes

Combine and drink cold in the morning. **Serves 2.**

Mandarinette • Tangerine drink

150ml/5fl oz fresh tangerine juice
juice of ½ lime
2 ice cubes

Combine and drink cold in the morning. **Serves 2.**

Pommette • Apple and orange juice

150ml/5fl oz unsweetened apple juice
150ml/5fl oz fresh orange juice
1 teaspoon cider vinegar

Combine and drink cold in the morning. **Serves 2.**

◆ FIBROUS DRINKS ◆

Pomme ◆ Apple

All kinds of apples can lend their different flavours to Cuisine Fraîcheur, and any good variety may be substituted for that given in a recipe so long as it is juicy and fresh. The virtues of the green cooking apple (or even cider or crab apples, if available) should not be overlooked: they can add a special tangy flavour to the juice of dessert or eating apples. Quinces, too, can be boiled, reduced to a pureé and mixed with unsweetened apple juice. This produces an aromatic drink rich in pectin, good for lowering cholesterol. There is no need to core or peel apples in juice-making. In fact, much of the flavour is in the skin; however, if you do not like this it may be strained out through muslin or a sieve.

Elixir de pomme à la menthe ◆ Apple elixir with mint

2 Cox's Orange Pippin apples
2 Bramley or Granny Smith apples
1 ripe crab apple (optional)
150ml/5fl oz water
1 tablespoon honey (optional)
pinch of ground cinnamon or cloves
slice of chilli
6 fresh mint leaves

Core and peel all the apples. Place the skins in a saucepan and add the water, honey, cinnamon and chilli. Boil for 10 minutes, then strain into a bowl. Cut the apples into wedges. Liquidise to a pulp with the strained liquid. Cool. If too thick, add enough water to make a drinkable consistency. Transfer the elixir to a jug containing 4 ice cubes and the mint leaves and serve. **Serves 2.**

Mûres et pomme ◆ Fraîcheur blackberry and apple

2 dessert apples, sliced with skin and pips
150g/5oz blackberries
150ml/5fl oz water
2 ice cubes

Liquidise all together. Strain, if liked. Serve in tall glasses, garnished with slices of lime. **Serves 2.**

Fraise et pomme • Fraîcheur strawberry and apple

2 dessert apples, sliced with skin and pips
150g/5oz strawberries, hulled
slice of green chilli
2 ice cubes

Liquidise all together. Strain, if liked. Serve in tall glasses. **Serves 2.**

Pomme citronelle • Fraîcheur apple and pear with lemon balm

1 juicy green apple, sliced with skin and pips
1 very juicy Comice pear, cored, peeled and sliced
150ml/5fl oz water
2 fresh lemon balm leaves
2 ice cubes

Liquidise all together. Serve garnished with a slice of lemon, lime or orange. **Serves 2.**

Grenadinette • Fraîcheur apple and pomegranate

2 apples, cored and sliced
1 pomegranate, peeled, or 1 tablespoon grenadine syrup
juice of 1 large orange
2 ice cubes
150ml/5fl oz soda water

Liquidise the apples with the pomegranate, orange juice and ice cubes. Top up with soda water and serve garnished with the slice of an orange and a few pomegranate seeds. Serves 2.

Prunes • Plums

The damson may have been brought to Britain from Damascus, Syria, by Crusaders in the time of Richard I. In 1542 someone wrote: '. . . damesyns eaten before dyner be good to provoke a man's appedyte.' The two best modern commercial varieties are Shropshire and Merryweather: get them as large and juicy as possible. They are rich in vitamins, minerals and fibre. Taken raw on their own they are rather sharp, but they combine beautifully with blander or sweeter fruits, such as apple or pear, to make excellent fools or drinks.

The Victoria plum as big as a peach is one of the finest desserts one could wish for to end a meal. The greengage is the sweetest of the white varieties.

Prunes de Damas aux poires • Damson and pear juice

150g/5oz damsons (stoned weight)
2 large, ripe Comice pears, peeled, cored and sliced
150ml/5fl oz water
juice of 1 orange

Liquidise together and serve with ice cubes in tall glasses. (An excellent aperient. Reduce or omit the water if you want a more concentrated drink.) **Serves 2.**

Prunes aux amandes • Fraîcheur prunes and almonds

150g/5oz large Californian prunes
150ml/5fl oz hot water
25g/1oz blanched almonds
100ml/4fl oz fresh orange juice
pinch of ground cinnamon

Soak the prunes overnight in the hot water. Remove the stones. Liquidise the prunes with the soaking water, almonds, orange juice and cinnamon. Serve cold first thing in the morning. (Another good laxative, used twice weekly.) **Serves 2.**

Fraîcheur de Reine-Claude • Greengage drink

150g/5oz greengages, stoned
150ml/5fl oz ginger ale
3 ice cubes

Liquidise all together and serve in tall glasses. Garnish with a slice of lime, cherries and mint leaves. **Serves 2.**

Papaye ◆ Papaya or Pawpaw

This is a fine fruit for fibrous drinks, with pleasant juice and a good texture. Its richness in enzymes, which aid digestion, makes it a good appetiser before a meal.

La papayade au citron vert ◆ Papaya and lime with soda

> 1 large ripe papaya, peeled, seeded and sliced
> juice of 2 limes plus a quarter-portion of their peel
> 150ml/5fl oz water
> 50g/2oz flaked almonds
> 1 teaspoon honey (optional)
> 2 ice cubes
> soda water to taste

Liquidise the papaya, lime juice and peel, water, almonds, honey and ice cubes. Serve in tall glasses, topped up with soda for a long drink. **Serves 2**.

La papayade au kiwi ◆ Papaya with kiwi

> 1 kiwi fruit, peeled
> 1 large ripe papaya, peeled, seeded and sliced
> 150g/5oz ripe gooseberries, or another kiwi fruit
> 150ml/5fl oz bitter lemon or tonic water
> 2 egg whites
> juice of 1 lemon

Liquidise all ingredients and serve in tall glasses. Garnish each with a slice of orange and two fresh cherries. **Serves 2**.

Framboises ◆ Raspberries

Raspberries have long been esteemed as the ambrosia of gastronomy. Recipes from old monasteries show how for centuries the fruit was used to make wine and liqueurs. Today, the culinary uses for raspberries are varied: for making wine and vinegar; as a purée in fools, sorbets and other desserts; and for topping in trifle and pâtisserie, notably the lovely Austrian Linzertorte.

Raspberries are rich in vitamin C and a number of nutrients. Be careful in buying after wet weather as damp fruit soon goes mouldy. Avoid containers that are stained at the base; the bottom layer of fruit could well be squashed. Of the many varieties the very best is Malling Notable – medium to large, bright red and deliciously sweet. In the diet, avoid the temptation of cream with them; try them with plain yogurt instead.

Framboises au jus d'ananas • Raspberry and pineapple juice

150g/5oz best quality raspberries
150g/5oz fresh pineapple (about 2 slices), peeled and cored
150ml/5fl oz fresh orange juice
1 teaspoon honey
2 ice cubes

Liquidise all ingredients and serve in tall glasses. This is a very refreshing drink with an afternoon snack. **Serves 4**.

Framboise fraîcheur • Raspberry shake

150g/5oz best quality raspberries
150ml/5fl oz fresh orange juice
75ml/3fl oz water
1 small dessert apple, sliced with skin and pips

Liquidise all ingredients. Strain, if liked, and serve with 2 ice cubes. This is an excellent mid-morning drink on a summer's day. **Serves 4**.

Rhubarbe ◆ Rhubarb

Rhubarb has been cultivated in Europe since the 14th century, and was treated as a vegetable in its early times rather than as a fruit plant. Introduced in England in the 18th century, it really became popular in Victorian times. In the herbarium, it has always been noted as a good, natural aperient. Very low in calories (only 6 per 100g/4oz), it contains vitamins A and C and minerals.

When buying, choose rhubarb that is fresh-looking and firm. Early rhubarb does not have to be peeled; just wash and chop it. Outdoor varieties have a stronger flavour and should be peeled: as you trim an end, the skin pulls off easily. Rhubarb can be poached and used in pies and tarts; or turn it into a purée to sauce fish, or for fools and jellies.

Nectar de Saleux à la rhubarbe ◆ *Rhubarb cup with strawberries*

450g/1 lb outdoor rhubarb, peeled and cut into finger-length pieces
150ml/5fl oz water
6 tablespoons honey
300g/10oz strawberries, hulled
150ml/5fl oz ginger ale
6 slices of cucumber, with skin

Simmer the rhubarb with the water and honey for 12 minutes or until very tender. Cool, then liquidise to a thin purée with 150g/5oz strawberries. Place in a jug with the ginger ale. Add the rest of the strawberries and the cucumber. Serve as a morning or afternoon drink with two or three ice cubes. **Serves 4.**

Fraîcheur au gingembre ◆ *Ginger fizz with pineapple and rhubarb*

225g/8oz outdoor rhubarb, peeled and cut into finger-length pieces
300ml/½ pint water
2 teaspoons honey
2 slices fresh pineapple, peeled and cored

15g/½oz fresh root ginger, peeled and sliced
150ml/5fl oz Indian tonic water

Simmer the rhubarb in the water with the honey for 12 minutes or until very tender. Cool, then liquidise to a purée. Add the pineapple and ginger and liquidise again. Serve in tall glasses, topped up with tonic and garnished with fresh borage flowers. **Serves 4.**

Jus de la Vigne ◆ Grape Juice

The cautious rules for wine-blending do not apply to grape juice, where that of several varieties may safely be put together to produce a well-balanced mixture. Some grapes may be too sweet for your taste and a drier or sharper sort may need to be added to get the desired flavour. Sometimes a small proportion of apple juice or lemon juice helps to remove any too-cloying tendency. On the other hand sultanas may be used to make an even sweeter juice. Grapes with a very distinctive flavour, like Muscatel, produce an excellent drink.

If you wish to take the short-cut of using bottled or concentrated grape juice, Cuisine Fraîcheur would find this acceptable, though the home-pressed juice is hard to beat.

Jus de la vigne aux pêches de Montreuil ◆ Grape juice cup with peaches

1 kg/2lbs seedless white grapes, stalks removed
2 ripe peaches, stoned and thinly sliced
150ml/5fl oz water
thinly pared rind and juice of 1 lemon

Press the grapes in a juice extractor, collecting the juice in a jug. Add the peaches, water, lemon juice and rind and 2 ice cubes. Leave to macerate 35 minutes in the refrigerator. Serve cold with a meal. Also makes a pleasant aperitif. **Serves 8.**

Fraîcheur mousseuse • Sparkling grape and cucumber refresher

1 kg/2lbs seedless Muscatel grapes
5 strawberries, hulled and sliced
4 slices of cucumber with skin
juice of 2 limes
thinly pared rind of 1 lime
300ml/½ pint sugar-free ginger ale

Press the grapes in a juice extractor and collect the juice in a jug. Add the strawberries, cucumber, lime juice and rind and 2 ice cubes. When ready to serve, mix in the ginger ale and serve with cold meals or at afternoon parties. **Serves 8.**

Cassis • Blackcurrant

Rich in vitamins and minerals, blackcurrants have long been regarded as an important medicinal fruit – to make a tisane or cordial for relieving colds, for example. Their robust flavour, sweet but with a nice astringency, also makes delicious drinks in combination with somewhat blander fruit.

In buying, look for firm, clean currants with a distinct gloss. Check that the base of the container is unstained. If you buy them on the stalk (usually cheaper), run a fork down the stalk to remove the fruit. They can be eaten raw as desserts, either on their own or in a baked pastry shell. The juice can be made into jellies, sorbets or blancmange. Bottled and concentrated juice may be used in drink recipes but needs diluting with water to a normal strength.

Cassis aux pommes • Blackcurrant and apple drink

2 dessert apples, sliced with skin and pips
150g/5oz blackcurrants, de-stalked
150ml/5fl oz water
2 ice cubes

Liquidise all together. Strain if liked. Serve in tall glasses, garnished with a slice of orange, lemon or lime. **Serves 2.**

Cassis au coing • Quince and blackcurrant drink

Quince is rich in pectin but above all it has a wonderful aroma which highlights the flavour of this delectable drink. If quince is not available use quince jelly just for the flavour.

150g/5oz blackcurrants, de-stalked, or 4 tablespoons blackcurrant syrup
150g/5oz fresh quince, quartered and cored but not peeled
150ml/5fl oz water
150ml/5fl oz soda water or ginger ale
juice of 1 lemon
2 ice cubes

Simmer the blackcurrants and quince in the water for 15 minutes or until tender. Cool, then liquidise the mixture. Strain if liked, and blend in the soda water and lemon juice. If using blackcurrant syrup, stir it in with the soda. Add the ice cubes and serve. **Serves 4**.

While some vegetable juices are delicious on their own, others no less valuable in nutrients are not so palatable. They need a little acidulation or brightening up, particularly for children.

The flavour of vegetable drinks can be improved with a variety of additions such as apple juice or herbs like chopped parsley, coriander, chives, mint and watercress. Also, some juices seem to help each other to show off their best. Carrots, being sweet and rich in carotene, make a very fine base for vegetable mixes, as do parsnips. Both combine well with the following: beetroot, cabbage, celery, cos lettuce, spinach and watercress. Cucumber with its skin can also be added to any of these to give the drink lightness. Watermelon goes well with carrots and tomatoes.

All root vegetables used for juice must be washed thoroughly and lightly scraped. As vegetable fibre can be rather dense for drinking it is better to use a centrifugal juice extractor – there are many brands on the market – to extract the juice, retaining the pulp for use in soups or purées. Make sure to add ice cubes to the drinks, not only to keep the chilled freshness but to prevent oxidation and discolouring.

Jus de carotte à la Trigonelle ◆ Fraîcheur with fenugreek and carrots

The seeds of fenugreek have been used medicinally all through the ages. This herb tastes nicely bitter, with a flavour similar to lovage and celery and a pleasant odour.

150g/5oz young carrots, scraped and grated
1 small stick of celery
sprig of fresh fenugreek
sprig of fresh parsley
small piece of fresh root ginger (the size of a grape), peeled
150ml/5fl oz water
50ml/2fl oz fresh lime or lemon juice
dash of Tabasco sauce

Liquidise all ingredients together, then pass through a fine strainer or juice extractor. Serve chilled in tall glasses. A good drink for mid-morning or before meals. **Serves 2**.

Cocktail de carottes aux abricots • Carrot and apricot cocktail

150g/5oz young carrots, scraped and sliced
150ml/5fl oz water
150g/5oz fresh ripe apricots, stoned
150ml/5fl oz fresh orange juice
1 teaspoon cider vinegar

Simmer the carrots in the water for 12 minutes or until tender. Cool, then liquidise the mixture with the apricots and orange juice. Add the vinegar and serve chilled with ice cubes. **Serves 6.**

Cocktail de tomate aux carottes • Fraîcheur with tomato and carrots

150g/5oz young carrots, scraped and grated
150ml/5fl oz orange juice
150g/5oz tomato, skinned, seeded and chopped
dash of Tabasco sauce

Soak the carrots in the orange juice for 10 minutes. Liquidise all ingredients together and strain through a nylon sieve. Serve chilled. **Serves 4.**

◆ MILK DRINKS ◆

The bland flavour of milk and the tanginess of fruit complement each other well and produce many delightful shakes and beverages. In the recipes we recommend the use of skimmed milk to keep the cholesterol level and calories down (a pint of whole milk contains 400 calories, but skimmed milk only half as much); some of the creamy taste does remain.

Two-thirds of a pint of milk is quite enough to supply an adult with the recommended daily intake of calcium. The casein in milk also supplies you with protein, and it gives phosphorus and other minerals, as well as vitamin B2 and lactose for energy.

The recipes include a section using soya milk and various nut milks; these will appeal to vegans or others wanting a pleasantly different milk beverage.

Fraise fraîcheur ◆ *Strawberry shake*

150g/5oz strawberries, hulled
300ml/½ pint skimmed milk
1 orange segment (blood orange, if possible)
2 ice cubes

Liquidise the ingredients and serve in tall glasses. **Serves 2.**

Ananasbana fraîcheur ◆ *Pineapple and banana shake*

1 slice of fresh pineapple, peeled and cored
1 ripe banana, peeled
300ml/½ pint skimmed milk
juice of 1 lime

Liquidise the ingredients and serve in tall glasses garnished with fresh borage flowers or 2 stoned cherries. **Serves 2.**

Charentaise ◆ *Charentais melon shake*

1 small Charentais melon
small piece of fresh root ginger (the size of a grape), peeled

300ml/ ½ pint skimmed milk
2 ice cubes

Halve the melon, discard the seeds and scoop the pulp and juice into a blender or food processor. Liquidise with the other ingredients. Serve in tall glasses garnished with a sprig of mint and a few cherries. **Serves 2**.

Passion de mon coeur ◆ Passion fruit drink

Passion fruits are imported from the West Indies, Brazil and Kenya. The fruit has a tough skin that is wrinkled and purply-brown; inside are juicy flesh and edible seeds.

2 passion fruits
juice of 1 lime
300ml/ ½ pint skimmed milk
2 ice cubes

Cut the passion fruits in half and scoop out the seeds and pulp with a spoon. Liquidise with the other ingredients. Serve in small glasses as the fruit is very expensive. Garnish each glass with a slice of lime or fresh mint leaf. A pleasant afternoon drink. **Serves 2**.

Lait de Soya ◆ Soya Milk

This is a very healthy alternative to skimmed cow's milk and can be readily used in all the milk shake recipes. It contains 18 per cent protein and no fat. Soya milk is now available in most supermarkets, but if you wish to make your own this is a simple matter.

Soak 150g/5oz dried soya beans overnight. Drain and rinse well to remove bitter flavour. Place in a saucepan with 600ml/1 pint of water, bring to the boil and simmer for 30 minutes. Top up the water level as it evaporates. Drain the beans and liquidise with 600ml/1 pint of cold fresh water. Strain the purée through a sieve, collect the milk and allow to cool.

The milk can either be used in fruit-flavoured milk shakes, or it makes a pleasant drink on its own with a little salt and honey added to taste.

The use of egg whites in cold fizzy drinks is quite common and every barman has many recipes featuring them. Egg whites stabilise drinks and beverages using citrus fruits. In a healthy diet the egg whites provide one amino-acid of the eight essential ones needed as part of our protein intake. Soya lacks this amino-acid, known as Tryptophane, hence the use of egg white in soya drinks.

Lait de soya aux mandarines ◆ Soya milk with satsuma

You can use tofu (soya bean curd) instead of soya milk for extra protein. Liquidise 25g/1oz tofu with 150ml/5fl oz water or fruit juice.

150ml/5fl oz soya milk
1 teaspoon honey
slice of fresh pineapple, peeled and cored
1 fresh and juicy satsuma, peeled and segmented
juice of 1 lemon
1 egg white
piece of fresh root ginger (the size of a grape), peeled
dash of Tabasco sauce

Liquidise all the ingredients. Serve in tall glasses with ice cubes, a few strawberries and a slice of lime or lemon. **Serves 2.**

Nutty Milk Drinks

Several kinds of nut, added in the liquidising process, can be used to give flavour and extra protein to milky drinks.

Cocolait ◆ Coconut milk

The coconut is unique in having its own milk, and I recall how wonderfully refreshing it was when I first came upon it in the Caribbean islands. Take the chance to try it if you see a coconut at the greengrocer's. Otherwise, a tasty substitute can be made, as follows.

75g/3oz desiccated coconut
600ml/1 pint water
25g/1oz skimmed milk powder

Simmer the coconut in the water for 5 minutes, then liquidise. Strain through a nylon sieve or fine strainer. Reheat, whisking in the skimmed milk. Either serve hot as a bedtime drink or chilled with ice cubes as a daytime beverage. **Serves 4 to 6.**

Amandine ◆ Almond milk

150g/5oz blanched almonds
300ml/½ pint water
juice of ½ lemon
1 teaspoon honey (optional)

Simmer the almonds in the water for 5 minutes. Liquidise while hot and allow to cool. When cold, add the lemon juice, a couple of ice cubes and the honey if you need a sweetener. Serve in tall glasses. **Serves 2.**

Noisettine ◆ Hazelnut milk

150g/5oz shelled hazelnuts in their skins
300ml/½ pint boiling water
small sprig of celery leaves
pinch of salt

Scald the hazelnuts in the boiling water. Cool in the water, then liquidise the mixture with the celery leaves. Season to taste and serve with ice cubes. **Serves 2.**

◆ HERBAL BEVERAGES ◆

The word *tisane* comes from the Latin *ptisana*, which was a decoction of barley popular in classical times. These herbal brews are highly important in the Love Apple Diet. They are pleasant and refreshing at any time of day and a healthy alternative to coffee and tea, being truly relaxing rather than stimulating. They can also be therapeutic for various ailments and this chapter will list some of these remedies.

In making a tisane, use fresh herbs if possible. They are more aromatic than dried herbs, though the latter will suffice if the fresh are not available. You allow 2 tablespoons of the fresh herb to each 600ml/1 pint of boiling water and infuse in a teapot or jug for 5 minutes. The flavour is improved by adding a slice of your favourite citrus fruit (lemon, orange, lime or tangerine) and a teaspoon of honey if you need it. In the summer, chilled tisanes make excellent refreshing drinks on their own. Or, with the addition of some diced fruit to your taste and perhaps a little sliced cucumber, a tisane can be the basis of a delicious punch. If you have ever wished that you had something more intriguing than orange juice to offer your guests who do not take alcohol, then a bowl of well-chilled tisane punch or fruit cup is the answer. Among the herbs ideal for fruit cups are marigold and clary flowers, hyssop and balm.

If you do not know tisanes well already, it is useful to familiarise yourself with just one or two initially, to help in liberating yourself from the tea and coffee habit. The Tisane Conil given here has been enjoyed in my family for some generations. The lime flower (linden) recipe is among the most popular in France (where the blossom is known as *tilleul*), especially with country people who drink it at bedtime. Bees are fond of the lime flower, and honey with its aroma is the world's best. The leaves exude a sweet substance which, though it can be a nuisance when it drips on city pavements, has the same composition as the sought-after manna of Mount Sinai. These tisanes are much more thirst-quenching than sweet drinks.

Boisson aux fruits ◆ *Tisane fruit cup*

Here is a recipe for a basic tisane fruit cup. With experiment you can vary it to suit your own taste as to strength and flavour.

16 fresh mint leaves
6 fresh lemon balm leaves
750ml/1¼ pints boiling water
2 tablespoons honey (heather flavour)
sprig of fresh heather (optional)
1 green dessert apple, sliced with skin
1 orange, sliced with skin
6 raspberries

Infuse the mint leaves and lemon balm in the boiling water in a teapot for 6 minutes. Stir in the honey and cool. Strain into a jug and add the remaining ingredients with some ice cubes. Garnish with 3 fresh mint leaves. **Serves 4**.

Fraîcheur Tisane Conil

2 tablespoons fresh mint or lemon balm leaves
6 thin slices of cucumber with skin
grated rind and juice of ¼ lemon
2 tablespoons honey
600ml/1 pint boiling water

Infuse the mint or lemon balm in the boiling water in a teapot for 5 minutes. Strain into a jug and add the cucumber, lemon rind and honey. Cool the mixture and add the lemon juice. **Serves 4**.

Tisane au miel ◆ Hot linden tea

2 tablespoons dried linden flowers
600ml/1 pint boiling water
4 slices of lime or lemon
1 tablespoon honey
4 fresh mint leaves

Infuse the flowers in the boiling water in a teapot for 5 minutes. Strain and serve in cups with a slice of lime and honey, plus mint for aroma. For a stronger brew, include the mint in the infusion period. **Serves 4**.

Les Tisanes Médicinales ◆ Herbal Remedies

For centuries many herbs, in the form of an infusion, have been taken to relieve certain ailments, and I believe this must be more then mere fancy. It is known that in their chemical composition some herbs do resemble expensive modern drugs. For example, the value of the humble poppy used as a pain-killer is beyond any doubt. My grandmother, a self-taught amateur herbalist, was always being sought out by villagers needing a remedy, and her simple infusions apparently gave relief when the village doctor could not help.

Below are listed some of the more familiar medicinal herbs and the conditions they are said to ease, sometimes according to a centuries-old reputation. We are not, of course, suggesting that devotion to herbal remedies is an alternative to a visit to the doctor, but as you re-educate your palate to raw foods, herbs will become important to you and it is interesting to learn their traditions.

Sage – astringent flavour; used for stomach upsets

Pennyroyal – eases pre-menstrual tension

Tansy – used for colic and gout

Fennel leaves and root – an aperient and diuretic

Dill – relief of flatulence and indigestion

Rue – very bitter flavour; said to aid sluggish circulations

Rosemary – for headache relief

Camomile – slightly bitter; used as a general tonic

Lime flowers – for indigestion or palpitation

There are also groups of herbs which are thought to give relief in more general forms of indisposition:

tonics and cleansers: nettle, mint, ginseng, rosemary, and the leaves of blackberry, raspberry and strawberry

soothers and soporifics: camomile, hops, lime flower, orange blossom, passion flower and red clover

fever-reducers: lime flower, peppermint, elderflower and yarrow

relief of colds and sore throats: leek syrup, rose hips, comfrey, aniseed, sage and liquorice

easing liverishness: angelica, agrimony and mugwort

diuretics: dandelion and celery seeds

Tisane camomile • *Camomile blossom tea*

Camomile is one of the most popular tisanes in France and elsewhere. It can relax the body and mind, and also prevent the kind of muscular cramps which often stop exhausted people from falling asleep. Drink four times a day as a general tonic and pick-me-up.

2 tablespoons camomile flowers (fresh or dried)
600ml / 1 pint boiling water
4 slices of lime or lemon with rind

Infuse the camomile flowers in the boiling water in a teapot for 5 minutes. Strain and serve in cups with a slice of lime or lemon. **Serves 4.**

◆ BEDTIME DRINKS ◆

Many people like a hot drink on retiring. Most of the tisanes will serve this purpose well, but if you prefer, there are also a number of hot milky drinks and delicious egg-nogs to enjoy. Egg yolk gives a drink some body; it should be mixed with the hot drink away from heat to avoid coagulation.

Lait à l'orge fermentée ◆ Malt milk

Extract of malt is available both in powder form and in syrup.

   1 tablespoon malt extract syrup
   150ml/5fl oz hot milk
   2 drops of vanilla essence

Dissolve the malt syrup in the hot milk and add the vanilla essence. Drink last thing at night. **Serves 2.**

Lait de poule ◆ Egg-nog

   2 egg yolks
   1 tablespoon honey
   1 teaspoon carob powder or grated carob bar
   150ml/5fl oz hot milk
   grated nutmeg

Place the egg yolks, honey and carob in a bowl and gradually whisk in the hot milk. Flavour with a little nutmeg and drink hot. **Serves 2.**

Lait de noisettes ◆ Hazelnut egg-nog

   225ml/8fl oz milk
   50g/2oz toasted hazelnuts, crushed
   1 tablespoon honey
   2 egg yolks
   rosewater (optional)

Heat the milk with the nuts, then liquidise to develop the nutty flavour. In a bowl, whisk the honey with the egg yolks. Gradually whisk in the nutty milk. A little rose water will improve the flavour. **Serves 3.**

La verveine sabayonnée ◆ Verbena tisane with egg yolks

The tisane must be hot but not boiling hot so the egg yolks do not curdle.

> 1 tablespoon fresh verbena (vervain)
> 150ml/5fl oz boiling water
> 1 egg yolk
> 1 tablespoon honey
> grated nutmeg

Infuse the verbena in the boiling water in a teapot for 5 minutes. Strain. Whisk the egg yolk with the honey in a bowl. Gradually whisk in the tisane. Flavour with a pinch of nutmeg. **Serves 2.**

Laitue fraîcheur ◆ Lettuce lullaby

Only a few vegetables go really well with milk but one of them is lettuce. The following recipe is one my grandmother used to prepare as a restful bedtime drink. It was known and used in Greek and Roman times as a gentle soporific. If you wish, add 50g/2oz ground blanched almonds to the mixture to enrich it with extra protein.

> ½ small lettuce with stalk
> 300ml/½ pint water and milk mixed
> salt to taste
> 1 tablespoon honey (optional)

Wash the lettuce leaves and drain well. Peel the stalk or core as it contains most of the milky liquid. Liquidise the leaves and stalk with the water and milk to make a thin purée. Season to taste and add the honey. Do not strain but drink as a cold soup at bedtime. **Serves 4.**

CRUDITÉS ET PÂTÉS
DIPS AND PÂTÉS

'Ah, *les beaux petits légumes!*' This was the way my dear grandma Mathilde fondly described the vegetables that reached her standard of perfection. They had to be very fresh, young and crunchy to pass her scrutiny. 'Eat, Jean,' she would say, plying me with a tender carrot or two, a fragrant spring onion or a few radishes. 'Taste them with your teeth like a young puppy chews a bone . . . '

Crudités always conjure up in my mind a vision of her luscious market garden in Picardy and its produce. Anyone coming anew to a mainly vegetarian diet should take every opportunity, as I did in boyhood, to rediscover all the subtle array of flavours and aromas to be found in vegetables that have come straight from the soil. It will add relish and interest to every meal.

Except for starchy tubers like yams and potatoes, all vegetables can be eaten in the raw state, and we tend to forget how splendid is the variety of choice – carrots, turnips, beetroot, celeriac, celery, fennel, cabbage, kohlrabi, onions, spring onions, broccoli, cauliflower, mushrooms, peppers and mooli, to name but a few. We can add all the familiar salad stuffs such as endive, radishes, Chinese leaves, chicory, cucumber, tomatoes, cress and radicchio. And virtually all the fruits and nuts, except for quince, can amplify the raw diet, either on their own or as a garnish.

In addition to raw dishes, this chapter offers a number of recipes for raw dips and pâtés, ranging from the simple to the complex. At its most basic, a peanut pâté or dip is made simply by liquidising toasted peanuts with just enough water to reduce them to a pasty substance.

In the healthy eating recommended by this book virtually all animal fats are avoided, and we suggest a number of ways of replacing this constituent by a better one. For example, avocado pulp, with its high unsaturated fat content, can be combined with other ingredients to make delicious dips. Instead of using oil in the pâté of smoked cod's roe we use soya milk and ground fresh nuts. Liver pâté containing custard apple pulp is another light and tasty innovation. All these show how easy it is to dispense with animal fat.

All pâtés are excellent for a quick snack or starter, spread on toast or crisp-bread, with lettuce or cucumber as garnish. They can also be a handy filling for tomatoes, celery sticks or tartlets. Dips can be consumed with sticks of carrot or celery, or the softer ones with pieces of chicory or Chinese leaves.

Oeuf surprise de kiwi • *Stuffed kiwi with egg and chilli*

The kiwi fruit or Chinese gooseberry comes in several varieties and is named after the wingless New Zealand bird whose whiskery body the fruit resembles. The fruit is rich in vitamins A, C and D, and has a powerful enzyme which can break down any protein. Added raw to cream or milk it will curdle them; it will tenderise fish or meat. The fruit is ripe if it gives slightly to pressure. It may be bought while still firm but will ripen quickly in a warm place.

Eaten raw, kiwis are pleasantly astringent, and deserve better than being merely an ornamental garnish. They may be halved, spooned out and eaten like avocado, and this gave me the idea for this egg and chilli pâté. In a healthy eating routine, seasoning with chilli helps to cut down on salt. If preferred, you can use 2 dashes of Tabasco sauce.

2 large ripe kiwi fruit
1 tablespoon sunflower oil
1 small shallot, peeled and chopped
1 small green chilli, seeded and thinly sliced
1 egg, beaten
1 tablespoon fromage frais (page 179)

Slice the top off each kiwi to produce a hat-like cover. Scoop out the pulp with a small teaspoon without damaging the skin. Reserve the pulp and skins.

Heat the oil in a pan and stir fry the shallot and sliced chilli until tender. Stir in the beaten egg and kiwi pulp and scramble for 2 minutes. Remove from the heat and liquidise until smooth with the cheese. Fill the kiwi skins with the mixture and replace the tops. Serve hot or cold in an egg cup. **Serves 2.**

Pâté de laitance à l'orange • Smoked cod's roe pâté with orange

Citrus fruit is an ideal accompaniment to any kind of fish. In this delicious smokey fish pâté, made without oil, the fine flavour of cod's roe harmonises well with the sharp sweetness of the orange segments used as garnish with lettuce leaves. Blood oranges belong to a variety known as Sanguine or Mori; they come to the market in winter, after the best-known orange variety, the Valencia.

Orange trees blossomed in the famed Hanging Gardens of Babylon as early as 800 B.C. and spread through Europe from the 16th century onwards. The orange of today is one of nature's marvels. It contains 13 different minerals and 10 vitamins, notably vitamin C. The rind holds 11 aromatics.

150g/5oz smoked cod's roe
juice of ½ lemon and ½ orange
50g/2oz shelled roasted peanuts
50g/2oz fresh breadcrumbs
100ml/4fl oz soya milk or plain low-fat yogurt
¼ teaspoon freshly ground black pepper
2 blood oranges
lettuce leaves
paprika

Remove the roe thoroughly from the skin and mix with the lemon and orange juices. Toast the peanuts in the oven for 5 minutes, or under the grill for 1 minute, until golden, then crush with a rolling pin. Soak the breadcrumbs and peanuts in the soya milk for 30 minutes. Liquidise the roe and breadcrumb mixture to a paste. Alternatively, a mincer may be used for a coarser mixture, or pass through a sieve. Season with pepper and chill, covered, for 1 hour.

Meanwhile, with a cannelle knife make a groove around the circumference of each orange. Insert the handle of a spoon between skin and flesh to remove the skin without tearing it, thus producing four orange-peel cups. Slice the orange flesh.

To serve, fill the orange cups with the pâté. Place each orange cup on a plate and surround by a few orange slices and a couple of lettuce leaves. Sprinkle a little paprika on the pâté. Serve with crispbread or French bread. **Serves 4**.

Pâté d'annone aux foies de volaille • Chicken liver pâté with custard apple

The custard apple, a tropical fruit, is oval-shaped and weighs between 225 and 450g (8oz and 1lb). The quilted skin can vary in colour from yellow to tan with red markings. The cherimoya, another variety of the species, has a scaly skin like a pine-cone. Custard apples can be eaten raw. Simply cut the fruit in half and spoon out the rich yellow-white pulp, discarding the brown seeds. The flavour resembles a cross between banana and pineapple. The pulp can be mixed with banana and cream to make a delicious fruit dip, or it can be liquidised with four times its volume of soda water for a refreshing drink. This pâté is wonderfully flavoursome and not so greasy as the usual liver pâté made with animal fat. If possible, buy livers from free range, corn-fed chickens.

    225g (8oz) chicken livers
    milk
    1 small shallot, peeled and chopped
    25g/1oz polyunsaturated margarine
    2 slices of chilli, or dash of Tabasco sauce
    50g/2oz cashew nuts, slightly toasted
    100g/4oz custard apple pulp
    good pinch of mixed spice
    salt

Clean the livers, removing all dark or discoloured bits; do not burst them. Soak the livers in milk for 30 minutes; drain and discard the milk.

Stir fry the shallot in the margarine for 2 minutes without browning. Add the livers, chilli and nuts and toss and cook for 5 minutes. Liquidise the mixture with the custard

35

apple pulp to produce a smooth paste. Add the spice and salt to taste, and pack into individual ramekin dishes. Cover and chill overnight. Serve with sippets of wholemeal bread or crudités of your choice. **Serves 4.**

Pâté de truite fumée au pamplemousse ◆ Smoked trout pâté with grapefruit

This delicious pâté was a speciality of the renowned Hermitage restaurant at Le Touquet where I did part of my training as a chef. It combines the subtle flavours of the trout with the tangy freshness of grapefruit to bring out the best of both.

Trout is a good source of protein, minerals and some vitamins. When fresh, it can be poached or grilled, or eaten raw after marinating in citrus juice. It has been a favourite dish of royalty, such as the Prince Regent when the great Carême was his chef, and Queen Victoria, who liked brown trout. Nowadays it is the pink-fleshed rainbow trout, introduced from North America, which is the favourite.

Grapefruit is rich in vitamins, minerals and trace elements. It plays an important part in the diet, for breakfast and other meals.

2 smoked trout, skinned and boned
1 small shallot, peeled and chopped
1 hard-boiled egg, shelled and sliced
150g/5oz fromage frais (page 179)
juice of ½ lemon
small bunch of fresh chives, coarsely snipped with scissors
4 lettuce leaves
1 grapefruit, peeled and segmented
150g/5oz bean sprouts
50g/2oz red pepper, cut into very thin strips
freshly ground black pepper

Mince the trout with the shallot and egg, and mix in the cheese. Blend in the lemon juice and chives. Place in individual ramekins, cover and chill. To serve, place the ramekins on individual plates. Arrange lettuce leaves and grapefruit segments neatly on the plates and sprinkle over them the bean sprouts, pepper strips and a little black pepper. **Serves 4.**

Pâté de lentilles aux carottes epicées • Ginger-flavoured lentil and carrot pâté

Lentils are one of the oldest foods in existence and are exceedingly nutritious, being rich in protein. They are largely used in soups, stews or purées; here they are made into a delicious pâté. Unlike other dried beans and peas, split red lentils do not require overnight soaking before cooking.

As for carrots, no Frenchman will ever forget the Battle of Crécy where a crop of carrots was ruined and our honour lost. As a result of this, in classical cuisine the term Crécy in a recipe title signifies that a dish contains carrot. Vitamins A and C are found in carrots and they contribute important dietary fibre when eaten raw.

The texture of this pâté can be softened to make a dip by adding some of the lentil cooking liquor.

150g/5oz split red lentils
150g/5oz carrots, scraped and grated
50g/2oz onion, peeled and chopped
2 garlic cloves, peeled and chopped
2 tablespoons olive oil
1 teaspoon Madras curry powder
1 tablespoon yeast extract
salt
good pinch of coarsely ground black pepper
juice of 1 lemon
½ piece of preserved ginger
5 tablespoons plain low-fat yogurt

Put the lentils and carrots in a pan with enough water barely to cover them. Bring to the boil, remove the scum and gently cook for 20 minutes until soft.

Meanwhile, stir fry the onion and garlic in the oil for 2 minutes. Sprinkle in the curry powder and cook a further 30 seconds, stirring.

Drain the lentils and carrots and mix with the curried onion mixture. Mash well and season with the yeast extract, salt, pepper and lemon juice to taste. Cover and chill well.

Liquidise the ginger and yogurt and blend into the lentil paste at the last minute. Serve in individual ramekins with crudités. **Serves 4**.

Pâté à l'ail aux pommes • Garlic and potato pâté

Garlic has been venerated from classical times for its remarkable range of culinary uses, as well as the almost magical healing powers credited to it. Homer tells us that it was to the virtues of garlic that Ulysses owed his escape from being changed by Circe into a pig.

Many cuisines would be lost without the beautiful capacity of garlic to enhance flavour. Rubbed on a crust of bread in the bottom of the bowl, its aroma permeates a green salad. It partners tomatoes well and is the essence of many wine sauces. Fish brushed with garlic paste is particularly delicious.

The curative properties of garlic have been amply proved ever since Roman soldiers used it to heal their wounds. I can personally testify to its effectiveness. As a child I was severely stung by a swarm of bees. My dear grandma, Mathilde, quickly mashed up a whole pound of juicy garlic with poppy seeds (a herbal morphia) and covered me with this poultice. The village doctor said it saved my life. I have also found garlic most effective for sciatica and rheumatism. A syrup of garlic or onion is a fine remedy for colds, asthma and sore throat: mix the juice of several cloves with honey, let it set for an hour and take it on a lettuce leaf or crust of bread.

225g/8oz potatoes, peeled and sliced
6 garlic cloves, peeled and crushed
1 small onion, peeled and chopped
2 tablespoons sunflower oil
juice of ½ lemon
1 egg, beaten
salt and coarsely ground black pepper

Cook the potatoes in boiling water for 20 minutes until soft. Drain and mash. Stir fry the garlic and onion in the oil for 1 minute without browning. Liquidise the mixture with the lemon juice and beaten egg and add to the potato purée. Season to taste. Serve this pâté either hot or cold, with crudités. **Serves 2 to 4**.

A Provençal variation of this dish is to add to the potato purée half its weight of cooked smoked haddock.

◆ HERB DIPS AND PÂTÉS ◆

Herbs are having a revival. They are being used more abundantly nowadays than in Escoffier's time, thanks to the cooks of Nouvelle Cuisine who employ them for their decorative appeal and aromatic fragrance. In Cuisine Fraîcheur and the Love Apple Diet we are also concerned with their therapeutic value – their importance for health.

Developing a knowledge of herbs and their uses can be very rewarding in enhancing the appeal of your food and drink. The first step is to build up a memory-bank of their different aromas. Simply squeeze the herb, sniff it intensely as you might savour the bouquet of a wine, and try to memorise its mix of scents and odours. Next you will develop your instinct for what herbs work best for a particular food, the kind of 'nose' possessed by the master-chef. Fruit cocktails offer pleasant practice. Your palate will tell you, for instance, that apple juice with mint, grapefruit juice with sage, and tomato juice with a little basil have a certain rightness about them.

Fresh herbs are invariably best, and it is well worth cultivating a herb plot in your garden or window-box. As your experience and nose will tell you, some dried or packeted herbs can be an acceptable second-best. Thyme and sage retain their fragrance well in dried form. With many others, however, too much of the essential has evaporated; parsley and chervil, for example, are poor value in dried form. Fresh parsley should never be washed *after* chopping, as some cooks do. Wash the whole stalk first and shake dry, then chop on a clean board, place the herbs in a cloth and squeeze dry. Take care to collect any juice for use in salad dressing or soup.

In the following recipes, we show how the right herbs can enrich the flavour of some fine pâtês. But first we review the great range of herbs and their uses.

Herbs are divided into pot herbs, sweet or aromatic herbs, and wild plants usable in cooking. *Pot herbs* include: parsley, purslane, tarragon, fennel, borage, chervil, horseradish, Indian cress, watercress, marigold, chives, onion and garlic. *Sweet herbs* include: thyme, sage, savory, mint, marjoram, basil, clary, rosemary, lavender, costmary, sweet cicely and dill (fennel fern). *Wild plants and herbs* include: charlock or wild mustard, ox-tongue or bugloss, hawkweed, burdock, willow-herb, fat hen or Good King Henry, sea-orache, sea-beet, samphire, saw-thistle, stinging nettle, chickweed and rocket.

In modern cooking, the range of herbs and vegetables used is always expanding. Examples of popular combinations include vichyssoise with chives; watercress sauce; sorrel omelette; pesto with pine nuts and basil; tarragon in béarnaise sauce and mint in the paloise sauce variation; dill sauce with salmon coulibiac; samphire with scallops; shallots with mussels; chervil with consommé; and the essential bouquet garni composed of bay leaf, parsley stalk, sprig of thyme and celery leaves.

The Use of Herbs and Aromatic Plants

Group 1 (herbs containing cineole)
Bay leaf: from the evergreen shrub, *Laurus nobilis*. Sweet and light in flavour with spicy undertone. Used in stock, soups and most stews, and with certain oily fish and tomato dishes. Also for dish decoration when green.
Rosemary: leaves, flowers and stems of the sweet-scented plant *Rosemarinus officinalis*. Pleasant and tenacious flavour. Used with fish and a large variety of vegetables and meats.

Group 2 (herbs containing eugenol)
West Indian bay: from a wild tree *Myrica acris*. Fresh and spicy flavour with strong clove character, warm and pungent with a bitter after-note. Used in sharp sauces and stock.

Group 3 (herbs containing thymol carvacrol)
Wild marjoram or oregano: the wild plant *Origanum vulgare*, found everywhere. Strong, fresh, sweet and spicy with a dominant flavour of eucalyptus. Warm and bittersweet. Used in pickles, soups, sauces and stews; with vegetables, pasta and rice dishes.
Savory: the plants *Satureja hortensis* (summer savory) and *S.montana* (winter savory), native to the Mediterranean countries. Sharp, sweet yet slightly bitter and not unlike thyme and sage. Used in soup, stocks, vegetable dishes and salads.
Thyme: from the common garden plant *Thymus vulgaris*. Very strong flavour with the marked thymol aroma. Used in the bouquet garni for all stocks and stews and for decorative purposes. Also good with fish and shellfish, as in moules marinières.
Mexican sage or oregano: *Salvia horminum*, from the Latin countries. Very strong, distinctive flavour. Used with all tomato dishes, chutneys and pickles; soups and stews; cereals, pasta and rice dishes and with vegetables.

Group 4 (the sweet herbs)
Basil: leaves and flowering tips of the plant *Ocimum basilicum*. A typically French herb with two detectable chemical characteristics – linalol and estragol. Sweet and spicy odour with a fresh, slightly balsamic undertone. Used mostly with fish, in tomato dishes and stews with beans. One of the ingredients of pesto, with pine nuts.
Marjoram: Southern Mediterranean species, commonly cultivated in herb gardens. Aromatic and spicy, not unlike nutmeg and cardamom with a bitter backnote. Less pungent than sage and can be used instead of it.
Parsley: from the herb family *Petroselinum*. Best in flavour when freshly chopped and used on the spot. Used in salads and stews, with all kinds of vegetables and in almost any dish with sauce or butter.
English sage: leaves of *Salvia officinalis*. Stronger flavour than marjoram and as good dried as when fresh. Used with other herbs in pâtés, in oily fish and white fish salads.

Group 5 (herbs containing thujone)
Dalmatian sage: a wild species of the common sage. Strong, sweet and astringent. Used in

meat dishes, certain fish pâtés and terrines, and with oily fish; and in vegetable casseroles.

Group 6 (the mint family)
Mint: many varieties come from the species *Mentha*, both wild and cultivated. These include spearmint (*Mentha spicata*), applemint (*M. rotundifolia* var. *suaveolens*) and peppermint (*M. X piperita*), perhaps the most familiar herb aroma. Uses are wide ranging, in salads, sauces, compound butters and mayonnaise (delicious with salmon, trout and other cold oily fish); with all the pulses, fresh peas, in soups with cucumber, and in the cucumber-garlic sauce, Raita; also with yogurt products, fruit salads, fruit cocktails, and in tisanes. New potatoes always need their little garnish of fresh mint. Very attractive either frosted or fresh as dish decoration.

Pâté d'herbes fines au yaourt • *Herb pâté with yogurt*

225g/8oz fromage frais (page 179)
150ml/5fl oz plain low-fat yogurt
1 tablespoon snipped fresh chives
1 tablespoon chopped fresh parsley
1 teaspoon chopped fresh tarragon leaves
1 garlic clove, peeled and finely chopped
juice of ½ lemon
good pinch of freshly ground black pepper

Beat the cheese and yogurt together in a bowl and blend in the herbs, garlic, lemon juice and pepper. (The garlic could be first liquidised in the lemon juice or squeezed garlic juice used.) Pack into individual ramekins, cover and chill well. **Serves 4.**

Pâté de concombre au yaourt • *Cucumber and minted yogurt pâté*

300ml/½ pint plain low-fat yogurt
50g/2oz walnut kernels
2 garlic cloves, peeled and chopped
freshly ground black pepper
6 fresh mint leaves, chopped
1 teaspoon chopped fresh parsley
150g/5oz cucumber, cut into very small cubes with skin

Liquidise yogurt, walnuts and garlic to a purée. Season with a little pepper and blend in the fresh herbs and diced cucumber. Leave for 30 minutes, and serve as a dip with crudités. **Serves 4**.

Fromage de soya oriental • Oriental soya cheese

1 spring onion, chopped, or 1 small onion, peeled and finely chopped
1 tablespoon sunflower oil
1 teaspoon curry powder
300g/10oz firm tofu, cut into small cubes
1 garlic clove, peeled and crushed
1 tablespoon soya or Worcestershire sauce
slice of fresh root ginger (the size of a grape), peeled
100ml/4fl oz water
slice of fresh pineapple, peeled, cored and chopped
juice of 1 lemon
1 teaspoon honey
1 teaspoon snipped fresh chives
3 fresh basil leaves

Stir fry the onion in the oil for 1 minute. Sprinkle in the curry powder and cook for a further 30 seconds. Add the tofu, garlic, soya sauce, ginger and water. Cook for 5 minutes, stirring occasionally, then liquidise to a purée with the pineapple, lemon juice, honey and herbs. Chill in a bowl, and serve in individual dishes as a dip with prawn crackers or matzos or fresh crudités. **Serves 4**.

Pâté de champignon de prairie à l'éstragon • Mushroom pâté with tarragon

Mushrooms are immensely valuable in a healthy diet. They contain more protein for their weight than almost any other vegetable. They are also richer in vitamins B1, B2 and B6 with only 7 calories per 100g (4oz). They contain no cholesterol or carbohydrate but have essential minerals like potassium, copper and phosphorus. No wonder the notables of ancient Rome, Egypt and China esteemed them as 'food for the gods'.

In preparing mushrooms, the skin of the larger sort (which are best for grilling) may be removed, but it is not necessary. Mushrooms should be washed quickly, drained well and wiped dry. The stalks can be saved for soups, sauces and stuffing. (See chapter 9 for other recipes on wild mushrooms.) If field mushrooms are not available, button or cup mushrooms may be used to make this pâté.

50g/2oz onion, peeled and chopped
2 garlic cloves, peeled and chopped
2 tablespoons sunflower oil
225g/8oz field mushrooms, chopped
25g/1oz fresh breadcrumbs or chopped walnuts
2 eggs, beaten
1 teaspoon tomato purée, or 1 small tomato, skinned, seeded and chopped
1 tablespoon chopped, mixed fresh parsley and tarragon leaves
good pinch of grated nutmeg (or mace) and black pepper mixed
salt or 1 teaspoon yeast extract
50ml/2fl oz plain low-fat yogurt

Stir fry the onion and garlic in the oil for 2 minutes without browning. Add the mushrooms and cook for 2 minutes. Blend in the breadcrumbs or walnuts. After 4 more minutes' cooking, beat in the eggs. Mix in the tomato purée or the tomato and chopped herbs and season to taste. Finally add the yogurt to produce a balance of acidulation and creaminess.

Pack the pâté into individual ramekins. Cover and chill. Serve with crudités, especially celery and carrot, or spread on toasted French bread. **Serves 4**.

The flavour of the pâté may be enhanced by adding 1 tablespoon mushroom ketchup with the tomato purée. To make a richer pâté, use 4 tablespoons of single cream instead of yogurt. If liked, garnish with sliced white mushrooms marinated in lemon juice for 10 minutes, and then dabbed with a little olive oil.

Pâté de maquereau au topinambour ◆ Mackerel pâté with Jerusalem artichoke

Mackerel is one of the cheapest fish of the tuna family, rich in protein and delicious when smoked. It can be marinated in lemon juice, then grilled or poached, and served cold with a salad (or it can be eaten raw after marinating in lemon or lime juice).

The Jerusalem artichoke is a very good winter vegetable, low in calories, rich in sodium, potassium, thiamin and vitamin C when uncooked. This vegetable was introduced to western Europe from North America in the early 17th century. Its rather strange name probably arose from a corruption of the Italian name for the sunflower artichoke, Girasole articiocco. When shopping, avoid small, bruised or broken tubers. Prime artichokes are fairly regular in shape and measure up to 10cm/4 inches long and 5cm/2 inches in diameter. They are best eaten raw – simply peel, wash and slice, and serve with lemon or lime juice. They can also be baked in their skins (after a good scrub), made into a purée or sautéed.

In this recipe the Jerusalem artichoke is used in two ways: first, some of the cooked vegetable is blended with mackerel in the pâté; secondly, raw artichoke adds its subtle flavour to the salad.

2 smoked mackerel, skinned, boned and minced
150g/5oz Jerusalem artichoke, peeled, cooked and mashed
2 sticks of rhubarb, peeled, diced and cooked until tender (3 minutes)
freshly ground black pepper
75ml/3fl oz plain low-fat yogurt
1 spring onion, chopped
1 hard-boiled egg, shelled and chopped
150g/5oz raw beetroot, peeled and grated
150g/5oz Jerusalem artichoke, peeled, cut into strips and marinated in lemon juice
4 lettuce leaves or some curly endive

Combine in a large bowl the minced mackerel flesh with the cooked artichoke and rhubarb. Season with black pepper (no salt is needed). Blend in the yogurt, spring onion and egg. Chill the mixture for 1 hour.

To serve, sprinkle some of the beetroot and raw artichoke on a lettuce leaf on each plate. Spoon the pâté into the centre. Serve as a starter, or use as a sandwich filling. **Serves 4**.

For a smoother pâté, put it through the liquidiser. Single cream can be used instead of yogurt.

Pâté chaud de saumon dans un nid de feuilles d'artichaut • Hot salmon pâté in a nest of globe artichoke leaves

The globe artichoke is among the oldest cultivated vegetables, originating in Asia but grown in southern Europe for centuries. It comes in two varieties, one purple and the other green. It is valuable in a diet, with a calorie-count of only 7 per 100g (4oz). This versatile vegetable can be boiled, baked, fried and stuffed (as in this recipe), and eaten hot or cold.

Globe artichokes are found in the shops from May to September, although they are probably best between July and August. The bought artichoke should look fresh, with stiff leaves that have a slight bloom to them and a few inches of stalk attached. Avoid artichokes that have fully open leaves or which have fuzzy, miscoloured centres, as these will have gone beyond their best.

4 globe artichokes
lemon juice
2 tablespoons plain flour
2 tablespoons oil
2 tablespoons wine vinegar
150g/5oz skinned salmon fillet
2 tablespoons cider vinegar

La soupe andalousienne · Pepper and tomato soup (page 54)

Above: Pascaline de kiwi au fromage · Kiwi and curd moulds (page 77)

Opposite: Truite tartare Tolstoy · Rainbow trout tartare (page 79)

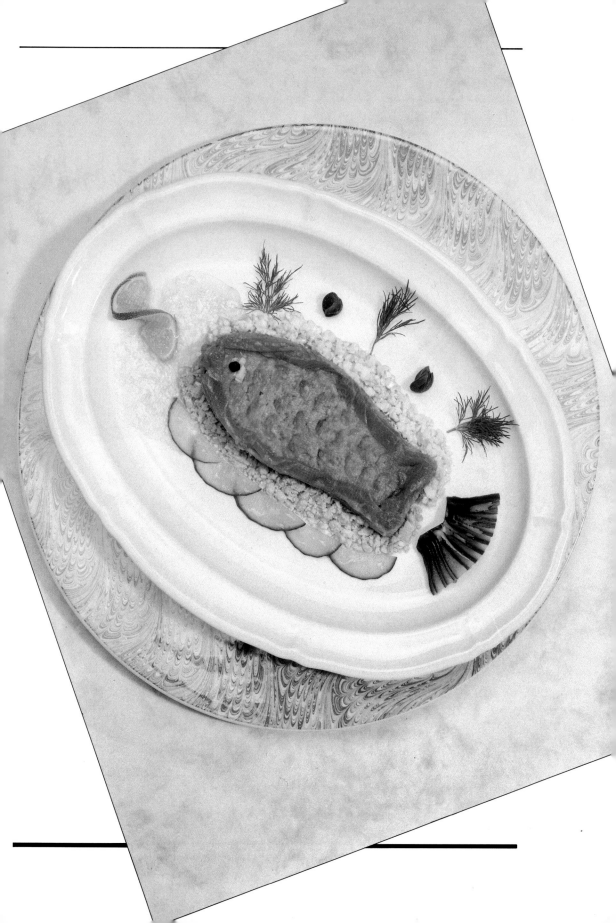

Above: Terrine de truite aux asperges ·
Rainbow trout loaf with asparagus (page 78)

Below: Les quatre purées hivernales ·
Winter vegetable purées (page 92)

sprig of fresh dill
freshly ground black pepper
75ml/3fl oz plain low-fat yogurt

Cut off the artichoke stalks two-thirds from the bottom and trim off the points from the outer leaves, leaving the top of each artichoke flat. Rub the cut surfaces with lemon juice to avoid discoloration. Mix the flour with 4 tablespoons of cold water into a paste. Blend this into 1.5 litres (2½ pints) of cold water. This is called a *blanc*. Add the oil and wine vinegar.

Bring the liquid to the boil, add the artichokes and simmer for 30 to 40 minutes or until a leaf comes away easily when gently pulled. Drain the artichokes upside down and when cool enough to handle, remove the hairy choke with a spoon to expose the bottom fleshy part or heart. You now have a cavity large enough to insert the filling. Keep the artichokes warm.

Place the fish in an earthenware dish. Add the cider vinegar, 75ml/3fl oz water and the dill sprig, and season well with pepper. Cover with greased foil or a lid. Bake for 10 minutes at 200 °C, 400 °F, Mark 6 (or poach on top of the stove using a metal dish). When cooked, liquidise the fish together with the poaching liquid, the dill and yogurt to reduce to a purée. Check the seasoning. Fill each artichoke with the pâté. Serve hot, or chilled, with lemon wedges. **Serves 4**.

Pâté de hareng saur aux courgettes • Kipper pâté with courgettes

Courgettes belong to the squash family, and are also known as zucchini and baby marrow. Though they have little nutritive value without the skin they can combine well with other ingredients, as in this tasty recipe, to produce a balanced dish. Home-grown courgettes are available from June to October, but imports from many countries make them available all year.

Usually at their best when 10 to 15cm (4 to 6 inches) long, courgettes can be bitter when longer or older and are then palatable only if cooked. They should be firm and shiny with a rich green colour and without blemishes.

Courgettes may be scrubbed but never peeled. They can be cut into fingers, sliced on a slant, or cut in half lengthways. Or, as in this recipe, they may be hollowed down the centre and filled with a cooked carrot.

225g/8oz kipper fillets
milk
2 shallots, chopped
2 tablespoons horseradish cream
75ml/3fl oz plain Greek-style strained yogurt

juice of ½ lemon
1 small garlic clove, peeled and finely chopped
75g/3oz mashed potatoes
1 tablespoon honey
1 teaspoon snipped fresh chives
freshly ground black pepper

garnish:
2 courgettes
2 spring carrots, scraped and parboiled for 4 minutes only

Soak the kipper fillets in milk for 15 minutes to remove excess salt. Drain and pat dry. Combine the kippers and remaining pâté ingredients in a bowl and leave to macerate for 30 minutes. Season with pepper, then liquidise to a paste. Put in a bowl, cover and chill for 1 hour.

Meanwhile, make grooves down the length of each courgette using a cannelle knife or lemon zester. Hollow out the courgettes lengthways with an apple corer to make a hole large enough to take a carrot. Put a cooked carrot in each courgette hole and blanch in boiling salted water for 2 minutes. Allow to cool.

Serve the pâté in a lettuce leaf in the centre of each plate. Slice the courgettes across on a slant and arrange neatly beside or around the pâté in an attractive pattern. Serve with sippets of wholemeal bread or crudités. **Serves 2 to 4**.

LES SOUPES FRAÎCHES
HOME-MADE SOUPS

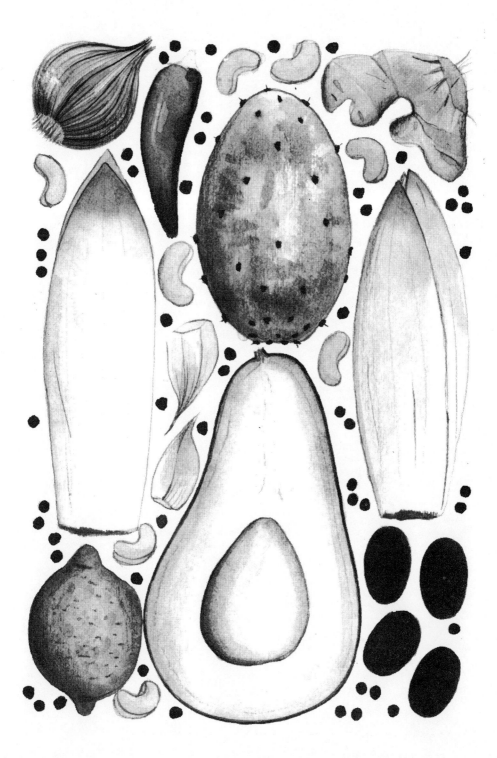

One charming country custom is the ritual of beginning a meal with a good bowl of soup, or it can be made into 'a meal in itself'. In France we say *manger la soupe* ('eat the soup') possibly because, as with country families like my own, the soup was made so thick with added ingredients, like the rich wholemeal bread my grandmother used to favour, that eating was a more accurate description than sipping or drinking.

Nourishing soups are an excellent dietary medium for young children, the elderly or invalids. When people have lost their appetite, or have difficulty in swallowing or digesting solid foods, then soup is ideal because the nutrients are well blended into the broth.

To make a soup, broth or consommé nourishing, it is desirable to add protein in the form of bread, vegetables, chicken, fish, eggs or cheese. Mostly these are added in cooked form, sometimes diced or grated, or liquidised into a purée for easier mixing with the broth. In the case of eggs, the yolks are usually blended with a little cream or milk and added to the soup away from the heat, then gently reheated without boiling to prevent curdling the soup. This gentle reheating is also necessary when adding yogurt.

Modern vegetarian soups make good use of nuts like peanuts, cashews, almonds and hazelnuts which can be toasted for better flavour, then ground or liquidised with the liquid.

A clear fish or meat consommé provides only a tiny amount of protein extracted from the source. A more nourishing soup will result from liquidising the protein foods mentioned above into cream soups, or eat them whole in a sort of peasant soup with beans, lentils, peas or bits of fish or meat if you are a meat-eater. As the following recipes show, there are so many good things to add that one could say the whole Garden of Eden may be served in a bowl.

Very up-to-date and nutritious are the refreshing cold soups, some of them uncooked like the Spanish gazpacho. The recipes here include a number of delicious examples of these raw-ingredient soups. They are best served freshly-made, when their flavour and nutrients are more intact. There is a selection of raw fruit soups, with intriguing new flavours and textures. Once you have tried one of these cold soups it will no doubt become one of your favourite starters or light meals.

We also present recipes which offer tasty dishes with the right amount of protein for a balanced meal, soups that can be served on their own with consequent saving of kitchen labour. Since they are a complete meal, not merely a starter, they can be eaten at any time of day you choose. Of course, if you are in good appetite, adjust the portion size and they can form part of a three-course lunch or dinner. The menu charts on p. 216–7 offer suggestions on the right balance of such a repast though the combination is left to you.

◆ RAW SOUPS ◆

Avocadine ◆ Avocado soup

Avocados originated in Central and South America where Aztecs and Incas prized them as food, and as a beauty aid on account of their natural oil content. Highly nutritious fruit, full of vitamins and some protein, avocados are now widely available all year round. There are several different varieties. The four principal ones imported are: Fuerte – oval, with dark green, roughish and spotted skin; Hass – smaller, with purple/black, rough and pebbly skin; Ettinger – oval, with bright green, shiny skin; and Nabal – plump and round with shiny green skin.

Avocados can be bought ready to eat, but if still firm, ripen them at home in a warm place such as the airing cupboard. To speed the ripening process, place in a bag with an apple. To test for ripeness cradle the fruit in the palm of your hand – when it yields to gentle pressure it is ready to eat. Once ripe, it should be eaten within 2 to 3 days.

To prepare an avocado, cut it in half lengthways, then gently twist the halves apart, loosen the stone with a knife and remove. If not serving immediately, rub the exposed flesh with lemon or lime juice to prevent discoloration, wrap closely and keep cool. Serve the avocado simply with a wedge of fresh lemon or lime, or filled with any of the following: fresh orange or grapefruit segments, diced fresh pineapple, diced tomatoes with chopped spring onion, raw sliced mushrooms tossed in vinaigrette sauce, diced marinated raw fish (see pages 105-6), chopped eggs, caviar, or mixed grated vegetables. The pulp of the avocado can be used as a spread on toast with ground toasted nuts, or mixed into any raw leaf salads. Also use the pulp instead of oil in any dressing.

1 ripe avocado, peeled and stoned
1 large tomato, halved and seeds squeezed out
2 spring onions (leave as much green stalk as possible)
small bunch of fresh fenugreek leaves, chopped (about 4 tablespoons)
100ml/4fl oz plain low-fat yogurt
⅛ teaspoon coarsely ground black pepper
salt
1 teaspoon cider vinegar
juice of 1 lime

Combine all the ingredients in a bowl, cover tightly and let them macerate for 30 minutes in the refrigerator. Liquidise to a thin purée. Chill in individual bowls and serve with savoury biscuits or matzos. **Serves 2.**

La soupe de figue de barbarie • Prickly pear potage

The prickly pear, sometimes known as Indian fig, is a member of the cactus family. It originated in South America, and it was Christopher Columbus who brought this fruit to Europe; it is now grown in the Mediterranean and other temperate regions. Limited supplies are imported into Britain from Italy and Mexico during early winter months.

The pear-shaped fruits are 7 to 8cm (about 3 inches) long and have a greenish-orange skin covered with tiny prickles. Handle them carefully, preferably with gloves.

To prepare a prickly pear, scrub it under the tap with a stiff brush to remove all the spines. Cut a slice from each end, then make a cut from end to end, taking care not to cut too deeply into the flesh. Peel back the skin completely to reveal the pinkish-orange flesh. This is normally eaten raw, sliced, with fresh lime or lemon juice which combine well with the sweet, aromatic flavour of the prickly pear. It can be cooked but loses its vital properties.

Prickly pear may be served raw and on its own as a breakfast starter, or it marries well with grapefruit in a fruit cocktail. A combination of prickly pear, peach, raspberries and orange makes a superb fruit salad.

1 ripe prickly pear, skinned and sliced
juice of 1 lime
150ml/5fl oz soya milk
50g/2oz fresh wholemeal or corn breadcrumbs
1 tablespoon cider vinegar
juice of ½ orange
1 teaspoon honey
slice of fresh root ginger (the size of a grape), peeled

Combine all the ingredients in a bowl, cover tightly and allow to macerate for 30 minutes in the refrigerator. Liquidise to a purée. Serve well chilled; to achieve the right temperature quickly, put the soup in your freezer for 15 minutes. Garnish the soup with a twisted slice of lime and two blood orange segments. **Serves 2.**

Délice de mangue frappée • Iced mango soup

Acclaimed as one of the most delicious and luxurious tropical fruits, the mango is known to have several thousand years of history as a food. (Buddha was said to have been presented with a mango grove to rest beneath.) I can still recall the way I was bowled over by the powerful, almost intoxicating aroma of this fruit when I first went ashore in the Caribbean nearly 50 years ago, when I was a young chef on a French cruise liner. In pre-war years the mango was not used in classical cuisine except as a chutney.

Mangoes vary a good deal in size, shape and colour, according to variety. They can be round, heart- or kidney-shaped and, when ripe, skin-colour ranges from yellow to orange or scarlet. Buy firm unblemished fruit and ripen at home in a warm place. They are best eaten when fully ripe, that is soft to the touch. Modern varieties, like Haydon and Tommy Atkins, are less fibrous and have thinner skins. The fruit is available all year round from many tropical countries. Mangoes are rich in vitamins, particularly vitamin A.

Mangoes are easy enough to eat once you know the secret of removing the stone. Put the mango, flat side down, on the chopping board. Cut a thick slice from the top of the fruit as near to the stone as possible. Turn it over and repeat the cut. The two halves can then be eaten as they are by scooping out the flesh. With their delicious sweet flavour, mangoes are best eaten on their own, but they also make an excellent addition to a fruit salad. Or they can be converted into lovely sorbets, mousses and – as you will find below – into a delectable soup. Green mangoes can be made into chutneys, too.

The soup here includes fresh tender spears of raw asparagus which are deliciously crunchy and palatable. As a little snack on their own they could be dipped into yogurt or an avocado dip. They blend very harmoniously with mango to create, to my taste, a most elegant new soup.

100g/4oz asparagus (about 4 thin spears)
1 ripe mango, skinned and stoned
100ml/4fl oz buttermilk
juice of 1 orange
slice of green chilli
mere pinch of sea salt

Make sure to use fresh, tender asparagus. Taste one spear raw first; peel the skin lightly if stringy, and cut into small pieces.

Combine the asparagus with the mango pulp, buttermilk, orange juice, chilli and salt in a bowl. Stir well, cover tightly and macerate in refrigerator for 20 minutes. Liquidise to a thin purée. Serve in a glass dish garnished with a sprig of fresh mint or a twisted slice of lime. **Serves 2.**

La soupe aux pêches Marie-José ◆ Peach soup with apple juice

Peaches are commercially divided into two classes – 'free-stones' and 'cling-stones'. The former, in which the flesh easily separates from skin and stone, are earliest and best for table use. They are akin to the nectarine, which is a cross between a Victoria plum and a peach. The cling-stone peach keeps longer in its fresh state than the free-stone and is the more familiar type in the shops. It is round and velvety, and its yellow skin is beautifully flushed with red when ripe.

Some people prefer to peel off the slightly bitter skin before eating a peach raw or poaching. Peaches are also available in dried form. In this diet we do not recommend canned peaches. Buy the fresh fruit unripe and let it mature at home in a warm place.

4 medium-size ripe peaches, stoned and sliced
150ml/5fl oz apple juice, pressed at the last minute
pinch of ground cinnamon
1 small stale bread roll, crumbled or cut into thin slices
100ml/4fl oz water
150ml/5fl oz buttermilk

Soak the peaches in the apple juice flavoured with the cinnamon for 20 minutes. Soak the stale roll in the water until soft. Combine all ingredients in a large bowl and mix well. Cover tightly and leave to macerate for 15 minutes. Liquidise the mixture to a thin purée. Serve well chilled in bowls garnished with a slice of peach, 2 raspberries and a mint leaf. If a sharper flavour is desired, add the juice of 1 lemon. **Serves 2.**

La soupe au melon aux raisins blancs • Melon soup with seedless grapes and buttermilk

Three kinds of melon are usually available, divided according to the colour of their flesh. First come the aromatic Musk melons with their orangey flesh – the cantaloup, citron, nutmeg and pineapple melons. Secondly, there are the big dark-green watermelons with red flesh and black seeds. Finally, there are the honeydew melons with white or pale green flesh. Varieties of this type include the Galia, sweet in flavour with white, net-like skin markings, the Ogen from Israel and Charentais from France. The Ogen and Charentais, from similar seed strains, are very sweet and have perhaps the finest flavour.

Test a melon for ripeness with gentle pressure at the stalk end. A ripe melon should also have an aroma, especially the Musk varieties. As with other fruit they can be bought firm and ripened at home.

Large melons can be first cut into wedges, then into smaller pieces in a boat shape. They may be garnished with a slice of orange, lemon or lime, plus a cocktail stick holding glacé cherries or grapes or banana. Serve well chilled.

1 small Ogen melon, or 225g/8oz wedge of watermelon, peeled and seeded
150ml/5fl oz buttermilk
150g/5oz seedless grapes
pinch of ground ginger, or a small piece of preserved ginger
1 teaspoon honey

Combine the melon flesh with the remaining ingredients in a large bowl. Cover tightly and leave to macerate for 20 minutes. Liquidise to a thin purée. Serve chilled, with mint leaves and a few sprigs of small seedless grapes as garnish. **Serves 2.**

La soupe andalousienne • Pepper and tomato soup

This gorgeous soup is one of my favourites. It brings to my palate the fine country aromas of Andalusia, a beautiful land where olive and orange groves mingle in the hot sun of the south. Another more personal reason for my liking this soup is that the small town of Conil there is a souvenir of my ancestors who were soldiers of fortune hired to fight baronial battles from Roman times to the French Revolution. I am glad that the more peaceful arts of the kitchen can turn the heavenly local ingredients into so many fine dishes.

The finest olives come from the area near Cadiz. The edible types are known as Queens; the Manzanilla variety is used for oil. Taken all round, this soup is probably the best of its kind for refreshing properties and richness in vitamin C.

1 small red pepper, cored, seeded and sliced
2 large tomatoes, cut into wedges
½ cucumber, sliced with skin
600ml/1 pint water
juice of 2 oranges
4 stoned green olives
1 small onion, peeled and sliced
1 slice of stale bread with crust
1 tablespoon cider vinegar
1 small green chilli, seeded and sliced
small sprig of fresh spearmint leaves
50g/2oz blanched almonds
100ml/4fl oz mayonnaise

Combine all the ingredients in an earthenware bowl, cover tightly and refrigerate overnight to allow the flavour to develop fully. Liquidise the mixture and serve in individual cups with a whirl of fresh mayonnaise piped over to form a garnish. Serve with crudités, such as cucumber, radishes, peppers, celery and mooli, cut into attractive sticks, and croûtons if desired. **Serves 8 to 10.**

This delicious cold soup will keep very well in the refrigerator.

Crème cressonière de Saleux • Watercress soup with goat cheese

When I was a child we used to gather fresh, wild watercress from the river that ambled slowly past my grandmother's home at Saleux in Picardy. Most watercress is cultivated now, of course, and you are lucky if you know a wild source in really clean water.

Watercress is a perfect ingredient to add piquancy to a salad, and is even better in this creamy-textured but uncooked soup formulated on Nouvelle Cuisine lines. It is a very healthy dish since the cress contains iodine, iron, phosphates, potash, calcium and vitamins A, C and E, with a low calorie count. Chopped watercress can also be used in omelettes, quiches, potato purée or in a baked potato instead of chives. It is an ideal garnish for fish, meat or poultry. In a hot potato soup add a bunch of liquidised raw leaves at the last minute to keep all the peppery flavour.

large bunch of watercress (use leaves only and thinner part of stem)
50g/2oz fresh goat cheese, crumbled
150ml/5fl oz buttermilk
150ml/5fl oz water
1 small slice of stale wholemeal bread
juice of 1 lemon
salt and freshly ground black pepper
1 tablespoon salted hazelnuts

Combine all the ingredients in a bowl, toss well and cover. Leave to macerate for 15 minutes. Liquidise to a thin purée. Serve in individual bowls garnished with a slice of lemon. **Serves 2.**

Crème de laitue au babeurre ◆ Lettuce and buttermilk soup

Lettuce has a long-standing culinary reputation, having probably been introduced to Britain by the Romans. It combines beautifully with buttermilk, the residue of cream or milk removed from the churn after butter-making. I prefer buttermilk to yogurt because it has a lower fat content than most yogurts, is highly digestible with diuretic properties, and is a cheap source of protein. Its slightly acid-creamy flavour is pleasant, and those who drink it regularly say it does wonders for the complexion.

1 medium-size lettuce with a good heart
small bunch of fresh chives
2 eggs, beaten
1 tablespoon mixed chopped fresh parsley and chervil
300ml/½ pint buttermilk
salt and coarsely ground black pepper

Separate the lettuce leaves. Peel the core stalk where the juice is stored and slice it. Liquidise all the ingredients to a thin purée with some of the buttermilk. Add the remaining buttermilk and season to taste. Serve very well chilled in earthenware bowls, with matzos, crispbread or wholemeal bread sippets. **Serves 2.**

La soupe d'endives aux noix et fromage • Chicory soup with cheese and walnuts

Do not be confused by the French word 'endive'. The chicory in this recipe is the compact, upright little salad vegetable with white-yellowish leaves wrapped closely as if to form one stem, and not the continental type of curly lettuce known as 'frisée'.

Chicory is a very welcome ingredient in Cuisine Fraîcheur, with its mere 9 calories per 100g/4oz and important nutrients like calcium, potassium and vitamin C when raw. The juice has tonic blood properties and is mildly aperient and diuretic. It is also known as a herbal remedy for stress. Chicory makes a pleasant addition to salads, just sliced across and tossed in a lemony-cheese dressing. It is nicely crunchy to use with dips; for this, cut the heads in half lengthways. For cooking, simply trim the root end a little and simmer in their own juice with lemon; or place in a little water and braise in the oven.

You will find this soup full of intriguing flavours. To make an amusing lunchtime guessing game, see if your guests can name all the contents!

2 heads of chicory, trimmed and sliced across
1 Granny Smith apple, cored and sliced
100g/4oz walnut kernels
50g/2oz fromage frais (page 179)
juice of 1 lemon
25g/1oz blue cheese such as Danish Blue, Roquefort or Stilton, crumbled
150ml/5fl oz apple juice
300ml/½ pint water
1 tablespoon cider vinegar
1 egg, beaten
50g/2oz fresh brown breadcrumbs or crushed ginger biscuits
1 spring onion, chopped, or 1 garlic clove, peeled and finely chopped
freshly ground black pepper

Toss all the ingredients together in a large bowl, cover and leave to macerate for 30 minutes. Liquidise to a thin purée and check the seasoning. Add more water if you prefer a thinner soup. Serve, well chilled, in individual bowls, with sticks of raw celery or carrot and a sprinkle of chopped parsley. **Serves 4.**

◆ HOT COOKED SOUPS ◆

La soupe calabrese aux noix d'acajou ◆ Broccoli soup with cashew nuts

Sprouting broccoli, much of it imported to Britain from the Continent, is often sold in the shops as calabrese. This delicate vegetable is much favoured with dips at cocktail parties and Nouvelle Cuisine has adopted it with gusto as a garnish for vegetable terrines, pâtés and mousses.

The green variety is available in May and June. The purple and white kinds along with Cape broccoli – which resembles a purple cauliflower – are in the shops in July and August. The essential when buying is freshness; avoid anything going yellowish. Shoots should look young and snap easily. The stalk is edible and should not be wasted. Eat on day of purchase.

Broccoli requires very little cooking. Make a double criss-cross slit in the end of the stalk and cook in very little boiling water, a maximum 5 to 8 minutes. Drain and serve immediately, with a light eggy or cheese sauce if liked.

1 medium-size onion, peeled and chopped
1 tablespoon sunflower oil
300ml/½ pint water
225g/8oz green broccoli, stalk cut into thin slices and florets left whole
150g/5oz cashew nuts
1 garlic clove, peeled
1 tablespoon chopped watercress
50g/2oz fromage frais (page 179) or tofu
salt and freshly ground black pepper

Stir fry the onion lightly in the oil until softened. Add the water and broccoli and simmer 7 minutes until almost tender. Add the cashew nuts, garlic, watercress and cheese or tofu. Cook 4 more minutes, then liquidise the mixture to a thin purée. If too thick, adjust with a little more water. Check the seasoning. Serve in individual soup bowls with an assortment of crudités: radishes, carrots, celery and fennel sticks. **Serves 3 to 4.**

La soupe de potiron aux abricots ◆ Pumpkin soup with apricots

Pumpkins were cultivated in North and South America before the Spanish arrived. They are of the same family as gourds and are used in many peasant-style dishes. They can grow to a huge size: one in 1881 is on record at 111 kg/245 lbs! Pumpkin is rich in vitamins A and C, and low *in calories. It comes into season in autumn. When selecting, ensure the flesh is moist.*

Pumpkin can be served as a vegetable purée, used in a mixture such as ratatouille, or combined with apple and ginger as a filling for tarts.

Fresh apricots, used in this recipe for flavouring, are very perishable and usually sold unripe. They will ripen quickly in a warm airing cupboard. Dried apricots may be used instead, but soak them first.

225g/8oz pumpkin pulp, diced
150g/5oz carrots, peeled and grated
1 small onion, peeled and chopped
100g/4oz ripe apricots, stoned
300ml/½ pint water
150ml/5fl oz buttermilk
salt and freshly ground black pepper

Simmer all the ingredients, except the buttermilk, until soft. Liquidise to a purée, then reheat. Blend in the buttermilk away from the heat, and adjust the consistency if too thick. Season to taste. Serve warm but not hot in individual bowls, with sticks of raw carrot as garnish. **Serves 4.**

Crème gauloise rabelaisienne • Gallic-style soup with herbs

I have named this delicious soup after François Rabelais, humanist, epicure, and authority on early dietary theory. His researches on food and the physical system were penetrating, strengthened by his professional training as a doctor.

His book, Gargantua and Pantagruel, *part satire, part fable, depicts enormous excesses of eating and drinking, and the sickness that goes with them. However, he was an apostle of something quite different – the proper enjoyment of food – and this is one of the underlying themes of Cuisine Fraîcheur. True enjoyment arises from a healthy pleasure in nourishing oneself wisely and well, and appreciating the bountiful and fresh ingredients that can go into this, such as those in this book. One of the Rabelaisian prescriptions for a healthful life was the use of salads, and he especially praised lettuce, which features in this recipe.*

1 lettuce with good heart
bunch of watercress, leaves only
100g/4oz sorrel leaves, stems removed
1 medium-size onion, peeled and sliced
50g/2oz polyunsaturated margarine, or 4 tablespoons oil
sprig of fresh savory
12 fresh mint leaves
1 litre/1¾ pints water

225g/8oz potatoes, peeled and thinly sliced
100g/4oz Brie, fresh low-fat plain yogurt or buttermilk
sea salt

Separate the lettuce, watercress and sorrel leaves, then cut into shreds. Stir fry the onion in the margarine or oil for 4 minutes or until translucent. Add all the leaves and herbs to the pan and cook for 4 more minutes. Add the water and sliced potatoes and simmer for 25 minutes.

Away from heat, mix in the cheese, yogurt or buttermilk, then liquidise the soup. Reheat and season to taste. **Serves 8.**

La soupe aux champignons et aux orties • Nettle and mushroom broth

Stinging nettles have been used as a wild vegetable for centuries. They contain chemical elements said to be good for sciatica and rheumatism and are a good blood purifier. To use as a vegetable simply blanch for 30 seconds in boiling salted water, drain and serve with nuts. It is best to pick the stinging nettle (Urtica dioca) when it is young, wearing gloves.

This soup is a meal in itself for the evening, perhaps followed by a slice of pineapple, half a ripe papaya, pear or apple.

225g/8oz button mushrooms, sliced
juice of 1 lemon
freshly ground black pepper
1 medium-size onion, peeled and chopped
2 tablespoons sunflower oil
2 handfuls of fresh nettles, chopped or shredded
600ml/1 pint water
1 vegetarian stock cube, or 1 tablespoon yeast extract
3 tablespoons oatmeal
75ml/3fl oz plain low-fat yogurt

Put the mushrooms in a bowl, sprinkle with the lemon juice and pepper to taste and toss to coat. Leave to marinate for 20 minutes while making the soup. Stir fry the onion in the oil for 4 minutes without browning. Add the nettles and stir fry for 3 minutes. Add the water and stock cube, bring to the boil and simmer for 12 minutes. Stir in the oatmeal and simmer 5 more minutes. Liquidise the soup until smooth. Whisk in the yogurt. Divide the mushrooms (with the marinade liquid) between two soup plates. Spoon over the soup. **Serves 2.**

This soup is eaten tepid, having a better flavour like that. It may be flavoured with a little chopped fresh marjoram at the last minute.

La soupe à l'ananas aux choux • Pineapple and cabbage soup

This recipe shows how the addition of succulent pineapple to a useful high-fibre vegetable like the cabbage can produce a most attractive dish, when on its own the 'greens' might be less than exciting. Pineapple not only enlivens the flavour of a savoury dish or a cole slaw, for example; its enzyme, bromelin, aids digestion in making the protein in the food easier to absorb.

To test a pineapple for ripeness, see if a leaf will pull away easily and press gently to check that the fruit is slightly soft. If unripe, suspend by a string in a warm place.

The best way to peel a pineapple is as follows: using a small sharp knife, take a thin slice from the base and discard it. Holding the leafy plume, make shallow cuts at an angle of 45° down each strip of 'eyes', first one way and then the other to make a wedge-shaped strip. These should pull away easily, leaving a zig-zag pattern. Trim off the plume, then slice and core the fruit.

Fresh pineapple can be liquidised with fresh root ginger, garlic and soya sauce to make a fine barbecue sauce – excellent with grilled fish, for instance. It can also be stir fried with mixed vegetables, blended in cole slaw, served with cream cheese, sliced mushrooms or prawns as an hors d'oeuvre, or made into tasty soups like this one.

4 slices of fresh pineapple, peeled and cut into fine shreds
150g/5oz white cabbage, shredded
1 small shallot, peeled and chopped
225g/8oz soft tofu
1 garlic clove, peeled
2 tablespoons soya sauce
1 small piece (about 15g/½oz) fresh root ginger, peeled
300 ml/10 fl oz water
salt and freshly ground black pepper

Combine all ingredients in a large bowl and leave to macerate for 45 minutes (in this period the fruit enzyme will be working on the protein to start the job of digestion for you). Liquidise the mixture and pour into a saucepan. Bring to the boil and boil for 5 minutes only. Season to taste and serve hot with toast, or chilled with sticks of celery. **Serves 4.**

Buttermilk can be used instead of tofu, but should be blended in away from the heat. Another variation is to omit the pineapple from the mixture and add it raw after the other ingredients have been cooked.

LES HORS D'OEUVRE CRÛS

RAW STARTERS

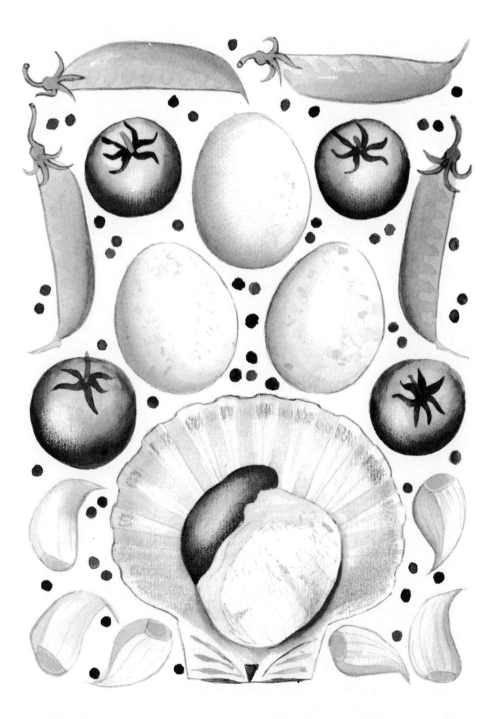

The hors d'oeuvre dishes in Cuisine Fraîcheur seem to me to show off the possibilities of raw food at their best, with their exciting variety of texture, taste and colour.

The use of fruit in starter courses is now well established. It can be a simple citrus fruit cocktail, a slice of melon, or papaya or fresh figs served with smoked fish, ham or poultry. At a gourmet gathering I have even served strawberries and lime with smoked salmon.

The recipes that follow show what appetising combinations can be made up with a little imagination, and by keeping in mind a few simple principles: choose ingredients that complement each other in a friendly way, such as partnering a tangy fruit with a blander fish, or select ingredients for texture contrasts as in crisp vegetables matched with softer elements.

The other guidelines will be familiar to most cooks. Make a point of having all ingredients as fresh as possible. Avoid soaking vegetables or salads in water; just rinse well, drain and pat dry with kitchen paper or a clean cloth. Do not cut up vegetables too much in advance of a meal; this affects the vitamin C content and risks discoloration.

While the dishes here are broadly called 'starters' there is no reason why they should not form a main course, either for the mid-day or evening meal or, in the right quantity, as a snack at any time. Hors d'oeuvre also make the perfect packed lunch for taking to a workplace, thus solving many of the problems of sticking to a healthy diet.

Les huîtres au caviar de saumon et salicornes ◆ Oysters and salmon caviar with samphire

All authorities on food, from Brillat-Savarin onwards, have agreed that cooking oysters is a culinary crime. Also, it is essential that oysters be really fresh, and served free of any suspicion of vinegary or spicy sauces. While too much kitchen interference with the dignity of the simple oyster is to be avoided, it may be discreetly mentioned that they can be turned into a delicious sauce by liquidising them with a little soured cream or plain yogurt, to be served with plainly poached or grilled fish.

The best French oysters, which originate from the Britanny coast, include the greenish-tinged Marennes, which are flat and derive their colour from the algae they feed upon, and the brown Belons. The finest British natives are from Colchester and Whitstable. All oysters have a strong muscle to close up their household against intruders, and this must be cut through with a knife to get them open (wear some protective gloves if you are not practised in the art). The soft part of the oyster, the liver, is composed largely of glycogen and this brings about the curious fact that the oyster is self-digestive, that is, digested by the human as soon as eaten.

Samphire, also known as St. Peter's herb, grows along marshy sea shores and has a pleasantly sharp flavour. It can be eaten raw or, if you find that too acidic, blanch it briefly.

100g/4oz samphire
4 oysters
½ shallot, peeled and chopped
2 tablespoons plain low-fat yogurt
coarsely ground black pepper
50g/2oz salmon caviar
1 hard-boiled egg, shelled and sieved or finely chopped

Wash the samphire well and drain. Alternatively, blanch it in boiling water for 30 seconds, drain and refresh in cold water; drain again well. Arrange the samphire on a plate.

Open the oysters, remove and reserve the bottom shells. Blend the shallot and yogurt and add pepper to taste. Place a spoonful of yogurt sauce in the bottom of each shell, put an oyster on top and add a teaspoon of caviar beside it, plus some egg. Serve very cold on the bed of samphire, which is very edible too. **Serves 1**.

Filet de hareng à l'ananas • Herrings with pineapple

I am one of those who regard herrings as one of the best things out of the sea. Rich in flavour, they are more nourishing than the most expensive poultry or meat, and almost as nutritious as salmon, at a fraction of the cost. Like the potato, the herring is one of those basic foods of history, keeping alive the common man and woman. For that reason, and their relative cheapness, this fine fish does not have a 'smart' image. This is certainly no reason to ignore them, rather the reverse. No true chef is snobbish about ingredients, being well aware that some of the best dishes in the kitchen repertoire were first devised by humble fisherfolk and peasants, people who knew a good mouthful when they tasted it.

Marinated herrings go back centuries, of course, in the form of pickled herrings. They have been making a come-back in Nouvelle Cuisine and, somewhat in that style, you will find that the recipe here makes a good starter. Some people, I know, are put off herrings by the imagined difficulties of preparation. This is solved by patronising a good fishmonger who will fillet them well, getting out the whiskery bones, and scale them for you.

Pineapple not only enlivens the flavour of a savoury dish such as this, it also aids digestion through the action of its enzyme, bromelin, which makes the protein in the food easier to digest.

4 scaled and filleted fresh herrings, each about 175g/6oz
150ml/5fl oz cider vinegar
150ml/5fl oz apple juice
1 tablespoon honey
salt and freshly ground black pepper
2 tablespoons single cream
150ml/5fl oz plain low-fat yogurt

2 sprigs of fresh dill, chopped
100g/4oz fresh pineapple, peeled and diced

Cut the fillets into 5cm/2 inch strips. Blend the cider vinegar, apple juice and honey in a saucepan. Add salt and pepper to taste. Bring to the boil, remove from the heat and allow to cool. Mix in the cream, yogurt, dill and pineapple cubes. Marinate the fish in this for 48 hours. Serve garnished with curly lettuce and sliced cucumber. **Serves 4**.

Bolée de céleri-rave aux graines de moutarde •
Celeriac with mustard sauce

Celeriac or 'turnip-rooted celery' was introduced to British kitchens in the 18th century from southern Europe where it had long been popular, having been developed from celery. The flavour of celeriac is like a combination of turnip and celery. It is a good source of minerals and vitamin C. Imported and home supplies are available from late September to April.

Celeriac can vary in size from that of a large cooking apple to a coconut; over-large specimens can tend to be woody or hollow. As much of the goodness lies just under the skin, this vegetable should be very thinly peeled and washed in water with a dash of white vinegar added to prevent discoloration. To cook, it may be cut into large cubes and boiled for 5 to 8 minutes, then served with any sauce you fancy. The French usually like it raw, cut into thin strips with a mustard mayonnaise, which I have modified in this recipe to reduce the oil content.

1 whole celeriac, peeled and soaked in water with a dash of white vinegar
50g/2oz walnut kernels, coarsely chopped
1 apple, cored and thinly sliced
1 spring onion, chopped, including much of the green
50g/2oz Edam cheese, cut into matchstick-size strips
1 tablespoon coarsely chopped fresh coriander leaves or parsley
4 lettuce leaves
2 radicchio leaves
1 head of chicory, thinly sliced

mustard sauce:
2 egg yolks
1 teaspoon made mustard with seeds
salt and freshly ground black pepper
6 tablespoons olive oil
6 tablespoons plain low-fat yogurt
¼ teaspoon celery seeds
juice of ½ lemon
1 tablespoon honey (optional)

First make the sauce. Place the egg yolks, mustard and salt and pepper to taste in a bowl. Very gradually add the oil, whisking in one direction only. Blend in the yogurt, celery seeds, lemon juice and honey. Alternatively, make the sauce in a blender or food processor. Transfer this sauce to a larger bowl and set aside.

Slice the celeriac to about the thickness of a potato crisp; a mandoline makes this easier. Cut the slices into thin strips and immediately blend into the sauce, along with the walnuts, apple slices and spring onion. Stir well, then mix in the cheese and coriander. Arrange the lettuce leaves and radicchio, alternately for colour contrast, on four plates or bowls with some of the chicory in each. Spoon the celeriac salad into the centre and serve cold. **Serves 4**.

La papaye à la Gauguin ◆ Papaya with smoked salmon and lime dressing

The painter Paul Gauguin lived on the island of Tahiti where the papaya, or paw-paw, thrives. It is said that the beauties he painted presented this fruit to welcome sailors ashore, so it became the local 'love-apple'. It is now grown in most tropical and sub-tropical regions. In flavour it bears resemblance to a mix of peach, melon and strawberry. It is rich in vitamin A, calcium and enzymes which aid digestion of protein.

Papaya should be available from good greengrocers or supermarkets all the year round. As it ripens the skin turns from green to a deep yellow. It is highly versatile on the table, making a pleasant breakfast alternative to grapefruit when served raw with wedges of lime, or as a starter or dessert with the evening meal. It goes well with smoked fish, poultry or ham, particularly with a dressing flavoured with fresh ginger. The green papaya is usually cooked with curry dishes.

    1 large ripe papaya, peeled, halved and seeded
    2 lettuce leaves, coarsely shredded
    1 lime (cut 2 slices and juice the remainder)
    50g/2oz cucumber, diced with skin
    1 teaspoon green peppercorns, coarsely crushed
    1 teaspoon raspberry vinegar (optional)
    50g/2oz smoked salmon, diced
    1 teaspoon coarsely chopped fresh mint

Slice each papaya in half lengthways, leaving one end uncut so that the slices will fan out without separating. Arrange each half thus prepared on a plate with the shredded lettuce and a lime slice. In a bowl, mix the lime juice with the cucumber and peppercorns. The raspberry vinegar may be added to increase sharpness, according to taste. Toss the mixture with the salmon. Spoon this sauce on the side of the plate and top with a sprinkling of mint. Serve chilled. **Serves 2**.

Les figues de France aux laitances de hareng • Fresh figs with herring roes

The fig is one of the most ancient plants, with many appreciations of its virtues in classical literature. Used fresh, it is a delicious and versatile fruit. When dried its sweetness content increases to 50 per cent and, like its companion the date, it is a useful substitute for sugar.

Ripe figs may be white, green, purple or black, according to variety. The skin and seeds are important fibre so avoid peeling the fruit if you can. Good restaurants often serve fresh figs with smoked fish, meat or cheese. They are best served raw, either in their natural state or marinated in orange or pomegranate juice. They may also be lightly poached in fruit juice.

The hors d'oeuvre presented here was a speciality of my late father's restaurants in France, and I am sure it will become a favourite of those who love soft roes as I do.

4 soft roes, preferably from fresh herrings (the fish can be grilled and used separately)
salt and coarsely ground black pepper
4 ripe purple figs
4 lettuce leaves
4 radicchio leaves
4 orange segments
4 lemon wedges

Place the roes, carefully washed and drained, on a metal tray. Season with a pinch of salt and plenty of black pepper and grill for 2 minutes until firm.

Make a criss-cross cut in the top of each fig and open up the four 'petals' like a flower. Arrange alternate leaves of lettuce and radicchio on four plates. Place a fig and a serving of roes on each, and garnish with an orange segment and wedge of lemon. **Serves 4.**

La pomme d'Adam au fromage blanc • Apple with cheese and walnut stuffing

Apples have been associated with good health for many centuries, and we could all benefit from eating rather more than the 11.5kg/25lbs per person per year we averagely consume. There must be good reasons why pagan gods, ancient myths and folklore have all associated the apple with well-being. The fact that apple pulp and rosemary were sold in the 16th century as a beauty cream called 'pomatum' shows that it has even had a reputation for external use.

Very tasty varieties are nowadays available all the year round, such as Cox's Orange Pippin, Granny Smith, Laxton's Superb, Golden Delicious, Bramley's and Discovery besides lesser-known types to seek out in country districts in autumn.

The apple is entirely at home in many dishes. It is a perfect little snack with a piece of cheese. It helps the flavour of salads like cole slaw and Waldorf. All citrus fruits go well with apple in a fruit salad (where the apple should be cored but preferably served with the skin on). Apple and blackberries, damsons and red or blackcurrants make a fine match. An easy little aid to losing weight is to eat an apple 15 minutes before a meal.

4 medium-size dessert apples
100g/4oz cottage cheese, blended with 1 tablespoon of plain low-fat yogurt to soften
1 small stick of celery, chopped
¼ red pepper, cored, seeded and chopped
1 tablespoon finely snipped fresh chives
8 walnut kernels, chopped
salt and freshly ground black pepper
celery seeds (optional)
1 small lettuce
1 large orange, peeled and segmented

Cut the apples in half, remove cores and scoop out some flesh from each to form a little cup. Dice the apple flesh thus removed. Place the cheese-and-yogurt mixture in a large bowl. Add the diced apple, celery, red pepper, chives and walnuts, plus salt and pepper to taste and a pinch of celery seed, if you have it. Blend all together well and fill each apple cup. Present on lettuce leaves garnished with orange segments. **Serves 4.**

Rondelles de pomme aux cacahouettes • Apple rings with peanut butter

Juicy, sharp-flavoured dessert apples, such as Granny Smiths, are best for this hors d'oeuvre. Proprietary peanut butter may be used if you really cannot spare a minute but I suggest you will find it more satisfying and very simple to make your own. (Would you agree with me that too many short cuts in the kitchen are a false economy? I think they spoil one's sense of craftsmanship, and the great pleasure in creating a good meal.)

100g/4oz shelled roasted peanuts
25g/1oz cottage cheese
2 tablespoons water
2 dessert apples, cored and sliced into thick rings
1 tablespoon toasted sesame seeds
1 teaspoon wheat bran
pinch of ground cinnamon
2 lettuce leaves
4 grapefruit segments

Liquidise the peanuts with the cottage cheese and water until quite smooth. For a coarser blend, use a pestle and mortar or rolling pin to crush the peanuts, then mix in the other ingredients. Spread the peanut paste thickly on each apple ring. Mix together the sesame seeds, bran and cinnamon and sprinkle over. Serve on the lettuce leaves, garnished with the grapefruit segments. **Serves 2**.

La salade ortanique ◆ Medley of pear, ortanique and sole fillets

The ortanique fruit, unique to Jamaica, is a cross between an orange and a tangerine, and has one of the highest juice contents of any citrus fruit. Supplies are imported into Britain from the end of January to April. Ortaniques are slightly variable in size, pale orange in colour, and may have blemishes which do not affect the flavour.

Ortaniques can be peeled and segmented like any citrus fruit. After removal of the pips, the sweet juicy flesh can be used in a fruit cocktail with avocado. It may also be used as a garnish for any fish, poultry or salad dish. Or, as in this recipe, it makes a flavoursome marinade for fish with a little lime added.

1 large sole, about 750g/1½lbs, filleed and skinned
salt and coarsely ground black pepper
2 ortanique fruits, one juiced and the other peeled and segmented
2 limes, one juiced and the other sliced
4 lettuce leaves
1 ripe Comice pear, peeled, cored and quartered

dressing:
1 spring onion, chopped
juice of 1 ortanique
juice of 1 lime
2 tablespoons olive oil or sunflower oil
1 teaspoon white or raspberry vinegar
1 teaspoon Dijon mustard

Cut the sole into thin strips. Season and place in a shallow dish. Combine the juice of one ortanique and one lime and pour over the fish. Marinate in the refrigerator for 4 hours, turning the fish occasionally.

Liquidise all the ingredients for the dressing together, with seasoning to taste.

To serve, drain the fish and arrange on the lettuce on four plates. Pour over the dressing. Decorate each portion with ortanique segments, twisted lime slices and a pear quarter. **Serves 4**.

Primeur de maïs aux pouces de soya océanique •
Baby sweetcorn and bean sprouts with king prawns

Baby sweetcorn are cobs harvested when very young and in prime succulence. They are so juicy you can eat them raw. They are available here, imported mainly from Kenya, from December to March. Highly nutritious, they contain good protein, fibre, mineral salts, and vitamins A, B and C. When shopping, look for fresh cobs with a protective husk around them; avoid corn which has gone a dull yellow colour.

Bean sprouts are available all the year round in most supermarkets. Very low in calories (35 per 100g/4oz) they are a good source of vitamin C plus some protein and fibre. Always rinse and drain bean sprouts, and preferably use on day of purchase or not long after.

8 baby sweetcorn
4 raw king prawns in shell
oil for brushing
salt and freshly ground black pepper
300g/10oz bean sprouts

dressing:
3 tablespoons plain low-fat yogurt
1 teaspoon Dijon mustard
small slice of fresh pineapple, peeled
15g/½oz piece of fresh root ginger, peeled
1 tablespoon soya sauce
1 teaspoon white vinegar
2 garlic cloves, peeled

Cook the baby sweetcorn in boiling water for 5 minutes. Drain and refresh under cold running water; drain again well.

Split open the king prawns lengthways and remove the black intestinal vein. Brush with oil and season. Grill about 5 minutes.

Meanwhile, liquidise the dressing ingredients together, with seasoning to taste. Cut the baby sweetcorn into small chunks and mix them in a salad bowl with the bean sprouts. Add half the dressing and toss together.

Arrange the salad and prawns on four plates and serve with the remaining dressing. **Serves 4**.

Coquilles Saint Jacques boulonnaise • Scallop, melon and ginger salad

The spicy, tropical flavour of ginger permeates this delicious concoction of good things. Ginger was one of those highly prized spices from the Orient when sea exploration was at its height.

When buying fresh root ginger, look for specimens that are roundish with almost kidney-shaped or knuckle-like knobbles. The skin should be a light reddish-brown colour. Choose samples that are up to 10cm/4 inches long and up to 1.5cm/⅔ inch thick. Ginger is best liquidised with a little lemon or pineapple juice before adding to whatever dish needs a ginger flavour, such as stir-fried vegetable and Chinese dishes, or liquidise with a little honey for melon, papaya and exotic fruit salads. In this recipe the ginger flavours the marinade for a truly excellent hors d'oeuvre.

225g/8oz shelled fresh scallops
4 thin asparagus spears, lightly scraped and cut into pieces
8 mangetouts, headed and tailed
½ Charentais melon, flesh cut into balls or cubes
4 cherry tomatoes

marinade:
small slice of fresh pineapple, peeled
piece of fresh root ginger (the size of a grape), peeled and sliced
2 tablespoons sunflower oil
2 garlic cloves, peeled
1 small shallot, peeled and chopped
2 tablespoons white vinegar
1 tablespoon honey
1 teaspoon French mustard
salt and freshly ground black pepper

Liquidise the marinade ingredients together, with seasoning to taste, and place in a large bowl. Slice the scallops if large. Add to the bowl with the coral, and leave to marinate for 3 hours.

If the asparagus spears are large, blanch them in boiling water for 2 minutes and drain. Add to the bowl with the mangetouts and marinate for a further 30 minutes.

Remove the ingredients from the bowl with a slotted spoon to drain and put on to four dishes. Arrange the melon and whole tomatoes on top. **Serves 4**.

Scallops may be blanched for 30 seconds if a slightly cooked flavour is preferred.

Roulade de truite saumonée florentine • Salmon trout and spinach roll

Young spinach leaves are very good eaten raw in a salad or, as in this dish, as a garnish for fish. When shopping, select spinach that looks clean and free of yellow or damaged leaves, hard stalks and flowering shoots. It is important to wash spinach in three waters to remove all trace of sand. Remove stalks and ribs and use the leaves only. When cooking, allow about 225g/8oz raw weight per serving and use little or no water. I also recommend you try it cooked in a dash of sunflower oil, which brings out the flavour well.

100g/4oz skinned salmon trout fillet
100g/4oz skinned plaice fillet
25g/1oz polyunsaturated margarine, melted
225g/8oz fresh spinach leaves, chopped
¼ red pepper, cored, seeded and chopped
1 tablespoon snipped fresh chives

marinade:
1 tablespoon white or cider vinegar
sprig of fresh dill
juice of 1 lime
juice of 1 lemon
pinch of grated nutmeg
salt and freshly ground black pepper

sauce:
75ml/3fl oz plain low-fat yogurt
75g/3oz fresh spinach leaves
3 fresh mint leaves or lemon balm

Slightly flatten the fish fillets with a knife blade. Combine the marinade ingredients, with seasoning to taste, and soak the fillets in it for 4 hours.

Drain the fillets well, lay on a pastry board and brush with the margarine. Make a layer of the salmon fillets on a piece of foil. Cover with the spinach leaves, then lay the plaice fillets on top. Roll up to make a Swiss roll shape and wrap tightly in the foil. Refrigerate or freeze for 15 minutes to firm the roll.

For the sauce, liquidise the ingredients to a purée and season to taste.

Cut the fish roll through the foil into finger-thick slices, then remove the foil. Pour a little sauce on to two plates and sprinkle with red pepper pieces and chives. Arrange the sliced roulade on each plate and serve. **Serves 2.**

Julienne aux oeufs de mouettes potagère • Gull's eggs and vegetable strips

Raw strips of vegetables such as leeks, carrots, turnips and celery have been part of the renaissance which has been going on in professional cooking. Sliced so finely they do not even need blanching, they add a natural garden flavour to dishes.

Leeks are a vegetable with an ancient history. They can be cooked and served in a vinaigrette sauce like asparagus, or mixed with cheese as a quiche filling. They are essential in good minestrone and in the leek-and-potato Vichyssoise with chives and cream. Choose medium-size leeks, trimmed of any wilted leaves. Store in an airy place or in the refrigerator, tightly wrapped.

1 stick of celery
1 small bulb of fennel, about 50g/2oz
1 leek
1 carrot, peeled
1 turnip, peeled
15g/½oz fresh root ginger, peeled
salt and freshly ground black pepper
2 smoked trout, skinned and filleted, or 100g/4oz smoked tuna
4 gull's eggs, boiled 10 minutes, shelled and halved
chopped fresh coriander

sauce:
45g/1½oz smoked cod's roe (peeled weight)
75ml/3fl oz plain, low-fat yogurt
1 tomato, skinned, seeded and chopped
celery salt

Shave the celery and fennel with a potato peeler. Cut the celery, fennel, leek, carrot, turnip and ginger into matchstick-size strips, thinner if you can. Combine and season to taste. Cut the fish into small strips and mix with the vegetables. Serve on to two plates.

Liquidise the sauce ingredients together and season to taste with celery salt and pepper. Pour some sauce over each serving. On top place two halved gull's eggs with an attractive sprinkling of coriander. **Serves 2**.

La poire au fromage herbacé • Pear with watercress and cheese sauce

Cottage cheese, made from skimmed milk, is a versatile ingredient in a healthy diet with its agreeable flavour, its low calorie count of 96 per 100g/4oz, and its ability to go well with most kinds of fruit and vegetables. My impression, though, is that many weight-watchers use it rather unimaginatively, serving themselves a dollop on a lettuce leaf as a token of dietary suffering. As this dish shows, there are more attractive ways of doing it justice.

Cottage cheese should be eaten very fresh, as close to the day of purchase as possible. I find that its flavour comes out best, as with all cheeses, if it is served at room temperature.

2 very ripe Comice pears
1 mooli, peeled and cut into matchstick-size strips, 100g/4oz peeled weight
2 Victoria plums, stoned and sliced

sauce:
50g/2oz cottage cheese or fromage frais (page 179)
50g/2oz leek, boiled 8 minutes
½ bunch of watercress, leaves only
25g/1oz Roquefort cheese
25g/1oz shelled roasted peanuts
juice of ½ lemon
grated nutmeg
freshly ground black pepper

Core the pears from the wider end, leaving the stem on as decoration. Cut a slice from the bottom of each so it will stand upright. Peel the fruit carefully and rinse in water acidulated with a little lemon juice for 1 minute, to prevent discoloration.

Liquidise the sauce ingredients to a thin purée, and season to taste with pepper and nutmeg. Pour a small pool of the sauce on to two plates. Place a pear on each. Garnish with strips of mooli and plums. A small curly lettuce leaf would also enhance the appearance of the dish. **Serves 2.**

LES ENTRÉES LÉGÈRES
LIGHT ENTRÉES

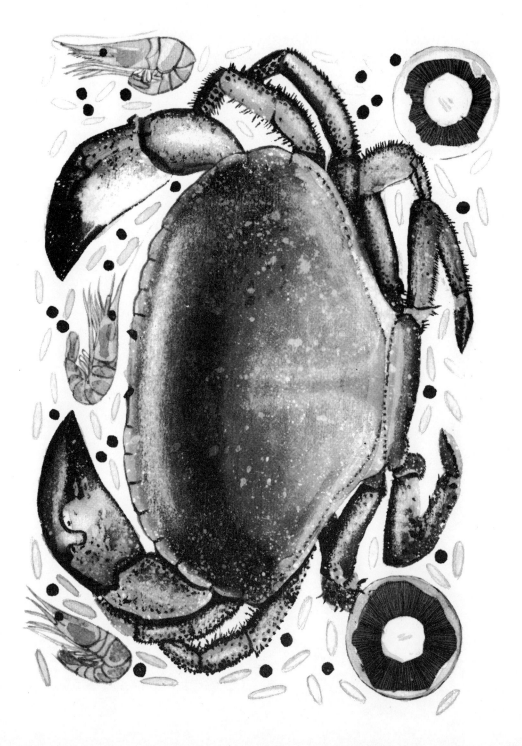

In classical cuisine, the light entrée was the delectable little made-up hot dish – the pride of the talented chef – served between the opening hors d'oeuvre or appetiser dish and the main course. These entrées used to concentrate on meat, especially offal, with vegetables more or less omitted. Chefs have been modifying this tradition for some time, in line with better thinking about diet, more often using fish, chicken or eggs in a variety of forms.

Here, for our semi-vegetarian Cuisine Fraîcheur, we have introduced some original concepts to carry this broadening out a good stage further, even turning the whole thing around in some ways to show how pleasing such light dishes can be when vegetables are given due prominence in partnership with permissible fish and white meats and the right weighting of aromatic herbs.

The dishes in this chapter follow the trend for individual portions to be served attractively on a medium-size plate. They are of value in adding essential protein to a high-fibre diet. Each can be served as a whole meal for those of smaller appetite, or a light snack for the gourmet, or as an interesting hot starter course.

Following our principles of healthier cooking, the cream once commonly used in these dishes has been replaced by low-fat yogurt. Poaching is preferred to deep-fat frying. Quiches and *bouchées* have been omitted because of the 50 per cent fat in puff pastry. Instead we can use scooped-out vegetables and fruit as containers to make many attractive small dishes which tempt eye and palate. A raw tomato stuffed with a hot filling is a typical example. Contrasting hot and cold ingredients in this way also enhances appreciation of fresher foods. Stuffed peppers and potatoes are also good in this context, though we have reserved recipes for them as main dishes in the Vegetarian section.

Another important feature of our light entrées is marinated raw fish. It is essential that fish to be prepared this way be very fresh. Buy only from a reputable fishmonger who has a good turnover, and take some care with the preparation of the fish. First wash it well in plenty of cold water and pat it dry, then put it into the marinade of vinegar and lime juice or similar acidic liquor and baste this well over the fish. Turn the fish three or four times during the marinating time to ensure it is sterilised. If you shrink from the idea of raw fish, remember that roll-mop herrings have been processed in just this way for centuries. It may even be that you will come to prefer the raw version to the cooked after you have had the new taste-experience of marinated trout, salmon trout and mackerel appearing in these recipes.

The smoked chicken dish also offers an alternative to the conventional cooking process. In other recipes we have given a new slant to familiar dishes to make them acceptable in Cuisine Fraîcheur, as in my version of Minced Fish with Chilli, which is a low-cholesterol echo of the old Chile con Carne with meat.

Pascaline de kiwi au fromage • Kiwi and curd moulds

This is a refreshing and nourishing little entrée made with the versatile kiwi fruit, and showing that it can be utilised as a savoury snack as well as a garnishing ingredient in many of the Fraîcheur recipes. If preferred, 1 teaspoon agar-agar may be used instead of gelatine; dissolve according to the instructions on the packet.

1 tablespoon powdered gelatine
6 tablespoons water
4 kiwi fruits, peeled and chopped
1 small tomato, skinned, seeded and chopped
225g/8oz curd cheese or fromage frais (page 179)
grated rind and juice of 1 lemon

garnish:
2 kiwi fruits, peeled and sliced
8 cherry tomatoes, preferably 4 red and 4 yellow
few fresh coriander leaves
4 sprigs of redcurrants

First dissolve the gelatine in the water.

In a saucepan, cook the chopped kiwis with the tomato over gentle heat for 5 minutes, stirring occasionally. Stir in the dissolved gelatine and cool.

In a bowl cream together the cheese and lemon rind and juice. Mix in the cooked kiwi mixture. Grease four 150ml/5fl oz capacity moulds, such as tumblers, with a little polyunsaturated margarine and fill them with the kiwi mixture. Allow to set for 2 hours in the refrigerator.

Turn out the pascalines on to four plates.

Garnish with sliced kiwi, cherry tomatoes and a few coriander leaves. On top of each pascaline place a sprig of redcurrants. **Serves 4.**

Terrine de truite aux asperges • Rainbow trout loaf with asparagus

The cherry tomato, no bigger than a walnut, is among the most flavoursome of its species, with a special sharp-sweet taste and aroma that has endeared it to exponents of Nouvelle Cuisine. In this recipe it perfectly complements the trout, which is among the most delicate-flavoured of fish.

In Cuisine Fraîcheur we recommend that tomatoes be eaten raw for maximum nutritional value, though they may also be cooked to make a coulis. Large fruit are very appealing to the eye and palate when stuffed with fish, eggs, minced vegetables, mushroom purée – all so easy to prepare.

¼ red and ¼ green pepper, seeded and diced
450g/1 lb fresh rainbow trout, well washed, filleted, skinned and minced
1 egg, beaten
6 tablespoons polyunsaturated margarine
150ml/5fl oz plain low-fat yogurt
1 medium-size shallot, peeled and finely chopped
8 small cabbage leaves, centre core removed
bunch of radishes
12-16 asparagus tips, cooked

sauce:
150ml/5fl oz plain low-fat yogurt
3 fresh mint leaves, chopped
1 tablespoon mango chutney or fresh mango pulp

Blanch the red and green pepper in boiling water for 30 seconds; drain and refresh under cold running water. In a large bowl, mix the peppers, minced fish, egg, margarine, yogurt and shallot. Chill in the freezer for 10 minutes while preparing the mould.

Parboil the cabbage leaves for 4 minutes, then drain and refresh under cold running water. Pat dry. Grease a sheet of foil with polyunsaturated margarine, then use the foil to line a 700g/1½lb oblong mould, such as a loaf tin or terrine. Cut the cabbage leaves into oblong pieces and use them to line the mould. Fill it with the fish mixture, pack down well and cover with greased foil. Place in a baking tin half-filled with hot water and bake at 200°C, 400°F, Mark 6 for 35 minutes. Allow to cool, then chill.

Turn the terrine on to a board and cut into finger-thick slices. Arrange on serving plates and garnish each with 2 or 3 radishes and 2 asparagus tips. Liquidise the sauce ingredients and serve a spoonful at the side of each plate. **Serves 6 to 8**.

Truite tartare Tolstoy • Rainbow trout tartare

1.1-1.4kg/2½-3lbs rainbow trout, well washed, filleted and skinned
juice of 2 lemons
1 tablespoon sherry vinegar
1 tablespoon honey
salt and freshly ground black pepper
grated rind of 1 lemon

garnish:
½ cucumber, halved lengthways and sliced
2 hard-boiled eggs, whites chopped and yolks sieved

lime slices
16 capers
sprig of fresh dill
fresh coriander leaves

sauce:
150ml/5fl oz mayonnaise or plain low-fat yogurt
2 capers
2 fresh mint leaves
1 tablespoon chopped fresh parsley
1 small gherkin

Place the fish fillets on a shallow dish and spoon over the lemon juice, vinegar and honey. Season to taste with salt and pepper and sprinkle on the lemon rind. Leave to marinate for 30 minutes.

Reserve four slices of the fish, about 25g/1oz each, for the garnish; mince the remaining fish, with the marinade, as coarsely or finely as you wish. Divide the minced fish into four equal portions.

Pat each portion into a flat oblong shape and mould it to resemble the form or outline of a trout in miniature size. (Alternatively, just mould into hamburger shapes.) Cut the reserved trout into very fine strips. Place these on the little 'trout' to outline the shape. Arrange on four plates.

Surround with sliced cucumber and egg whites and yolks, and garnish with lime slices, capers, dill sprig and coriander leaves.

Liquidise the sauce ingredients together and serve with the trout. **Serves 4.**

Filet d'anguille fumée aux deux choux • Two-cabbage salad with smoked eel and peanut dressing

The humble cabbage deserves every respect in a healthy diet for its high-fibre content, low calories (only 20 per 100g/4oz) and tastiness when treated with the right accompaniments. It has become popular in various forms of cole slaw salad, and can be most appetising with a nice garlic dressing.

All kinds of cabbage descend from the Wild or Sea Cabbage, native to various coastal regions of Europe. Its name comes from the Latin caput (head). It was well liked by the Romans who introduced it to Britain.

In shopping, look for really fresh and crisp specimens, with well-packed leaves. The base of the stalk is a good checking-point: it should be clean and not slimy. Red cabbage should have a good bloom to it.

150g/5oz white cabbage
150g/5oz red cabbage
1 red onion, peeled and chopped or shredded
small bunch of Chinese leaves, separated (about 4 leaves)
1 green and 1 red apple, cored and sliced
150g/5oz smoked eel fillet, cut into thin strips
75g/3oz walnut kernels
large bunch of corn salad leaves, leaves not separated
1 hard-boiled egg, yolk sieved and white finely chopped

dressing:
3 tablespoons sunflower oil
2 tablespoons raspberry or wine vinegar
50g/2oz shelled roasted peanuts
1 teaspoon made English mustard
salt and freshly ground black pepper

Core the two cabbages and cut into thin shreds. Place the shreds in two separate bowls. Liquidise the dressing ingredients and add half to each bowl. Toss well. Leave to marinate for 1 hour, then mix half the chopped onion into each kind of cabbage.

Place a Chinese leaf on each of four plates and top each with a little heap of both salads. Garnish with red and green apple slices. Arrange the eel strips in a criss-cross pattern on top and around. Add a few walnuts, a leaf of corn salad, and a sprinkle of egg white and yolk. **Serves 4**.

Pepperonade au poulet fumé et champignons acidulés • Peppers with smoked chicken and mushrooms

Peppers are one of the more recent salad vegetables to become popular here. Increasing quantities are now grown in British glasshouses, besides imports from many countries, so they are available all the year round.

Unlike chillies, these sweet peppers do not have a hot taste. The red pepper (the ripe form) is sweeter than the green, so the choice depends on your taste and the intended use. Milder varieties, yellow, purple and white in colour, are nowadays reaching the shops.

The inside seeds and membrane should be removed before cooking the pepper or using it in salads. In this high-fibre diet we recommend leaving the skin on. But if this does not suit, put the pepper briefly under the grill until it blisters, then peel. The pepper can play a tasty part in salads, light Gazpacho-type soups, omelettes, pilaffs, or in ratatouille with aubergines and tomatoes. It makes an excellent light dish when stuffed with rice, fish, minced meat or poultry and oven-baked. The calorie-count is only 15 per 100g/4oz, with plenty of vitamin C.

½ red, ½ green, and ½ yellow pepper (the remaining halves can be used
    in a soup or pilaff)
breasts of 1 smoked chicken
150g/5oz mushrooms, sliced
1 small red onion, peeled and cut into thin strips
½ piece of preserved ginger, cut into thin strips
1 round lettuce, to serve

dressing:
150ml/5fl oz plain low-fat yogurt
3 leaves of fresh mint, chopped
1 small green chilli, seeded and sliced, or Tabasco sauce to taste
1 teaspoon seed mustard
salt and freshly ground black pepper

Remove the seeds and membrane from the half peppers and cut into matchstick-size strips. Cut the chicken breasts into roughly bite-size pieces. Combine the peppers, chicken and other salad ingredients in a bowl. Liquidise the dressing ingredients. Add to the salad and toss. Leave to marinate for 30 minutes.

In four glass bowls, arrange two or three lettuce leaves as a nest and fill with the salad. **Serves 4**.

Petit ragoût de salsifis aux moules safranées ◆ Salsify with mussels in saffron sauce

Looking like a long, slender parsnip with an earthy skin, salsify has soft white flesh when cooked, with a flavour reminiscent of oysters (hence its popular name, the oyster plant). From medieval times on, it has been enjoyed as a vegetable in much of Europe but it rather fell out of fashion in Britain. This is a pity as it is a useful ingredient. I have partnered it here with mussels to make a dish that should intrigue you and your guests.

    Salsify is mainly imported from France and Belgium, from October to late spring. Choose salsify that is free of damage or discoloration and treat with care to avoid 'bleeding'. Scrape rather than peel and place immediately in a little salted water to which a dash of white vinegar has been added to prevent them turning black. Salsify can be served raw in a light yogurt mayonnaise with mustard seeds or in a garlic dressing, or in a light seafood sauce like this one.

450g/1 lb salsify, scraped
1 teaspoon plain flour
50ml/2fl oz sunflower oil
2 garlic cloves, peeled and chopped
2 medium-size shallots, peeled and chopped
½ teaspoon curry powder
5 strands of saffron
150ml/5fl oz apple or white grape juice
2 tablespoons cider vinegar
75ml/3fl oz water
sprig of fresh thyme
1 tablespoon chopped fresh tarragon
5 spinach leaves, shredded
450g/1 lb fresh mussels, scrubbed
75ml/3fl oz plain low-fat yogurt mixed with 1 teaspoon cornflour
salt and freshly ground black pepper

Cut the salsify into finger-size pieces and drop into a pan of boiling water. Simmer for 5 minutes, then remove from the heat. Mix together the flour and 1 teaspoon of oil and stir into the water; this forms a skin on the salsify and helps to keep it white. Drain and set aside.

Heat the remaining oil in a large saucepan and stir fry the garlic and shallots for 1 minute. Stir in the curry powder and saffron and cook 30 seconds. Add the fruit juice, cider vinegar, water, the herbs and spinach. Bring to the boil and simmer for 4 minutes. Add the mussels, cover and cook for a further 5 minutes until they open, shaking the pan occasionally.

Remove the thyme and all the mussels. (Discard any mussels that are still closed.) Set the mussels aside. Liquidise the sauce with the yogurt mixture, then pour into a clean pan. Simmer for 4 minutes, stirring. Add the salsify to the sauce and season to taste. Simmer for a further 5 minutes. Meanwhile, remove the mussels from their shells. Keep warm.

Fold the mussels into the salsify mixture. Serve in individual soufflé or ramekin dishes, with toasted French bread or toast fingers. If possible, present the small dishes on plates lined with paper doilies. **Serves 4**.

Royal Crécy aux fèves des Marais • Broad beans with baked egg pudding

Broad beans are one of the oldest cultivated vegetable and a great favourite of many, especially when the beans are young enough to be eaten with the pods. Unfortunately, few other than keen gardeners will manage to acquire them in that state. However, broad beans have become more popular since chefs began taking the trouble to remove the skin of each bean, which takes away the slightly bitter after-taste. Prepared like this I have used them in my pâtés and terrines instead of expensive pistachio nuts.

Broad beans show up well in salads, as a vegetable garnish or in a light entrée. They are rich in protein so little of that element needs to be added.

450g/1 lb broad beans in the pod
50ml/2fl oz cider vinegar
1½ tablespoons honey
small piece of preserved ginger
225g/8oz young carrots, scraped and cut paper-thin

egg pudding:
4 large eggs, beaten
1 small tomato, skinned, seeded and finely chopped
600ml/1 pint milk
1 garlic clove, peeled and chopped
salt and freshly ground black pepper

Cook the beans in boiling water for 5 minutes. Drain and shell, then skin each bean. Set aside to cool.

Liquidise the vinegar with the honey and ginger. Marinate the sliced carrots in this for 1 hour.

For the egg pudding, beat the eggs well in a bowl. Cook the tomato in a small pan for 3 minutes to evaporate the moisture, stirring frequently. Cool, then blend into the eggs with the milk, garlic and salt and pepper to taste.

Grease four 150ml/5fl oz metal pudding basins with polyunsaturated margarine. Fill the moulds with the egg mixture and place in a baking tin half-filled with hot water. Bake at 200°C, 400°F, Mark 6 for 35 minutes or until the egg mixture is set.

To serve, arrange a ring of broad beans around the edge of four plates and put a ring of carrots inside them. Pour a little of the carrot marinade over the beans. Turn an egg pudding out into the centre of each plate. On each pudding place a tomato rose (made from tomato skin) or three carrot slices. Garnish with a little chopped parsley or coriander and preserved ginger strips. **Serves 4**.

Tartelettes de foies de volaille aux navets nouveaux • Chicken liver tartlet with spring turnips

Turnips have been eaten for many centuries. The Saxons used both roots and leaves, often cooked as my Grandma did in an iron cauldron, with whatever meat or poultry was around. What a long tradition some of our cooking methods have, and how often they are the best!

Prime young spring turnips can be eaten raw with a French dressing of oil and vinegar or with yogurt and lemon. Or they can be a garnish to delicious entrées such as this fine liver tartlet. Turnip tops can be used raw in salads or cooked like spinach. Prime turnips feature in many stews and casseroles or can be mashed with potatoes or served with grills. They are rich in minerals and vitamins. Early turnips are usually sold six to a bunch and washed. Globular varieties are said to have more flavour but this is a matter of personal preference. Avoid maincrop turnips that are spongy or otherwise in inferior condition. Baby turnips can be just scrubbed without peeling; older types must be peeled.

450g/1 lb small turnips, peeled if necessary
grated nutmeg
salt and freshly ground black pepper
1 egg yolk
3 tablespoons plain low-fat yogurt
2 tablespoons lemon juice
8 individual pastry cases, approx 10cm/4 inches diameter, baked
225g/8oz chicken livers, sliced
3 tablespoons sunflower oil
75g/3oz button mushrooms, thinly sliced
4 tablespoons consommé or stock
8 young spinach leaves
few sprigs of watercress

Cut the turnips into pieces. Put in a pan with water to cover, a generous pinch of nutmeg and salt and pepper to taste. Bring to the boil and simmer until the turnips are tender. Drain thoroughly and mash with the egg yolk, yogurt and lemon juice. Keep hot.

Warm the pastry cases in a 200°C, 400°F, Mark 6 oven.

Meanwhile, fry the chicken livers in the oil until sealed but still pink in the centre. Add the mushrooms and seasoning and simmer steadily for a further 3 minutes. Stir in the consommé, and let bubble briskly for 1 minute.

Fill the pastry cases with turnip purée and top each one with the chicken liver mixture. Arrange on a large serving platter and serve hot, garnished with spinach leaves and watercress. **Serves 8.**

Omelette Confucius • Crab and Chinese leaf omelette

Though Chinese leaves or cabbage have recently become popular in the West, they have been on record as eaten in their home country as early as the 5th century. They are now imported from Israel, Holland and Spain as well as homegrown. The two varieties available are a long one and a round or oval specimen. About 700g/1½lbs is an average weight so shops sometimes sell half a head. Obviously choose examples that look really fresh.

Chinese leaves are valuable in salads, stiff enough to use with dips, or like bean sprouts may be briefly cooked in a quick stir fry.

A good fishmonger will dress a crab for you, ready to eat. If it is a case of do-it-yourself, a 900g/2 lb crab can be boiled in 30 minutes. If you wish, use the white meat only for a combination dish like this and reserve the dark meat to make a crab pâté with other cooked fish.

1 small head Chinese leaves, or ½ big one (6 leaves)
small piece of fresh root ginger (the size of a grape), peeled and sliced
4-5 tablespoons sunflower oil
salt and freshly ground black pepper
4 eggs
1 tablespoon mixed chopped fresh coriander and mint leaves
1 small shallot, peeled and chopped
150g/5oz white crab meat
1 teaspoon sesame seeds, toasted

With a rolling pin, flatten four Chinese leaves and place on a platter about 25cm (10 inches) in diameter. Liquidise the ginger with 1 tablespoon of oil. Season to taste with salt and pepper and sprinkle this dressing over the leaves. Finely shred the remaining two Chinese leaves.

Beat the eggs in a bowl with the herbs and seasoning. Heat 2 tablespoons of oil in a heavy 20cm/8 inch frying pan. Stir fry the shallot and shredded Chinese leaves for 2 minutes, then add the egg mixture. Cook until just set and golden brown on the bottom, then carefully turn the omelette over, without breaking it, and brown the other side.

Slide the omelette on to the platter over the Chinese leaves and cut into four quarters. Keep hot.

Stir fry the crab meat in a small pan in the remaining oil until hot. Place a serving on each piece of omelette and sprinkle over the sesame seeds. The garnish could be a courgette blossom, samphire stems or halves of cherry tomatoes. Serve hot. **Serves 2.**

Purée de poisson aux flageolets mexicaine ◆ *Minced fish with green flageolets and chilli*

The chilli, a favourite ingredient in much Asian and Caribbean cuisine, can lend a little excitement to a dish when used with discrimination, as in this recipe. Chillies come in two main varieties. One is long, thin and very hot while the other is shorter with a milder flavour. Unless you have a very robust palate do not put uncooked chilli directly on the tongue as it is so hot, and do not touch the sensitive eye area or lips when preparing chillies. Red chillies are simply a riper version of the green. Most chefs use the latter, but it is hard to detect the difference between them. The hotness can be reduced by removing the seeds as in this dish.

2 red mullet, each 225g/8oz, filleted and skinned
2 large tomatoes, each about 100g/4oz
2 eggs, beaten
2 garlic cloves, peeled and chopped
50ml/2fl oz sunflower oil
1 medium-size red onion, peeled and chopped
1 green chilli, seeded and sliced, or 3 dashes of Tabasco sauce
75g/3oz canned drained flageolet beans
10 spinach leaves
juice of ½ lemon

stock:
about 225g/8oz fish trimmings, including head, bones and skin of mullet
1 small onion
1 carrot, peeled and sliced
1 stick of fennel or 1 teaspoon aniseed
600ml/1 pint water
salt and freshly ground black pepper

Boil the stock ingredients for 20 minutes, then strain through muslin or a fine sieve. Cook the fish fillets in the stock for 5 minutes only. Drain and allow to cool, then chop.

Make two tomato 'cups' for the fish mixture by cutting off the top and scooping out the pulp and seeds. Discard the seeds, and add the tomato pulp, eggs and garlic to the fish. Liquidise together to a paste.

Heat the oil in a sauté pan and cook the onion and chilli for 2 minutes without browning. Add the beans and the fish mixture. Stir quickly to scramble until firm but creamy. Season with a little salt and remove from the heat.

Spread the spinach leaves on two plates to cover all except the plate edge, and sprinkle with the lemon juice. Fill the tomato cups with the fish mixture and put in the centre of each plate. Serve immediately. If you prefer the tomato cooked, fill the cups and bake in the oven at 200°C, 400°F, Mark 6 for 5 minutes. **Serves 2.**

Flan de poireaux au blanc de volaille • Chicken and leek flan

The culinary term 'flan' in France means a baked egg custard with various flavourings or ingredients such as vegetables, meat, fruit or fish, and with or without a pastry base. The little entrées here are moulded in individual oval dishes and are turned out after being cooked.

Eggs are an important ingredient in Cuisine Fraîcheur and, of course, have multiple uses. An average size 4 egg (weight 57.5g/2oz) contains high quality protein, vitamins A, B2 (riboflavin) and D, besides iron, calcium, thiamin and nicotinic acid. A fresh egg can be judged by the firm, jelly-like nature of the white. This makes it easier to fry or poach than a stale egg since the yolk is firmly encased and will not break.

1kg/2lb 2oz white of leeks
4 tablespoons sunflower oil
4 tablespoons water
2 chicken breasts, skinned, boned and minced
4 eggs, beaten
150ml/5fl oz plain low-fat yogurt
salt and freshly ground black pepper
grated nutmeg

sauce:
2 tablespoons sunflower oil
100ml/4fl oz water
½ bunch of watercress, leaves only
100ml/4fl oz plain low-fat yogurt

Set aside four leeks for the sauce, and slice the remainder thinly. Cook the leek slices in the oil for 4 minutes without browning. Add the water, bring to the boil and simmer for 2 minutes only. When cool, blend in a bowl with the minced chicken, beaten eggs and yogurt. Season to taste with the salt, black pepper and a pinch of nutmeg or mace if desired.

Grease six earthenware or metal moulds of 150ml/5fl oz capacity with a little poly-unsaturated margarine and fill with the leek mixture. Place the moulds in a baking tin and add hot water to come about halfway up the moulds. Bake at 210°C, 405°F, Mark 6/7 for 20 to 25 minutes. Remove from the oven and allow to rest for about 5 minutes.

Meanwhile, prepare the sauce. Slice the reserved leeks. Heat the oil in a pan and add the leeks and water. Cook for 5 minutes or until soft. Liquidise with the watercress and yogurt. Season to taste with salt, pepper and nutmeg.

To serve, pour the sauce into the centre of six plates and turn each flan out on to it. Decorate with a sprig of parsley, watercress or curly lettuce if you wish. **Serves 6.**

Chayote aux langoustines sur mâche douce • Christophine with scampi and corn salad

Chayote is a member of the gourd or marrow family that grows in profusion in tropical climates. It is roughly pear-shaped, usually with a ridged green skin, though smooth and white varieties are now seen. The flesh is firm and very pale green and its delicate flavour reminds me of squash. In the U.K. you will usually find this vegetable at bigger supermarkets or West Indian shops. Chayote also goes by other names such as christophine, vegetable pear, or chow-chow.

Preparation and use is much the same as for marrow or courgettes. They are delicious stuffed with fish, chicken or eggs. To serve on its own, simply peel, slice and cook in a little water for 8 minutes or until tender, and serve with a peppery vinaigrette, an egg sauce or mayonnaise.

Langoustines, or Dublin Bay prawns, are sold as scampi when without the shell. You can either buy cooked prawns and remove the flesh from the tail or buy frozen raw scampi and cook as indicated here.

1 medium-size chayote
4 tablespoons sunflower oil
1 small red onion, peeled and chopped
1 green pepper, cored, seeded and sliced
½ medium green chilli, seeded and sliced
3 fresh tarragon leaves, chopped
1 tablespoon tomato purée, or chopped pulp of 1 large tomato
4 button mushrooms, sliced
juice of 2 limes
salt and freshly ground black pepper
25g/1oz plain flour
ground ginger
225g/8oz raw scampi
2 large radicchio leaves, shredded
2 corn salad leaves
50g/2oz shelled roasted peanuts, crushed and slightly toasted
1 tablespoon mixed chopped fresh parsley and dill

Cook the chayote in its skin in boiling water for 20 minutes; drain. Cut in half and remove the seeds. Scoop out a little of the flesh from each half to make a cavity for the stuffing. Chop the scooped-out flesh and set it aside. Keep the chayote shells warm.

Heat half of the oil in a pan and stir fry the onion, green pepper, chilli and tarragon for 4 minutes without browning. Add the tomato purée or pulp, chopped chayote flesh, mushrooms and lime juice. Cook for 2 more minutes. Season to taste with salt and pepper and remove from the heat.

Season the flour with salt and ginger and use to coat the scampi. Heat the remaining oil in a frying pan and cook the scampi for 4 minutes, turning once to brown evenly. Drain away surplus oil, if any, and stir in the sauce. Fill the cavity in the chayote halves with the mixture, piling it up.

Arrange the shredded radicchio and corn salad on two plates, with a chayote half on each. Sprinkle on the crushed toasted peanuts and freshly chopped herbs. Serve hot
Serves 2.

Galettes de panais à l'églefin ◆ Parsnip and haddock cakes with tomato

Parsnips are native to Britain and have been cultivated since Roman times, though their size and quality has naturally been greatly improved by breeding. They were the traditional accompaniment to roast beef and were served with salt cod on Ash Wednesday. Parsnip wine has been made by country people for centuries. The French rather haughtily regarded them as food for the pigs, but young chefs have now brought them back into high esteem across the Channel too.

In selecting top quality parsnips (lesser kinds may be adequate for soups) choose those with no fangs or blemishes. Avoid any with soft brown patches on the shoulders or that have become dried and wizened.

2 medium-size parsnips, 225g/8oz total weight
225g/8oz fresh haddock fillet, skinned and minced
3 small shallots, peeled and chopped
50g/2oz fresh brown breadcrumbs
2 eggs
salt and freshly ground black pepper
3 tablespoons sunflower oil
2 large tomatoes, skinned, seeded and chopped
1 teaspoon tomato purée
1 small chilli, seeded and sliced, or 3 drops of Tabasco sauce
2 fresh basil leaves, chopped
1 teaspoon cornflour mixed with 3 tablespoons water

Peel and slice the parsnips. Cook in boiling water for 15 minutes. Drain and, when cool, mash to a purée. Combine the parsnip purée and haddock in a bowl with 2 of the shallots, the breadcrumbs, eggs and seasoning.

For the tomato sauce, heat the oil in a pan and stir fry the remaining shallot for minutes. Add the tomatoes, tomato purée, chilli and basil. Cook for 10 minutes, then thicken with the cornflour mixture. Boil 3 more minutes to a jam-like thickness, stirring frequently. Season and keep warm.

Grease a baking tray with oil. Drop eight small heaps of the fish mixture like small pancakes at regular intervals on it. Grill for 4 minutes on each side or until brown.

To serve, place two spoonfuls of tomato sauce on each plate with two 'galettes' arranged beside it. The garnish could be a twisted lemon slice and a little lettuce. **Serves 4 (small portions)**.

Galettes de pomme au carvi • Potato cakes with caraway

When unexpected guests turn up, it is often useful to be able to produce a dish that is special yet needs no fuss, using ingredients that are always to hand – potatoes and an onion for example. This is one of my own household's nice surprises for visitors who 'just dropped in' – and who invariably ask for the recipe. The galettes can be flavoured with other seeds such as anise or celery seeds, but I find the caraway seeds the tastiest aromatic for them.

450g/1 lb potatoes, peeled and grated finely into a pulp
1 small onion, peeled and grated
2 eggs, beaten
50g/2oz wholemeal flour
½ teaspoon baking powder
75ml/3fl oz buttermilk or plain Greek-style strained yogurt
50ml/2fl oz water
½ teaspoon salt
freshly ground black pepper
1 teaspoon caraway seeds
4 tablespoons sunflower oil

In a bowl combine all ingredients except the oil to produce a thickish batter. Heat the oil in a 20cm/8 inch frying pan. Drop in a large spoonful of batter for each cake, cooking four at a time. The cakes will be about 2.5cm/1 inch in diameter. Cook for 1 minute on each side or until crisp and golden. Repeat until all the batter is used. Sprinkle on more salt if wished and serve hot. **Makes 18 cakes.**

Choux-rave aux champignons tomatés • Kohlrabi with mushrooms and tomatoes

Kohlrabi is a hybrid member of the cabbage family, sometimes called a 'turnip-cabbage'. It reached Europe in the 16th century, possibly from the East, and became widely popular in some countries. But it has never quite won a name for itself in Britain or the United States. This is a pity as it is a good vegetable, hot or cold, with a nutty flavour.

The leaves may be treated like spinach, but it is the round base stem that is generally used.

This can be white, light green or purple in colour. Buy only young ones, no bigger than an orange. They are usually cooked in the skin and peeled afterwards; some people prefer steaming for maximum flavour. Kohlrabi can be served hot, either plain or with peanut butter or cheese sauce; or allow to cool and blend with mayonnaise; or, if very young, serve raw, finely sliced, with corn salad, celery and onions.

2 small kohlrabis
6 anchovy fillets
2 spring onions, chopped
2 large tomatoes, skinned, seeded and chopped
6 shelled walnuts, chopped
2 tablespoons sunflower oil
1 tablespoon cider vinegar
2 garlic cloves, peeled and chopped
3 fresh tarragon leaves, chopped
salt and freshly ground black pepper
225g/8oz mushrooms, sliced
8 lettuce leaves

Cook the kohlrabis, in the skin, in boiling water for 35 minutes.

Meanwhile, desalt the anchovies by soaking in a little warm water for 15 minutes. Drain, pat dry and dice. Mix the anchovies in a bowl with the spring onions, tomatoes, walnuts, oil, vinegar, garlic, tarragon, and salt and pepper to taste. Fold in the sliced mushrooms. Arrange the lettuce on two plates and spoon the mushroom mixture on them.

Drain the kohlrabis. Peel and cut into slices or strips. Arrange on top of the mushrooms and sprinkle with a little chopped parsley. **Serves 2.**

Les quatre purées hivernales • Winter vegetable purées

A selection of Nouvelle Cuisine-style vegetable purées, with their different colours, flavours and textures, stimulates the taste buds and is very impressive served at a special meal or dinner party.

225g/8oz each swede, parsnips and carrots, all peeled and roughly chopped
225g/8oz Brussels sprouts, trimmed
4 tablespoons soured cream
2 eggs, beaten
45g/1½oz polyunsaturated margarine
salt and freshly ground black pepper
100g/4oz firm mashed potato (optional)

pinch of grated nutmeg
finely grated rind of ¼ small lemon
1 teaspoon toasted and roughly chopped pine nuts
1 teaspoon roughly chopped blanched almonds
¼ teaspoon coriander seeds

Cook the vegetables individually in boiling salted water until tender and drain thoroughly, then mash or purée in a liquidiser. To each vegetable purée add 1 tablespoon soured cream, one-quarter of the eggs and margarine, and salt and pepper to taste. If the purées are too slack to be moulded, beat one-quarter of the mashed potato into each. To the swede purée add the nutmeg and lemon rind; to the parsnip purée add the toasted pine nuts; to the carrot purée add the blanched almonds; and to the sprouts add the coriander seeds.

Reheat the purées, in separate pans, in a bain marie (a larger pan of hot water). Use an ice-cream scoop to serve, putting a scoop of each purée on each plate. Serve hot, garnished with a sprig of tarragon, or a fine julienne of raw carrot and swede. **Serves 4**.

Oignons de Bretagne aux pignons • Stuffed onions with pine nuts and prawns with pumpkin sauce

It is hard to imagine what cuisine would be like without the great onion family. All the way from the robust peasant stew to the refined classical dishes flavoured by the mild shallot, this vegetable has lent its varied but always appetising character to cooking to an extent perhaps unmatched by any other.

Though not especially nutritious in themselves, onions have a very healthy proportion of vitamins and mineral salts, and they are a must in Cuisine Fraîcheur. Salads or dips can be easily enhanced with the addition of onion. Raw chopped onion can be sprinkled over cooked root vegetables; or onion can be liquidised and added to any kind of dressing. More nutrients are preserved if onions are baked or boiled with the skins on, but these should of course be removed before serving.

2 large Spanish onions
50g/2oz pine nuts
25g/1oz sultanas, soaked in hot water for 10 minutes and drained
50g/2oz fromage frais (page 179)
100g/4oz peeled cooked prawns

sauce:
1½ tablespoons sunflower oil
150g/5oz pumpkin pulp, diced small
1 large carrot, peeled and chopped

1 small onion, peeled and chopped
1 teaspoon tomato purée
1 teaspoon honey
150ml/5fl oz water
good pinch of turmeric
salt and freshly ground black pepper

Bake the onions in their skins at 200°C, 400°F, Mark 6 for 35 to 40 minutes or until soft.

Meanwhile, prepare the sauce. Heat the oil in a pan and stir fry all the vegetables together gently for 10 minutes, stirring from time to time. Add the tomato purée, honey and water. Bring to the boil and simmer for 12 minutes or until the vegetables are very soft. Liquidise the sauce, then reheat. Add the turmeric and season to taste. Keep warm.

Peel the onions. Squeeze each onion to remove the centre core and form a cavity. Chop the core and mix with the pine nuts, sultanas and cheese. Fill the onion cavities to the top. (If any filling remains, spread on toast for another snack.)

Pour the sauce on to two plates and arrange an onion in the centre. Arrange the prawns around the onion and serve. **Serves 2.**

Filets de lotte en cocotte au fenouil • Monkfish with Provençal sauce and fennel

The long history of fennel shows that it was enjoyed by ancient Egyptians, Greeks and Romans, and esteemed for its medicinal properties. The edible part of fennel is the bulbous lower part or root that has the appearance of celery. The aromatic fern part is used to flavour fish stocks or as a garnish. Choose well-rounded specimens of pale green or white colour.

To prepare for salads, cut the bulb in half lengthways and then across in very thin slices. For cooking, leave the bulb in halves and cook in a little boiling water with a pinch of salt (15 minutes at boiling point). Drain and serve hot with a sprinkling of ground coriander or nutmeg, or sauces like a yogurt sauce or this Provençal sauce.

150g/5oz fish heads, bones and trimmings
1 red onion, peeled and chopped
1½ tablespoons sunflower oil
2 garlic cloves, chopped
2 large tomatoes, skinned, seeded and chopped
1 teaspoon tomato purée
6 fresh tarragon leaves
450g/1 lb monkfish fillet
salt and freshly ground black pepper
1 fennel bulb, thinly sliced

Put the fish trimmings and a little of the onion in a pan, cover with water and bring to the boil. Simmer for 20 minutes, then strain the stock. Reserve 300ml/½ pint.

Heat the oil in a pan and gently stir fry the remaining onion and the garlic for 3 to 4 minutes. Add the tomatoes and tomato purée and cook 1 more minute. Add the reserved stock slowly and simmer the sauce for a further 12 minutes. Add the tarragon leaves.

Cut the monkfish fillet into strips 6cm/2½ inches long and 2cm/¾ inch thick. Add the fish to the sauce and poach gently for 8 minutes. Add moderate seasoning.

Arrange the sliced fennel on four plates, with a central hollow like a nest. Fill with the fish mixture. Sprinkle over a little of the chopped fennel fern and serve. **Serves 4.**

If you find the raw fennel too crunchy, you may cook it in boiling water for 5 to 8 minutes, but it will lose some of its aromatic fragrance.

Crème d'aubergines aux mangetouts • Aubergine dip with mangetouts

Aubergines originated in southern Asia but are now also grown in Europe. When raw, they contain 14 calories per 100g/4oz, and provide dietary fibre especially if you use the skin where the flavour is concentrated. They may be deep purple or white, or a mixture of the two, and come in several shapes and sizes. Choose aubergines that are plump and firm with a smooth glossy skin.

Before cooking aubergines, slice them and soak in cold water, or sprinkle with salt and leave to drain for 30 minutes. Either method will draw out the bitter juices.

Mangetouts, or sugar peas, are a blessing in a semi-vegetarian diet. The whole pod is edible, and only minimal preparation is needed since they have no tough lining like the shellable pea. Now imported from several countries as well as home-grown, mangetouts have the merit of availability through the year.

Choose pods that look bright green and juicy. The tiny bumps of the peas should not be too prominent (indicating an older pod). To prepare, simply top and tail, pulling away any string from the edges.

Eat them raw with dips, as in this recipe. Or, if preferred softer, just blanch in boiling water for 30 seconds, refresh in icy water and drain well. Or they can be stir fried Chinese-style (maximum 1 minute) without blanching. They contain protein and 67 calories per 100g/4oz.

1 large aubergine, sliced
50ml/2fl oz sunflower oil
50g/2oz shelled roasted peanuts
1 garlic clove
juice of ½ lemon
1 tablespoon tahini (sesame seed paste)
salt and freshly ground black pepper

1 teaspoon honey (optional)
225g/8oz mangetouts, tailed

Soak the aubergine slices in cold water for 15 minutes to eliminate the bitter juice, then pat dry. Spread out on a baking tray, brush with the oil and grill for 5 minutes on each side.

Liquidise the aubergine slices (with skin), adding the peanuts, garlic, lemon juice and tahini, which will thicken the paste. Add a light seasoning and the honey if wished. Serve warm in small ramekins with the raw mangetouts, which each person uses to eat the dip. **Serves 4.**

This creamy aubergine dip can also be served with other crudités such as Chinese leaves, mooli, celery and fennel. It is an excellent filling for raw tomatoes, or a spread on bread or toast.

Quenelles de merlan aux deux radis • Whiting dumplings with radish and mooli, and horseradish sauce

Radishes come in several colours and varieties. Their piquant crispness has long made them part of the hors d'oeuvre tray or a nibble with drinks. In 1598, the playwright Ben Jonson wrote of them: 'We will have radishes to taste our wine . . . '

In summer, the familiar red radishes are sold in bunches of a dozen, or cleaned and pre-packed in supermarkets. Mooli, or white radish, is a parsnip-shaped member of the radish family. It has a smooth white skin and regular shape. It was part of the rations of the Egyptian labourers working on the Great Pyramid. Mooli is bitter and can be cooked but is usually best served raw in dressing. It is available all year round in the U.K, with supplies from Holland, Kenya and Italy. To prepare mooli for salads, peel and wash well in cold water. The leaves of young mooli can be cooked like spinach. Japanese cooks know it as diakon and use it in many raw fish recipes.

450g/1 lb whiting, filleted, skinned and minced
1 egg, beaten
50g/2oz polyunsaturated margarine
1 small shallot, peeled and chopped or liquidised with the juice of 1 lemon
1 teaspoon chopped fresh tarragon
25g/1oz fresh breadcrumbs
salt and freshly ground black pepper
about 300ml/½ pint fish stock (page 102)
1 mooli, about 100g/4oz
bunch of red radishes
¼ small cucumber, peeled, halved lengthways and sliced

sauce:
75ml / 3fl oz plain low-fat yogurt
75ml / 3fl oz ready-made horseradish cream
1 teaspoon sweet made English mustard

Combine in a mixing bowl the minced fish, beaten egg, margarine, shallot, tarragon, crumbs and seasoning. Divide the mixture into 12 egg-shaped balls, using a little flour to ease handling. Place these quenelles in a greased flameproof baking dish, adding fish stock up to the top of the quenelles. Poach for 8 minutes or until they float. When ready, remove with a slotted spoon and keep warm.

Meanwhile, liquidise the sauce ingredients and season to taste with pepper.

Peel the mooli, cut it in half lengthways and then slice across, as with the cucumber. Wash the red radishes and slice.

On four plates place two spoonfuls of sauce and two quenelles and surround with concentric rings of cucumber, red radishes and mooli. Decorate the quenelles with sprigs of rosemary. **Serves 4**.

Lamettes de maquereau macéré au jus de pomme et de mûres • Cold raw mackerel with apple and blackberry

This recipe brings back fond memories of my childhood blackberrying expeditions in the woods and fields of Picardy. There is something very satisfying about coming home with a basket brimming with this toothsome fruit. Blackberries have several colourful local names such as bramble-berries, bramble-kites and lawyers. The juice is a good tonic, rich in vitamin C and potassium.

Select fruit that is firm, dry and black. If buying ready picked, avoid stained punnets – evidence of a crushed bottom layer. In Cuisine Fraîcheur the fruit is used raw, even in a pie. If mixed with apple, that is cooked separately and the blackberries are delicately blended later. In this recipe the tang of the fruit contrasts well with the slight oiliness of the fish.

1 large mackerel 450g/1lb, skinned and filleted
salt and freshly ground black pepper
small bunch coriander leaves
few coriander seeds
150ml/5fl oz apple juice
2 tablespoons white vinegar
1 tablespoon sesame oil

1 Granny Smith (or similar dessert apple), cored and sliced
225g/½lb blackberries
4 small spring onions
few sesame seeds

Cut the mackerel into very thin slices (like smoked salmon). Place them in a shallow dish and season with salt, pepper and a few chopped coriander leaves and seeds. Blend the apple juice and vinegar with the sesame oil. Pour this over the mackerel, cover with greaseproof paper and chill overnight.

Next day arrange the mackerel slices on two plates with some of the strained marinade. Decorate with overlapping apple slices and a heap of blackberries. Cut the spring onions in frills at both ends, then soak them in water until the ends curl back like petals. Place them on the side of the plate and sprinkle a few sesame seeds on the apple and decorate with more coriander leaves. Serve well chilled with wholemeal bread or crispbread. **Serves 2.**

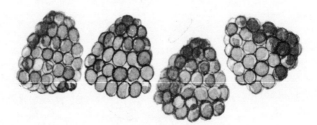

LES PLATS MARITIMES
SEAFOOD DISHES

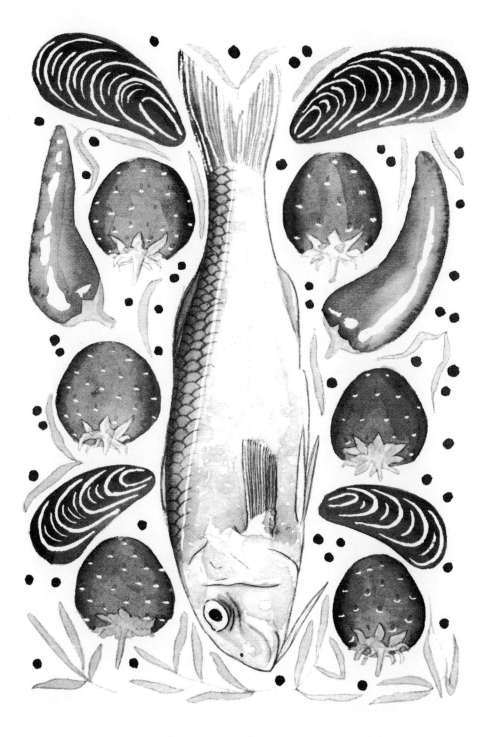

This chapter offers some of the most appetising dishes in Cuisine Fraîcheur. Anyone who has avoided fish in their diet because of the supposed need for troublesome preparation or 'frying tonight' smells around the kitchen may be surprised to find how agreeable it can be to make some of the following dishes, using modern methods. And you will see how much more beautiful a fish dish can look on the table when compared with the traditional lump of plain or battered white fish.

Fish and its preparation has fascinated me since my childhood upbringing in the great fishing-port of Boulogne, where every day I could see the silvery catch landed and, within hours, magically converted into some of the fine speciality dishes on the menu of my father's quayside restaurant. Ever since my apprenticeship days I have seen fish-cookery as more adventurous and rewarding than the meat side; and I still find fish a wonderfully adaptable ingredient now that I put the emphasis on its contribution to healthy eating.

One of several still relatively novel ideas found in these recipes is that of serving raw fish which has first been marinated in fruit juice, a mustardy sauce or similar pickling agent. This method has largely been borrowed by the chefs of Nouvelle Cuisine from an esteemed Japanese tradition. Such dishes are light, extremely digestible, easy to make and look good. As my recipes show, they are a way of discovering the delicate natural flavours of such fish as salmon, trout, sole, sea bass and other high-quality fish. And, of course, there is the added treat of being spared much cooking time and the old greasy washing-up. So long as the fish is good and fresh, the marinade will make the fish safe to eat: it is really the same process that has been used to pickle raw herring for centuries.

Happily, the selection of fish on sale at good fishmongers has been improving. Thanks to fish-farming, very fresh trout are available all year round, and almost any recipe for bass, mullet, carp or salmon can be adapted for using trout.

Fish are important in giving Cuisine Fraîcheur its healthy balance. They are a valuable source of good-quality protein and minerals, and of vitamins A, B, D and E. Fish contain no connective tissue like meat so are never tough or indigestible, and the fats are of the low-cholesterol type. The other health advantage which appeals to a growing number of semi-vegetarians is that fish are definitely 'free range' and spared the artificial hormones and dubious methods involved with battery chickens and penned calves.

This cuisine applies a number of particular ideas to improving the dietary quality of fish-cookery while keeping maximum quality and appeal to the eye. You may be able to adapt these methods to your own recipes. There are, for example, combinations of fish with the more delicate vegetables and fruit, whose tangy flavours give a pleasing contrast. Compositions of fish and shellfish bring out the subtly different tastes and textures of both components. The old cream-laden dressings have been replaced by light, herby sauces using yogurt and other non-fattening ingredients. Instead of pastry, with its 50 per cent fat content, we use low-fat pancakes or other attractive containers for fish stuffings such as peppers or spinach leaf wrappings.

All these devices will help to conserve your health and your time. I have put an emphasis on presentation because fish lends itself so well to a charming appearance, and a few minutes spent in arranging a dish with its garnish can turn a routine meal into a great pleasure.

Bolée bretonne • Breton fish soup

This fine soup is a reminder of my time doing military service aboard a French destroyer before the war as an officers' cook, when this dish was a favourite of the wardroom mess. The essential in its preparation is a really good, home-made fish stock. Once you have that, nicely clarified, any fish can be added with suitable herbs to aromatise it. I have refined and improved the recipe over the years and served it both hot and cold at banquets and other functions with great success.

4 raw Dublin Bay prawns
4 small shelled scallops
225g/8oz cod fillet, skinned and cut into 2.5cm (1 inch) cubes
1 teaspoon lemon juice or white vinegar
1 teaspoon honey

basic fish stock:
1 red onion, peeled and sliced
1 tablespoon sunflower oil
750g/1½lbs fish trimmings (bones or heads from sole, cod, turbot, trout, plaice)
1 garlic clove, peeled and crushed
1 carrot, scraped and sliced
slice of fennel, chopped
1 stick of celery, sliced
sprig of fresh thyme
1 teaspoon aniseed
1.5 litres/3 pints water
150ml/5fl oz white grape juice

to clarify:
225g/8oz minced cod fillet
1 egg white
juice of ½ lemon

Peel the prawns and set aside. Reserve the heads and shells to make the stock. In a large saucepan, stir fry the onion in the oil for 3 minutes. Put in the prawn heads and shells, fish trimmings, garlic, carrot, fennel, celery, thyme and aniseed. Cook for 4 more minutes, then add the water and grape juice. Bring to the boil and simmer for 35 minutes.

Cool the stock for 10 minutes, then strain through a fine mesh or nylon strainer. You should have about 1 litre/1¾ pints of very good stock. Allow to cool completely.

To clarify the stock, mix the minced cod with the egg white and lemon juice. Blend with the cold stock. Reheat slowly over a low heat until the whole mass of minced fish coagulates as a crust on top. Simmer very gently for 20 minutes without disturbing, then carefully remove the fish crust and pass the stock again through a nylon strainer. The resulting fish consommé should be clear. Discard the minced cod crust. Add the lemon juice or vinegar and honey.

Take a quarter of the fish consommé and place it in a shallow pan. Bring gently to the boil, then add the prawns, scallops and cubes of cod. Poach for 4 to 5 minutes.

Heat the remaining fish consommé separately and pour into soup plates. Add the seafood using a slotted spoon and top up the plates as necessary with more consommé. Garnish each serving with two basil or mint leaves and a slice of lime floating in the soup. Serve with Chinese prawn crackers. **Serves 4.**

Soupe de truite provençale Paul Cézanne • Cold trout and vegetable soup

My great-great-uncle, Maxime Conil, was married to Rose Cézanne, sister of the celebrated Impressionist painter, Paul Cézanne. Maxime and Paul held opposite views on almost everything except food and the importance of it being really good. In one of those little anecdotes that are passed on in families, I was always told of their rare but mutual agreement that this delicious cold fish minestrone was better than a bouillabaisse. The recipe has been in my family's cooking repertoire for generations. Served cold, with ice cubes, it is very much a summer starter. As an alternative to trout, try it with mackerel, when you can get it really fresh.

1 trout, 350g/12oz, skinned and filleted
juice of 2 lemons
juice of ½ orange
1 teaspoon white vinegar
salt and freshly ground black pepper

broth:
600ml/1 pint water
50g/2oz stale bread, crumbled
2 garlic cloves, peeled and chopped
4 stoned green olives
1 tablespoon olive oil
1 green chilli, seeded and sliced
1 red onion, peeled and chopped
50ml/2fl oz plain low-fat yogurt
1 tablespoon tomato purée or ketchup
2 fresh basil leaves
2 fresh mint leaves

garnish:
50g/2oz fresh sweetcorn kernels, cooked 3 minutes and drained
25g/1oz red pepper, seeded and diced
25g/1oz green pepper, seeded and diced
1 large tomato, skinned, seeded and chopped
25g/1oz cucumber, diced

Wash the trout fillets in cold running water to remove all traces of blood. Cut the fish into tiny cubes (5mm/¼ inch or less) and place in a shallow dish. Add the lemon and orange juices, vinegar and seasoning and toss to mix. Leave to marinate for 3 hours.

Place all the broth ingredients in a large container and refrigerate for 3 hours.

When ready to serve, liquidise the broth. Add the sweetcorn, peppers, tomato, cucumber, and fish with its marinade. Serve in a soup tureen and add one ice cube and a sprinkling of chopped fresh parsley or coriander to each serving. **Serves 4**.

Les coquilles St Jacques Côte d'Opale • Scallops with mushrooms, tomatoes, yogurt and basil

Scallops are an excellent shellfish with tender and delicately-flavoured meat. They come in three sizes: the Mediterranean scallop, the Queen scallop and the largest, Pecten maximus. The familiar ribbed shell used to be worn by early pilgrims to show that they had been to the Holy Land.

A scallop should be closed tight at time of purchase as a sign that it is fresh. They are also sold frozen already shelled, but these tend to be a little tough. Scallops can be served raw with vinaigrette, or lightly poached for 2 minutes and served with many sauces, such as tomato, curry, or cream. They can be grilled, fried, used in stir fry oriental dishes or made into kebabs with other fish and prawns.

To prepare, remove the black beard and gravel bag. Cut out the edible parts, that is the white nut of meat and the red coral, and wash well under the tap. If they are very large cut them across in half.

1 tablespoon sunflower oil
1 small shallot, peeled and chopped
small sprig of fresh thyme
150ml/5fl oz unsweetened pineapple juice
4 large shelled scallops, cut into 5mm/¼ inch slices
salt and freshly ground black pepper
ground ginger
2 curly lettuce leaves
red and green lettuce leaves
150g/5oz mushrooms, sliced
2 large tomatoes, skinned, seeded and cut into cubes
8 fresh chives, snipped with scissors
50ml/2fl oz plain low-fat yogurt
4 fresh basil leaves, chopped
juice of 1 lemon

Heat the oil in a shallow pan and stir fry the shallot with the thyme for 30 seconds. Add the pineapple juice and bring to the boil. Poach the scallop slices in the liquor for 2 to 3 minutes. Season to taste with salt, pepper and ginger.

Arrange the lettuce leaves attractively on two plates. Sprinkle the mushrooms, tomato and chives over the leaves. Place the scallops on top with a little of the poaching liquor poured over. Blend the rest of the liquor with the yogurt and basil and serve separately. Lastly, squeeze the lemon juice over the fish. **Serves 2**.

Truite marinée à la moutarde • Raw trout with mustard and yogurt dressing

Many kinds of fish are suitable for serving raw after salting, such as is done to make Gravadlax or, marinating in a fruit juice or other acidic liquid. So long as the fish is very fresh, it is a perfectly safe, sterile and tasty way of presenting them. All over the Pacific islands people have eaten fish marinated in lime juice for centuries. The Scandinavians and Far Eastern people have likewise farmed fish and eaten them in similar fashion. The delicate flesh and flavour of the trout is ideal for this purpose.

If you find this dish appealing, then it is worth noting that it can be served in endless variations by changing the garnish: tangerines or orange segments, or salad stuff like mooli, red radishes, grated celeriac or carrots can all be used. The ever-useful mustard, in the milder Dijon form, adds a nice piquant bite to the dish.

1 large rainbow trout, 750g/1½lbs, skinned and filleted
sprig of fresh dill, chopped
1 tablespoon honey
1 tablespoon salt
grated rind and juice of 1 lime
grated rind and juice of 1 lemon
1 teaspoon Dijon mustard
75ml/3fl oz plain low-fat yogurt
¼ small green chilli, seeded and chopped

garnish:
75ml/3fl oz soured cream, whipped lightly
1 teaspoon red lumpfish caviar or roe
6 slices of lime, twisted, or fresh rosemary sprigs
½ cucumber, halved lengthways and thinly sliced
1 papaya, peeled, seeded and sliced
fresh coriander leaves

Wash the trout fillets in cold running water to remove all traces of blood. Pat dry. Prepare the seasoning by mixing together the dill, half the honey, the salt and lime and lemon rinds. Rub the fish fillets on both sides with the mixture, wrap in foil and refrigerate for at least 6 hours or overnight. Next day, rinse the fish under cold running water to remove surplus salt, then cut into tiny 5mm/¼ inch cubes.

In a bowl, combine the mustard with the yogurt, remaining honey, lime and lemon juices and chilli. Mix well and toss the fish in this sauce.

To serve, place a 6cm/3 inch pastry-cutter on each plate to act as a mould. Fill it with the fish mixture. Top with a little whipped soured cream, level with a palette knife and carefully lift off the mould. This should leave the filling looking like a little sand-castle. Add a touch of lumpfish roe and a twisted slice of lime. Surround each moulded fish with alternate rows of cucumber and papaya and add about 5 coriander leaves per plate. Serve well chilled. Keep any remaining mixture for a salad another day. **Serves 6.**

Les moules à la nouvelle boulonnaise • Mussels in new Boulogne style

Mussels used to be termed the 'poor man's oyster', but nowadays some fish gourmets rate them above oysters for their fuller flavour. My family has been cooking and serving mussels in scores of ways for generations. My brother Pierre had a popular 'Relais Routier' café-hotel near Lille where he served mussels cooked with chips as is the fashion in Belgium and Holland. The biggest varieties are imported into the U.K. from there, the British regulations being that mussels cannot be sold in the shell below a length of about 5cm/2¼ inches.

There are a host of ways of serving mussels: raw, with lemon, like oysters; grilled with garlic butter; stuffed with spinach and other herbs; in curry sauce; as part of Spanish paella with rice; or in several ways with white wine (excluded from Cuisine Fraîcheur). I dedicate this dish to my home town, Boulogne.

1½ tablespoons sunflower oil
1 small red onion, peeled and chopped
1 spring onion, chopped
1kg/2lbs 2oz fresh mussels in the shell, scrubbed
1 garlic clove, peeled and crushed
1 teaspoon cider vinegar
150ml/5fl oz water
8 sprigs of fresh tarragon
50g/2oz fresh spinach, shredded
juice of 1 lemon
1 egg yolk
1 teaspoon cornflour
4 tablespoons buttermilk or soured cream
salt and coarsely ground black pepper

Heat the oil in a large saucepan and stir fry the onion and spring onion until soft without browning. Add the mussels, garlic, vinegar and water. Cover and boil for 5 minutes until all the mussels open. (Discard those which do not.)

Strain off the liquor through a fine sieve into a small saucepan. Add the tarragon, spinach and lemon juice and bring to the boil. In a bowl, mix together the egg yolk, cornflour and buttermilk. Add 4 spoonfuls of the hot liquor, then stir this mixture into the remaining liquor in the pan. Cook gently, stirring constantly, until it is of a thin custard consistency. Season to taste.

Serve the mussels into two hot soup plates and pour the sauce over. Add a sprinkling of finely chopped fresh parsley, tarragon and mint. Provide a side plate for discarded shells and a soup spoon for drinking the sauce – or mop it up with crusty French bread as they do in Boulogne. **Serves 2.**

Caviar de thon aux choux parfumés à l'orange • Creamed tuna fish with orange cole slaw

The tuna or tunny fish is the giant of the mackerel family, sometimes attaining a weight of 136kg/300lbs. Though more common in southerly seas, it finds its way into the British catch too, and can sometimes be bought fresh at the more adventurous sort of fishmonger's. Canned tuna makes a quite acceptable dish if the fresh sort is difficult to get, or you can substitute fresh salmon or mackerel fillet.

Tuna meat is flaky, pleasantly mild in flavour, and ranges in colour from deep cream to pink. It can be bought packed in oil or brine, or smoked cut into slices, in air-tight packs. It is excellent in salads, such as the French Salade niçoise, or as a filling for sandwiches. Here the fish combines deliciously with a sharp and fruity cole slaw salad.

1½ tablespoons sunflower oil
2 shallots, peeled and chopped
1 garlic clove, peeled and chopped
225g/8oz fresh tuna fillet, skinned and diced, or drained canned tuna
1 large tomato, skinned, seeded and chopped
¼ teaspoon curry powder
50g/2oz walnut kernels, chopped
salt and freshly ground black pepper
50g/2oz fresh white or brown breadcrumbs
50ml/2fl oz plain low-fat yogurt
juice of ½ lemon
juice of ½ orange
1 orange

cole slaw:
150g/5oz white cabbage, shredded
1 shallot, peeled and chopped
juice of ½ orange
juice of ½ lemon

Heat the oil in a sauté pan and stir fry the shallots and garlic for 30 seconds. Add the fresh tuna and tomato and cook for 5 minutes. Sprinkle in the curry powder, walnuts and seasoning and cook 1 more minute. (If using canned tuna, add it now.) Remove from the heat and cool a little, then liquidise to a paste with the breadcrumbs. Mix in the yogurt and fruit juices. Check the seasoning and chill well.

Combine the cole slaw ingredients with seasoning to taste.

Using a zester, pare very fine strips of rind from the orange. Peel the orange and separate it into segments.

Divide the tuna 'caviar' between four plates and add two spoonfuls of cole slaw to each. Sprinkle with the orange rind strips and a little chopped fresh parsley, and garnish with the orange segments. **Serves 4**.

Filet de sole charentaise Conil ♦ Fillets of sole with charentais melon

The flesh of the sole is white, delicate in flavour and very firm. As a table fish it ranks second only to turbot. It comes in several varieties of which Dover Sole is the best; lemon sole and other kinds are more like plaice.

In selecting sole, the gills should be bright, the skin rather viscous and slimy. The fishmonger will skin and fillet it for you. That may also be an opportune moment to ask for the bones for making fish stock. Bones will keep well in your freezer, well-wrapped in a polythene bag, and so will the stock when you have made it. There are many recipes for sole. Some of the most famous are: Bonne Femme, baked with shallots and mushrooms; Walewska, with crawfish and cheese sauce, created for Napoleon's mistress, Maria Walewska; Normande, with oysters; and Colbert, fried in egg and breadcrumbs, created in the reign of Louis XIV.

8 sole fillets, skinned
salt and freshly ground black pepper
2 tablespoons chopped fresh mint
300ml/½ pint white grape juice
1 Charentais or Ogen melon
150ml/5fl oz plain low-fat yogurt
½ teaspoon cornflour

Sprinkle the fillets with salt and pepper to taste and half the chopped mint. Roll up each fillet and place in a deep frying pan. Sprinkle over the remaining mint and add the grape

Romance de la mer · Medley of fish, shellfish and vegetables with two sauces (page 114)

Above: Suprême de poulet Liotro · Chicken breast with blood orange (page 130)

Right: Chiffonade de légumes à l'Indochine · Chinese-style stir fried vegetables (page 188)

Above right: Comète de riz aux fruits de mer· Rice stars and seafood kebabs (page 118)

*Salade florale · Green salad with
flowers (page 160)*

*Champignonnade de truite arc en ciel · Rainbow
trout and mushroom salad (page 159)*

juice. Cover and poach gently for about 12 minutes until the fish is just tender.

Meanwhile, halve and seed the melon. Using a parisienne cutter or melon baller, scoop out the melon flesh into balls. Scrape out any remaining flesh attached to the skin (for adding to the sauce).

Using a slotted spoon, lift out the cooked sole fillets and keep warm on a serving dish. Add the scraped-out melon flesh to the poaching liquor and boil until reduced by about half. (If the melon flesh is too firm use a liquidiser.) Blend the yogurt and cornflour in a bowl and mix with the fish liquor. Gently simmer for 5 minutes.

Spoon a little sauce in the middle of the fish and garnish with the melon balls and a sprig of mint. Serve the rest of the sauce separately. **Serves 2**.

Tresse fermière aux deux truites • Plaited trout fillets

In the old days the technique of combining different kinds of fish for the table by plaiting them together was usually applied to whiting or sole fillets, which were then deep-fried. Many younger chefs have made this more elaborate, giving such plaited dishes names like 'mosaic' or 'tapestry'. Since such a method can produce a charming presentation of a meal, especially useful when you have guests, we adapt it to Cuisine Fraîcheur in this recipe using two kinds of trout of slightly different colouring. The flesh of the brown trout can vary from white to a pronounced rosy colour while the rainbow is pinkish.

When choosing your fish always look for a bright and sparkling skin with a silvery or golden sheen. Flesh should be firm and elastic with a sweet smell. The eyes should shine and the gills be bright red. If you can, buy the fish on the day of the meal to ensure freshness.

To fillet a trout, take a sharp knife and remove the head from the gutted fish. Snip the backbone behind it with a pair of kitchen scissors. Now slip the knife between the ribcage of the fish and its flesh. Keeping the blade flat against the bones, work in smooth strokes down the side of the fish towards the tail. Turn the fish over and repeat the process. To skin the fish, hold the tail with a cloth (skin side down on the board) and scrape the knife along the skin to free the flesh.

1 rainbow trout, about 450g/1lb, filleted and skinned
1 brown trout, about 450g/1lb, filleted and skinned
salt and coarsely ground pepper
8 spinach leaves
small sprig of fresh dill, chopped
1 small tomato, skinned, seeded and chopped

sauce:
150ml/5fl oz fish stock (see page 102)
2 strands of saffron
1 teaspoon cornflour, mixed with 5 tablespoons buttermilk or soured cream

Cut the fillets into finger-thick strips 8cm/3¼ inches long. There should be eight strips of each kind of trout. Season the strips.

Blanch the spinach leaves in boiling water for 30 seconds. Refresh, drain and pat dry. Remove the central rib of each leaf.

Wrap the strips of brown trout separately in the spinach leaves to make tubular shapes. Interweave four of these green tubes with four of the pink rainbow squares. Wrap this plait carefully in foil. Repeat to make a second plait.

Heat water in a steamer with a handful of seaweed for aroma, if available, then place the fish parcels in the top part or on the rack. Cover with lid and steam for 8 minutes.

Meanwhile, put the fish stock and saffron in a pan and bring to the boil. Gradually stir in the cornflour and buttermilk mixture and simmer until thickened. Season and strain.

Pour a little pool of sauce on each plate. Unwrap the fish plaits carefully and place on the sauce. Sprinkle dill and neatly diced tomato over the sauce for colour contrast. **Serves 2.**

Les crêpes bretonnes ◆ Baked seafood pancakes

Pancakes are a very welcome addition to Cuisine Fraîcheur. They avoid the 50 per cent fat of pastry and have better protein, and they can be made very quickly and served with a variety of delicious fillings, whether as snacks, a light lunch, or something bigger. This recipe, which presents an assortment of smoked and raw fish and vegetables parcelled in Breton crêpes, is one I have often served as a main fish dinner.

In Brittany pancakes are called galettes *and are cooked on a griddle referred to as a* galetien. *These delicate pancakes have been made the same way, with wholemeal or buckwheat flour, since Roman times. You can either use milk, water or beer. I think half water and half milk produces a good batter. For a spongier mixture add ¼ teaspoon baking powder and 1 teaspoon potato starch. Buttermilk or sour milk is recommended for a lighter mixture.*

pancake batter:
100g/4oz wholemeal flour
1 tablespoon cornflour
pinch of salt
2 eggs
150ml/¼ pint buttermilk
150ml/¼ pint water
1 tablespoon chopped fresh parsley
sunflower oil, for frying

filling:
50g/2oz cooked rice
1 egg, beaten

2 tablespoons plain low-fat yogurt
25g/1oz each cooked peas, beans and diced carrot
1 mushroom, sliced
50g/2oz white fish fillet, poached for 1 minute and flaked
1 teaspoon chopped fresh dill
1 shallot, peeled and chopped
salt and freshly ground black pepper
225g/8oz smoked tuna fish or salmon (4 large slices)
4 large leaves of chard, spinach or sorrel

sauce:
2 tablespoons plain low-fat yogurt
1 teaspoon sunflower oil
1 teaspoon cider vinegar
juice of ½ lemon
juice of ½ orange
1 teaspoon finely chopped onion
1 teaspoon chopped gherkin
1 teaspoon chopped fresh dill
¼ teaspoon made mustard

Combine the pancake batter ingredients and stir until smooth. Heat a teaspoon of oil in a 16-18cm/6½-7 inch omelette or pancake pan. When the oil is very hot, pour in about 4 tablespoons of batter and tilt to coat the pan thinly and evenly. Cook on both sides for 1 to 2 minutes. Turn the pancake on to a sheet of greaseproof paper to cool. Use up the batter to produce about four pancakes in all.

In a large bowl blend the rice with the egg and yogurt. Add the cooked vegetables, mushroom and flaked white fish. Flavour the mixture with the dill, shallot and seasoning to taste.

On a board place a large slice of smoked tuna. On top of it place a chard leaf and one-quarter of the rice and fish mixture. Roll up the tuna into a neat parcel. Place the parcel on a pancake and roll up once more. Neatly wrap the pancake in well-greased foil, sealing the edges tightly. Repeat the operation to use up all the pancakes and filling. Bake in a 200°C, 400°F, Mark 6 oven for 12 to 15 minutes.

Meanwhile, make the sauce by liquidising the ingredients together.

Unwrap the rolls and serve on to four plates, with a garnish of two lettuce leaves, lemon slices and a slice of green apple with the skin. Serve with the sauce. **Serves 4.**

Truite saumonée aux feuilles de betterave • Baked trout stuffed with mushrooms and chard

The chard used in this recipe is often sold as spinach though its leaves are a good deal wider with a prominent white rib when mature. When young, it is very useful for wrapping stuffing mixtures or in salads and egg dishes. If cooking the chard separately, it is best to steam the leaves whole and cut them up afterwards.

Chard is known in French as bette or poirée and features on our menus as bette à cardes. Rich in potassium and calcium, it is ideal for a slimming diet. It can be eaten raw, or cooked with savoury cheese or curry sauces, or used as filling for pizza, quiches, tarts and omelettes.

2 rainbow trout, about 450g/1lb each
6 large chard leaves, central rib removed
salt and freshly ground black pepper

stuffing:
2 tablespoons sunflower oil
25g/1oz shallot, peeled and finely chopped
1 garlic clove, peeled and finely chopped
150g/5oz mushrooms, finely chopped
1 chard leaf, chopped
2 tablespoons fresh wholemeal breadcrumbs
50g/2oz polyunsaturated margarine
2 eggs, beaten

sauce:
small sprig of fresh dill, chopped
75ml/3fl oz plain low-fat yogurt
50ml/2fl oz mayonnaise

First, bone the two trout as follows: Cut open the underside of the fish from gills to tail, using a sharp knife. Open out, flesh side down, and press firmly all along the backbone with your thumbs. Turn the trout over and lift out the complete backbone, using a knife to loosen side bones. Snip the head end of the bone with scissors.

Blanch the 6 large chard leaves in boiling water for 20 seconds. Drain and cool in ice water. Drain well and pat dry with a cloth. Divide the leaves in half and arrange them, slightly overlapping, in two rows on a board. They should match the length of the trout. Lay the trout on top and season to taste. Cover with greaseproof paper and set aside while preparing the stuffing.

Heat the oil in a pan and stir fry the shallot and garlic for 30 seconds. Add the mushrooms and cook for 2 minutes. Remove from the heat and mix in the chopped chard leaf, breadcrumbs, margarine and eggs. Put half the stuffing on to one side of each trout and fold over the other side of the trout to restore its original shape. Wrap the chard leaves around the fish, ensuring they are well covered. Wrap the fish again in oiled foil, sealing the edges tightly.

Place the fish in a baking tray with 100ml/4fl oz of water. Bake in a 200°C, 400°F, mark 6 oven for 20 minutes. Meanwhile, mix together the ingredients for the sauce. Serve the fish piping hot in the foil which is removed by the diner. Serve with the dill sauce.

An alternative method, as in the illustration, is to bake the trout in a tray without the foil. Just brush sunflower oil over the leaves, cover with a lid and bake for the same length of time.

For a garnish, scrape 2 carrots, groove lengthways with a cannelle knife and slice across. Marinate with 8 small sliced mushrooms in the juice of 1 lemon and a little sunflower oil. Arrange the mushrooms on top of the fish and the carrots around it with fresh coriander leaves in between. Near the end place a little julienne of carrot strips. **Serves 2.**

Blanc de turbot aux nectarines • Turbot with nectarines and spinach

Many consider the turbot to be the finest fish to come out of the sea, along with its cousin, the brill. It is rounder in shape and much larger than the plaice and its spots are smaller and more numerous. It can reach a hefty size of about 13.6kg/30lbs, but 3.6kg/8lb fish are about the average.

Turbot is cut into steaks for grilling or poaching, and is often served with a Béarnaise sauce when grilled and Hollandaise when poached. The whole fish can be stuffed with a fish soufflé mixture and baked – a spectacular dish when prepared this way. It has become a favourite fish for Nouvelle Cuisine, like bass and red mullet, and is sometimes served only half-cooked or even raw in thin slices.

2 turbot fillets, 150g/5oz each, cut into 3 slices
225g/8oz fresh spinach leaves, centre ribs removed
1 teaspoon sunflower oil
grated nutmeg
salt and freshly ground black pepper
lemon juice
2 nectarines, seeded and sliced

sauce:
1 teaspoon cornflour
4 tablespoons Greek-style strained yogurt or soured cream
75ml/3fl oz fish stock (see page 102)
2 egg yolks
1 ripe avocado, peeled and stoned
juice of 1 orange
juice of ½ lemon
piece of fresh root ginger (the size of a grape), peeled
pinch of chilli powder

Wrap the fish fillets in a piece of oiled foil. Place this parcel in the top of a steamer, cover and steam for 3 to 5 minutes.

Meanwhile, brush the spinach with the oil, season with nutmeg, salt and pepper to taste and sprinkle over a few drops of lemon juice. Arrange the spinach on two plates to cover almost completely, except the edge.

For the sauce, mix the cornflour with the yogurt or soured cream in a bowl. Bring the fish stock to the boil, stir in the yogurt mixture and simmer gently for 3 minutes. Whisk in the egg yolks. Heat gently for 30 seconds, then remove from the heat. Liquidise the avocado with the orange and lemon juices and the ginger and add to the pan. This will thin it to the right consistency. Season with the chilli powder and salt to taste.

To serve, place three pieces of fish fillet in a triangular shape over the spinach on each plate. In the centre pour a little pool of the sauce. Beside each piece of fish place two slices of nectarine, using one whole nectarine per portion. If you wish you can sprinkle a few blanched orange rind strips on the fish, or a fine julienne of preserved ginger or fresh carrot. **Serves 2**.

Romance de la mer • *Medley of fish, shellfish and vegetables with two sauces*

This dish looks most attractive, even romantic, on the table, in the way it combines a number of delicate colours. It is easy to prepare and extremely tasty, and should tempt anyone's appetite. The two sauces, one pink and one white, derive from Nouvelle Cuisine and show a pleasing contrast of aroma, flavour and colour which has been well received at some of our best, fashionable restaurants.

You can now buy good quality ready-cleaned mussels from Holland. The fishmonger will open the scallops for you.

2 shelled scallops, sliced
juice of 1 lemon
1 teaspoon sunflower oil
salt and freshly ground black pepper
450g/1lb fresh mussels in the shell, scrubbed
225g/8oz cod fillet, skinned and cut into 2.5cm/1 inch cubes
1 teaspoon paprika

stock:
150g/5oz fish bones and trimmings
150ml/5fl oz white grape juice
150ml/5fl oz water
1 teaspoon vinegar
1 small onion, peeled and sliced

rosemary sauce:
small sprig of fresh rosemary
1 teaspoon cornflour mixed with 5 tablespoons soured cream

pepper sauce:
4 tablespoons sunflower oil
2 garlic cloves, peeled and crushed
¼ red pepper, seeded and chopped
1 large tomato, skinned, seeded and chopped
1 teaspoon cornflour mixed with 2 tablespoons soured cream and 2 tablespoons
water

Put the scallops in a bowl with the lemon juice and oil. Season to taste. Marinate for 15 minutes.

Meanwhile, prepare the stock. Bring the ingredients to the boil and simmer for 15 minutes; strain. Divide the stock in half.

Put one portion of stock into a saucepan. Add the mussels, cover and boil for 5 minutes. Remove the mussels and discard the shells; set the mussels aside. Strain the stock.

The stock thus enriched by the flavour of the mussels is the basis for the rosemary sauce. Add to it the sprig of rosemary and reboil. Strain to remove the rosemary, and return the stock to the pan. Add the cornflour and soured cream mixture and simmer for 3 minutes, stirring. Season to taste. Set aside.

For the pepper sauce, heat the oil in a pan and stir fry the garlic for 30 seconds. Add the red pepper and tomato and cook for 3 minutes. Then add the remaining stock and boil for 5 minutes. Liquidise. Reheat and thicken with the cornflour and soured cream mixture. Add seasoning and keep warm.

Reheat the rosemary sauce and poach the scallops and cod cubes in it for 3 minutes. Remove the seafood with a slotted spoon.

Pour the two sauces beside each other on to an oval platter. Garnish with spinach, chicory and fresh coriander leaves at each end. On the spinach leaves place the cod cubes and sprinkle with paprika. Next to the cod arrange the mussels. In the centre of the dish, on the red sauce, place the scallops. **Serves 2.**

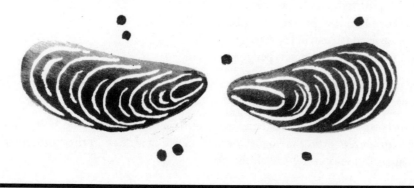

Loup de mer à la vapeur aux rameaux de salicornes • Sea bass steamed with seaweed garnished with samphire

Among the fish-cookery lessons we have learned from Japan, apart from the healthiness and pleasure of raw fish, is to steam fish for the bare minimum of time. This preserves maximum flavour. Adding seaweed to the steaming liquid is another excellent oriental idea. If you cannot get fresh seaweed, there are many kinds of dried seaweeds available in health food shops. These include wild nori or laver, kombu and kelp.

Marsh samphire is a seashore plant, collected at a number of points along the coasts of Britain. It is rich in soda and was once used in the manufacture of soap and glass – hence its other name glasswort. It has a pleasant, lemon-acidic flavour. It can be eaten fresh and raw but is even better if blanched for 30 seconds, when your palate will tell you why it is called 'asparagus of the sea'. When fresh, it should be a vivid green, firm, brittle and juicy. It is often used as a garnish for steamed fish.

Sea bass is a fish of the mullet family, now very fashionable. It is often baked with a bunch of fresh fennel inside its belly, but it is also delicious steamed as here. The flesh is very firm. It requires some acidulation with it, best provided by lime or lemon, a green salad, or a mixed salad with citrus fruits.

1 litre/1¾ pints water
450g/1lb fresh seaweed, or 100g/4oz dried seaweed
bunch of fresh thyme
few slices of fennel
1 teaspoon aniseed
2 sea bass fillets from the tail, about 175g/6oz each, scaled but with skin left on
2 sprigs of marsh samphire, blanched for 30 seconds

sauce:
2 tablespoons sunflower oil
150g/5oz fennel, thinly sliced
1 shallot, peeled and chopped
1 tablespoon plain flour
300ml/½ pint fish stock (see page 102)
50ml/2fl oz plain low-fat yogurt or buttermilk
pinch of ground turmeric (optional)
salt and freshly ground black pepper

First prepare the sauce. Heat the oil in a saucepan and stir fry the fennel and shallot over low heat for 5 minutes. Add the flour and stir well; cook for 30 seconds more.

Add the fish stock gradually, stirring constantly, and bring to the boil. Liquidise the sauce to a thin purée. Add the yogurt away from the heat. Stir in the turmeric if you want a yellow sauce and season to taste. Keep hot.

Put the water and most of the seaweed in the bottom of a steamer. Add the thyme, fennel and aniseed and bring to the boil. Season the bass fillets and wrap them in well-oiled foil. Place in the top of the steamer with the remaining seaweed as a lining. Steam for 6 minutes.

To serve, place the fish skin-upwards on two plates. Beside it place a spoonful of sauce. Garnish with the samphire and a little heap of raw, crisp carrot, swede and fennel cut in fine julienne. **Serves 2**.

Etoile de riz aux crevettes • Rice star with prawns

The versatility of rice gives it a deserved place in Cuisine Fraîcheur. It is one of the oldest grown crops, and at least half the world's population depends on rice for half its calorie intake. There are several thousand varieties of rice, but they can be divided into three major types: short grain, medium grain and long grain – the latter being the kind most bought in Europe. Many people seem to have difficulty in cooking rice well. To those with this problem I need do no more than recommend the short-cut I take myself, which is to use the finest quality rice which comes from the United States and is marketed under the brand name Uncle Ben's. It is available in packets of long grain, wholegrain, and mixed long grain and wild rice.

The flavour of this rice dish is enhanced by fresh, ripe mango. The prawns for the garnish should be cooked at the last moment, if possible.

600ml/1 pint fish stock (see page 102)
1 tablespoon turmeric
100g/4oz whole grain rice
50g/2oz peas, cooked
1 tablespoon finely chopped red pepper
salt and freshly ground black pepper
12 large Mediterranean prawns, cooked and peeled
2 mangoes, peeled, stoned and cut into slivers
1 okra, sliced crossways

sauce:
1 small onion, peeled and chopped
1 small stick of fennel, chopped
1 garlic clove, peeled and chopped
2 tablespoons sunflower oil
1 tablespoon curry powder
1 tablespoon plain flour
300ml/½ pint fish stock (see page 102)
1 tablespoon tomato purée
50ml/2fl oz mayonnaise

Put the fish stock and turmeric in a pan and bring to the boil. Add the rice, stir and cover. Simmer gently for 20 minutes, then drain. Combine with the peas and red pepper, and season to taste with salt and pepper. Oil the inside of a small star-shaped mould, about 10cm/4 inches across or 75g/3oz capacity, and fill with the rice while it is still hot. Turn out a rice star on to each plate.

For the sauce, stir fry the vegetables in the oil for 2 minutes. Add the curry powder and flour and cook for 30 seconds. Stir in the fish stock and tomato purée, bring to the boil and simmer for 12 minutes. Strain the sauce and season. Whisk in the mayonnaise.

Pour a pool of sauce on to the side of each plate. Add the prawns and slices of mango and okra, and garnish each plate with a slice of lime. **Serves 4**.

Plain boiled rice is usually cooked in five times its volume of water. The surplus water can be discarded. When cooking rice in stock, it is worth bearing in mind that rice absorbs two and a half to three times its volume of liquid depending on how quickly the liquid evaporates. For example, 150g/5oz of rice boiled in 750ml/1¼ pints of water produces 450g/1lb of cooked rice, and leaves 300ml/½ pint of surplus liquid. If the rice is baked, as for pilaff, there is no need to put more than three times its volume of liquid.

Comète de riz aux fruits de mer • Rice stars and seafood kebabs

225g/8oz rainbow trout fillet, cut into 2.5cm/1 inch squares
225g/8oz monkfish fillet, cut into 2.5cm/1 inch cubes
16 button mushrooms
1 red and 1 green pepper, cored, seeds removed, cut into 2.5cm/1 inch squares
1 medium-size onion, peeled and quartered, with layers separated into wedges
4 ripe apricots, halved and stoned
4-8 lime slices
little sunflower oil
salt and freshly ground black pepper
1 carambola, sliced, to garnish
75ml/3fl oz mayonnaise blended with a little tomato purée or chopped fresh
    tarragon and basil, or lemon wedges

rice:
4 tablespoons sunflower oil
1 small onion, peeled and chopped
2 garlic cloves, peeled and chopped
150g/5oz long-grain rice
½ teaspoon turmeric

550ml/18 fl oz water or fish stock
sprig of celery leaves
sprig of fresh thyme
50g/2oz cooked peas
50g/2oz cooked sweetcorn kernels

First prepare the rice. Heat the oil in a saucepan and stir fry the onion and garlic for 1 minute without browning. Add the rice and stir well for 30 seconds. Sprinkle in the turmeric and pour in the water or fish stock. Bring to the boil and add the celery leaves and thyme sprig. Simmer gently for 20 minutes.

Meanwhile, thread the fish, mushrooms, peppers, onion pieces, apricot halves and lime slices on skewers, alternating ingredients and colour. Sprinkle with oil and seasoning. Grill for 8 minutes on a foil-lined tray, turning to cook evenly.

When the rice is ready, stir in the peas and sweetcorn and season to taste. Pack the rice mixture into well-greased individual star-shaped moulds and turn out on to four plates. Add the kebabs to the plates and garnish with carambola. Serve with the mayonnaise or wedges of lemon. Serves 4.

Mousse de truite aux deux fruits ◆ Trout mousse with kiwi and strawberries

Salmon trout, also known as sea trout, has a pale pink flesh and is perhaps more delicate in flavour then either trout or salmon. It makes a perfect summer dish when poached whole in a court bouillon, then skinned and served either hot with Hollandaise or cold with mayonnaise. New potatoes with fresh mint and a little lemon are a good accompaniment, while cucumber and dill are the customary garnish. Salmon trout is in season from March to August. Good rainbow trout, mostly from fish farms, is available all year round, so if necessary, rainbow trout could be used in this recipe.

1 fresh salmon trout, about 1.5kg/3lbs, skinned, filleted and well washed
225g/8oz fromage frais (see page 179)
50ml/2fl oz Greek-style strained yogurt
25g/1oz powdered gelatine, soaked in 75ml/3fl oz cold water
75ml/3fl oz boiling water
dash of Tabasco sauce
salt and freshly ground white pepper
6 kiwi fruit, peeled and sliced on a slant
12 strawberries, hulled and halved

marinade:
2 kiwi fruit, peeled and sliced
1 teaspoon grated lemon rind

juice of 1 lemon
juice of 1 lime
1 tablespoon distilled white vinegar
1 tablespoon sunflower oil
¼ teaspoon made English mustard
1 teaspoon honey

Liquidise the marinade ingredients and cover the fish fillets with it in a shallow dish. Leave to soak overnight in the refrigerator, turning the fish three times. Drain the fish. Slice half the trout fillets very thinly with a sharp knife as you would smoked salmon; set aside. Mince the remaining fish fillets and put into a bowl. Add the cheese and yogurt and mix well.

Dissolve the soaked gelatine in the boiling water. Allow to cool, then blend with the minced fish mixture. Season with the Tabasco, and salt and pepper to taste. Refrigerate for 2 hours.

Divide the fish mousse into 6 portions and shape them like eggs. Wrap each in a slice of salmon trout. Arrange on 6 plates. Garnish each with kiwi slices and two strawberry halves. Arrange sprig of dill and a twisted slice of lime on top of each mousse. No sauce is needed with this delicate dish. **Serves 6.**

VOLAILLE ET VERDURE
POULTRY WITH VEGETABLES & FRUIT

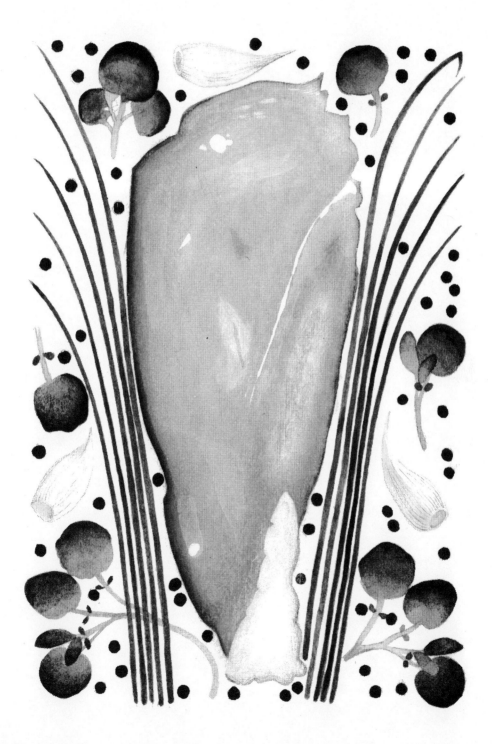

In gastronomy, *volaille* is the collective term for feathered birds raised on farms, that is chickens, ducks, geese, guinea fowl and turkey. Some may be surprised to learn that these days it also includes pigeons and quails which are also farm-bred for their eggs and meat. Cuisine Fraîcheur has a strong preference for free-range birds and eggs; they do thrive better in the open air, and our palates will appreciate the difference when enjoying the cooked product.

I have also brought rabbit into these recipes because the best preparations of it are not dissimilar to those for poultry. Rabbit is one of the most highly-esteemed ingredients of French and Spanish cookery – almost with the prestige of roast beef in England – the basis of numerous dishes good enough to delight any gourmet. Perhaps the British have been a little snobbish about rabbit, with so many around and thus relatively cheap, just as the French were once rather uppity about the parsnip. But rabbit, like pigeon, is gradually creeping back into fashion again as British chefs of Nouvelle Cuisine (like us of Cuisine Fraîcheur) try to be objective about the merits of good food, regardless of its humble origins. As for any false belief that rabbit is not easy to get, you may like to know that there are 2,000 commercial rabbitries in Britain (while France, remarkably, has ten times that number).

This chapter really provides the *pièces de résistance*, or main dishes, for the Cuisine Fraîcheur diet. Not surprisingly, chicken slightly predominates among the recipes, for the good reason that it is such an excellent and versatile meat, the world's most-eaten fowl, and the basis of hundreds or thousands of recipes in the global cook-book from the great *suprêmes* of French *haute cuisine* to the peasant stew.

If chicken has a fault it is that its meat can be rather bland, and few modern gourmets like it in stodgy cream sauces any more. But like the other white meats, it lends itself admirably to combinations – as illustrated in the following recipes – with crisp raw vegetables, slightly sharp and tangy fruits, an interesting cheese sauce, fruit vinegars, or a sweet-and-sour borrowed from oriental cuisine.

Chicken and turkey in particular are relatively low in fat. To reduce the fat (and improve the flavour) during cooking try these tips: 1) eat very little of the skin or, if desired, remove it entirely before cooking; 2) grill, roast or poach rather than fry; 3) use lemon or lime juice, spices or herbs to flavour the skin instead of butter, margarine or other fat. Insert herbs such as thyme, rosemary, sage or tarragon into a bird before roasting.

In selecting, note that poultry should generally have a fine white skin and flesh. A yellow skin used to indicate an over-fat bird, but nowadays is more likely to be the golden-coloured maize-fed chicken which has a delicious flavour both in its meat and eggs. Generally, very young birds are more tender but tend to have less flavour while old birds are tougher and tend to end up in the stock-pot for consommés and *pot-au-feu*. So, depending on the nature of the dish, a compromise on the right size is often desirable. Both chicken and turkey are also sold jointed which avoids the tedium of carving and wastage.

Poulet en gelée • Jellied herb chicken

This style of chicken poached and served cold in jellied stock, or aspic, is far more succulent than the usual stew and just the right dish for serving outdoors on a summer's day.

1 oven-ready chicken, about 1.5kg/3½lbs
½ lemon
1 bay leaf
1 small onion, peeled
few cloves
few black peppercorns, crushed
handful of parsley stalks
4 teaspoons powdered gelatine
150ml/¼ pint dry white grape juice
1 tablespoon cider vinegar
½ teaspoon turmeric (optional)
3 tablespoons chopped fresh parsley
1 tablespoon each chopped fresh basil, tarragon and chives
salt and freshly ground black pepper

chicken stock:
225g/8oz chicken carcass, bones and skin
1 carrot, peeled
1 leek, coarsely chopped
bunch of fresh thyme
600ml/1 pint water

First, make the stock. Put the ingredients in a saucepan and bring to the boil. Cover and simmer for 1 hour. Strain.

Put the chicken into a pan with the lemon half, bay leaf, onion stuck with cloves, peppercorns and parsley stalks. (Other herbs can be added if wished.) Put in enough stock to come half-way up the chicken, adding a little water if necessary. Cover and bring to the boil. Simmer 20 minutes. Cool the chicken in the stock, then remove it. Strain the stock; there should be about 600ml/1 pint. Set aside.

Remove the leg joints from the cooked chicken. These can be kept for another dish; or, if preferred, the leg-meat can be stripped off the bones and served with the jellied chicken.

Remove the remaining meat from the chicken, discarding all skin and bone, and chop it.

Put 4 tablespoons of the chicken stock into a small bowl with the gelatine; stand in a pan of hot water and stir until the gelatine is dissolved. Stir this liquid into the remaining chicken stock with the grape juice and vinegar. Add the turmeric to colour, if liked. Cool until it becomes a syrupy jelly. Stir in the chicken, chopped herbs and seasoning. Pour into a 900ml/1½ pint mould and chill until set.

Turn out the set jellied chicken carefully on to a serving dish. Surround with sprigs of curly lettuce and fresh coriander leaves to garnish. **Serves 4 to 6**.

Suprême de volaille au vinaigre en brochette • Chicken kebab, flavoured with fruit vinegar

While mild-flavoured chicken dishes can be enjoyable, there are times when this bird benefits from a little spicy excitement, as Indian and other cuisines have found. You will find that this dish has an intriguingly spicy effect with its combination of curry powder and fruit vinegar, to give an aromatic sharpness. Nouvelle Cuisine is fond of assisting poultry with a slightly acidic sauce in this way. But I recall that my grandmother, who kept a hundred free-range chickens roving willy-nilly about her country homestead, often prepared a sort of chicken fricassée with a vinegar overtone. So the idea is not new and must have some right instinct about it.

4 boneless chicken breasts, 175g/6oz each
juice of 1 lemon
2 tablespoons raspberry vinegar
2 tablespoons plain low-fat yogurt
2 garlic cloves, peeled and crushed
1 tablespoon curry powder
salt and freshly ground black pepper
100g/4oz mushrooms
1 small red pepper, cored, seeded and cut into squares
1 small green pepper, cored, seeded and cut into squares

Cut the breasts into 2.5cm/1 inch square pieces. Combine the lemon juice, vinegar, yogurt, garlic, curry powder and seasoning in a dish. Marinate the chicken in this mixture for 12 hours or overnight.

Trim the mushroom stalks level with the caps. Thread the meat, peppers and mushrooms on long kebab skewers. Grill for 10 minutes under a medium heat, turning to cook evenly. Baste occasionally with the marinade during cooking.

Serve garnished with lemon wedges, sliced peaches and lettuce leaves. **Serves 4**.

Escalopine de dindonneau aux fruits citronés ◆ Turkey escalope in buttermilk sauce with citrus fruit

Turkey escalopes, taken from the breast are now being used in the same way as veal escalopes, which means there are many recipes to choose from: egg-and-breadcrumbs (Viennoise), with banana (Maryland) or pineapple (Caribbean style) or with cheese and ham (Cordon Bleu). The escalopes should be batted out with a wooden mallet (see method below) to make them thinner: a good single portion is about 100g/4oz.

You will find that buttermilk gives a slightly piquant flavour to the sauce which blends well with poultry. Buttermilk is becoming a popular replacement for fattier cream or even yogurt. Green peppercorns can be found canned in various supermarkets; they are milder than black or white types.

4 turkey escalopes, 100g/4oz each
2 tablespoons seasoned flour
1 orange
1 grapefruit
1 lime
1½ tablespoons sunflower oil

sauce:
2 small shallots or 1 red onion, peeled and chopped
10 green peppercorns
150ml/5fl oz unsweetened apple juice
1 teaspoon cornflour
150ml/5fl oz buttermilk
salt
ground mace

Place the escalopes between sheets of polythene or greaseproof paper and gently bat out to make them thinner. They will not tear if first brushed with a little oil or water. Cut each escalope into two pieces. Coat in the seasoned flour, shaking off excess.

Using a zester, pare thin strips of rind from the orange, grapefruit and lime. Blanch in boiling water for 4 minutes and drain. Peel and segment the fruit. Set the segments and strips of rind aside.

In a large shallow pan, fry the escalopes in the oil for 4 minutes on each side. Remove and keep warm. In the same pan, stir fry the shallots and peppercorns for the sauce for 2 minutes. Add the apple juice and boil for 3 minutes to reduce the liquid by half. Stir the cornflour into the buttermilk and pour this mixture gradually into the pan, stirring. Bring to the boil and simmer for 4 minutes. Season to taste with salt and mace.

To serve, arrange the escalopes in a pool of sauce on each plate. Sprinkle over the strips of rind and garnish with the fruit segments. **Serves 4.**

Terrine de poulet verdure • Chicken and spinach terrine

Perfect for summer days, this kind of terrine is both light and satisfying. It is also very tasty as a sandwich filling for a lunch-box or picnic, or as a quick snack with a salad. This is a three layer terrine with a spinach filling in the middle.

3 tablespoons sunflower oil
700g/1½lbs chicken meat, minced
1 garlic clove, peeled and crushed
1 teaspoon green peppercorns
salt and freshly ground black pepper
1 tablespoon powdered gelatine
4 tablespoons water
25g/1oz shelled and skinned pistachio nuts
25g/1oz fromage frais (see page 179)
175ml/6fl oz plain low-fat yogurt

spinach filling:
450g/1lb spinach, cooked, drained and chopped
150ml/5fl oz plain low-fat yogurt
2 egg yolks
2 teaspoons powdered gelatine
3 tablespoons water
grated nutmeg

sauce:
200ml/⅓ pint Greek-style strained yogurt
bunch of watercress
1 garlic clove, peeled and chopped
4 tablespoons unsweetened apple juice

Heat the oil and fry the minced chicken for 5 minutes without browning. Add the garlic, green peppercorns and seasoning to taste. Cook briskly for 1 minute, then liquidise the chicken mixture until smooth. Dissolve the gelatine in the water; add to the mixture. Mix in the pistachio nuts, cheese and yogurt. Set aside.

For the spinach filling, combine the spinach with the yogurt and egg yolks. Dissolve the gelatine in the water, and blend it in. Season to taste with salt, pepper and nutmeg.

Place a layer of the chicken mixture in a 900g/2lb capacity oblong terrine. Allow to set for 1 hour in the refrigerator. Cover with the spinach filling and finish with the rest of the chicken mixture. Chill for 2 hours until set firmly.

For the sauce, liquidise the yogurt, watercress and garlic until smooth. Add the apple juice and seasoning.

Turn out the terrine carefully on to a platter. Cut into thick slices and serve each slice on a pool of sauce. Sprinkle a few green peppercorns or coriander seeds in the sauce. **Serves 8 to 10.**

Poulet à la marocaine • Moroccan chicken

This is a very palatable Arab dish that greatly pleased clients when I introduced it at the Athenaeum Hotel restaurant in London in the Fifties. Its basis is couscous or semolina, which cooks in 8 minutes and is richer in protein than rice, being made from durum wheat. To add to its variety include sultanas, almonds and chopped red peppers, with a wedge of red watermelon as side garnish. Thus presented, it can look a feast.

1 oven-ready chicken, about 1.5kg/3½lbs
8-10 large fresh mint leaves
salt and freshly ground black pepper
ground ginger
paprika
ground cumin (optional)
50g/2oz soaked prunes, stoned and chopped
75g/3oz fresh apricots, stoned and chopped
3 tablespoons pine nuts
½ teaspoon mixed spice
1 garlic clove, peeled and crushed
5 tablespoons sunflower oil
pinch of powdered saffron
chilli powder
225ml/8fl oz chicken stock
150g/5oz couscous
1 tablespoon tomato purée
50g/2oz seedless raisins
2 teaspoons rosewater
4 courgettes, sliced and marinated in lemon juice for 5 minutes

Ease your fingers between the skin and flesh of the chicken breast and insert the mint leaves at intervals. Move the skin back into position. Season the chicken inside and out with salt, ginger and paprika. Add some cumin, too, if liked.

Mix the prunes and apricots with half the pine nuts, half the mixed spice and seasoning and put this into the cavity of the bird.

Liquidise the remaining pine nuts with the garlic and 1 tablespoon of oil to obtain a paste. Flavour it to taste with the saffron, ground ginger, chilli powder and remaining mixed spice. Brush or spoon this mixture all over the chicken and chill for 1 hour.

Roast in a 200°C, 400°F, Mark 6 oven for 45 minutes, basting frequently with a little of the stock.

Meanwhile, cook the couscous according to the instructions on the packet.

When the chicken is ready, remove it from the tin. Joint the chicken, and set the joints aside in a warm place with the stuffing. Bread up the back of the chicken and place it in a saucepan with the remaining stock and the drippings from the tin (skimmed of all fat). Bring to the boil and simmer for 10 minutes; strain. Stir in the tomato purée and seasoning to taste. Keep this sauce warm.

Place the couscous in a baking dish and dry in the oven for 5 minutes. Separate the grains with a fork, then blend in the raisins, rosewater, remaining oil and seasoning to taste.

To serve, place a spoonful of couscous on each plate and garnish with the marinated raw courgettes and a few leaves of coriander and mint. Add the chicken joints and stuffing, and serve the sauce separately. **Serves 4**.

Poulet et mangue en brochette • Chicken and mango kebab

Mango contains juices with an enzyme that can tenderise meat or poultry, though this is barely necessary with the highly digestible chicken.

I recommend the simple kebab skewer, which comes in various lengths, as a very useful piece of equipment in this cuisine. Using all kinds of poultry, other white meat or fish, the cook can improvise an attractive variety of kebabs with the addition of chunks of fresh vegetables or fruits.

4 chicken breasts, skinned and boned
4 tablespoons olive oil
juice of 2 fresh limes
2 tablespoons chopped fresh mint
1 teaspoon honey
2 large ripe mangoes
salt and freshly ground black pepper

Cut the chicken breasts into even-sized cubes. Mix the olive oil, lime juice, chopped mint and honey in a bowl and stir the chicken in this marinade until evenly coated. Cover and chill for 1 or 2 hours.

Peel and stone the mangoes and cut into chunks similar to the chicken pieces. Thread chicken and mangoes alternately on to 4 long kebab skewers. Brush with the marinade and a little extra oil if wished and season. Grill for 5 or 6 minutes on each side, basting again before turning. Serve on a bed of rice tossed with toasted almonds. **Serves 4**.

Suprême de poulet Liotro • Chicken breast with blood orange

This chicken, poached in a stock of orange juice and water, is best served with a sauce using one of the good brands of mayonnaise on the market. One I venture to recommend is Renshaw Conil mayonnaise which I helped to devise and which was rated among the best by a panel of expert caterers. Compare it to others and make your own judgement.

I suggest a blood orange here – such as the new variety Liotro – because they are sweeter than ordinary oranges. The tablespoon of white vinegar added to the stock slightly acidulates it and makes the dish more savoury.

4 large chicken breasts
600ml/1 pint water
225g/8oz chicken giblets
grated rind of 1 orange
juice of 2 blood oranges
1 tablespoon distilled white vinegar
salt and freshly ground black pepper
4 blood oranges

sauce:
50ml/2fl oz mayonnaise
50ml/2fl oz plain low-fat yogurt
grated rind and juice of 1 blood orange
2 drops of orange blossom essence
2 spring onions, chopped

Remove the skin and bones from the chicken breasts. Set the breasts aside, and put the skin and bones in a saucepan. Add the water, giblets, orange rind and juice and vinegar, with seasoning to taste. Bring to the boil, cover and simmer for 20 to 30 minutes. Strain.

Return the strained stock to the pan, add the breasts and poach gently for 20 minutes. Cool in the stock in the refrigerator or, for speed, 20 minutes in a freezer. The stock will set to a soft jelly.

For the sauce, combine the mayonnaise with the yogurt and flavour with the orange rind and juice, orange blossom essence and spring onions.

Using a zester, thinly pare the rind from one orange in thin strips. Blanch these in boiling water for 2 minutes and drain. Peel and segment all the oranges.

To serve, slice the jellied chicken breasts and arrange on four plates. Garnish with the orange segments, orange rind strips and a few coriander leaves. Serve the sauce separately. **Serves 4.**

Poulet cressonière • Chicken with watercress sauce

Watercress is another of those herbs whose slightly pungent pepperiness can bring out the best in chicken, as in this attractive cold dish.

I recommend only buying watercress that has a grower's label attached; this should ensure that it comes from supervised and clean water. It should naturally be of a vivid green colour to prove its freshness.

Whenever I use watercress I am reminded of its high place in country lore. The celebrated herbalist, Culpeper, advocated watercress soup to cleanse the blood in the spring, and country folk swore by it for the cure of rheumatism or relief of hiccups. Fashion-conscious women in the 17th century crushed the leaves to make a sort of face-pack for the removal of freckles. However, I must say that I prefer to see it on the plate.

4 chicken breasts, poached (see Poulet en gelée, page 124)
bunch of watercress, divided into sprigs
75g/3oz curd cheese
300ml/½ pint chicken stock
50g/2oz spring onions
1 garlic clove, peeled
salt and freshly ground black pepper
1 tablespoon snipped fresh chives
350g/12oz courgettes, shredded or sliced
juice of 1 lemon

Skin the chicken breasts. Liquidise the watercress sprigs, curd cheese, chicken stock, spring onions, garlic and seasoning to taste until smooth. Stir in the chives. Spoon this watercress sauce on to plates and place the chicken on top.

Mix the courgettes with the lemon juice and arrange around the chicken. Sprinkle over a few more chives. **Serves 4**.

Tranche de pintade aux deux sauces fruitées • Guinea fowl with kiwi and mango sauces

Guinea fowl has been in the cuisine from ancient times. It is simply a domesticated game bird and has a delicate, tender and gamey flavour – better than chicken or turkey if it has been fed well. The meat tends to dry in roasting so it needs frequent basting.

The two sweet-and-sharp fruit sauces here bring out the quality of guinea fowl well. The breast of the bird forms the centre of the dish while the legs are turned into a pâté to go in a thin crust of puff pastry (only 50g/2oz of pastry per portion, a minimal amount of fat).

131

1 oven-ready guinea fowl, about 1kg/2¼lbs
salt and freshly ground black pepper
1½ tablespoons sunflower oil
100g/4oz puff pastry
beaten egg yolk, to glaze
50ml/2fl oz plain low-fat yogurt
1 mango, peeled, stoned and sliced
1 kiwi fruit, peeled and sliced
8 black grapes, halved and seeded

kiwi sauce:
1 shallot, peeled and chopped
3 tablespoons sunflower oil
2 kiwi fruit, peeled
50g/2oz spinach leaves
2 fresh mint leaves
½ teaspoon cornflour dissolved in 2 tablespoons water

mango sauce:
1 shallot, peeled and chopped
3 tablespoons sunflower oil
1 mango, peeled and stoned
75g/3oz swede or yellow turnips, peeled and diced
100ml/4fl oz water
1 teaspoon turmeric
½ teaspoon cornflour dissolved in 3 tablespoons water

Season the trussed guinea fowl inside and out and brush with the oil. Roast at 220°C, 425°F, Mark 7 for 30 minutes, basting occasionally with a little stock or water.

Meanwhile, roll out the pastry to 3mm/⅛ inch thick and cut out four rounds or ovals with an 8cm/3 inch diameter cutter. Place on a greased baking tray. Score the shapes with a criss-cross pattern using the prongs of a fork or back of a knife. Brush with the egg yolk. Let rest in the refrigerator for 20 minutes, then bake for 15 minutes at the same temperature as for the bird. Remove and cool.

To make the mousseline, scrape the meat from the legs of the cooked guinea fowl, discarding the skin, and chop it or mince it finely. Add the yogurt and seasoning to taste and keep warm. Keep the rest of the guinea fowl warm.

For the kiwi sauce, stir fry the shallot in the oil for 1 minute. Add the kiwi fruit, spinach and mint. Cook for only 2 minutes, then season and liquidise. Thicken with the cornflour mixture, boiling for 3 minutes. Keep warm.

For the mango sauce, stir fry the shallot in the oil for 1 minute, then add the mango, swede and water. Simmer until the swede is soft. Add the turmeric and seasoning, and liquidise to a purée. Thicken with the cornflour mixture as above.

To serve, pour equal quantities of each sauce on to two plates, one in the centre and one to the side. Place a piece of pastry on each plate and top with mousseline. Cover with another pastry piece. Cut the breasts, without skin, into eight thin slices, thus allowing four slices per portion. Arrange on the plates. Garnish with mango and kiwi slices and grapes. **Serves 2.**

Méli-mélo de fruits et dinde ◆ Tutti-frutti turkey

The turkey has been familiar on British tables for about three centuries, having been acclimatised from North America. It quickly replaced other fowls of the air in esteem and, right from the start, has been given its special Christmas place. The best turkey to buy is a free-range hen, seven to nine months old. Its breast should be broad and plump and its flesh very white.

Turkey deserves a change from the traditional cranberry sauce, and you will find the fruit-and-yogurt dressing used here gives this useful and nutritious bird a fresh sparkle; indeed, it could be used with any kind of poultry.

1 tablespoon sunflower oil
450g/1lb boneless turkey breast, skinned and cut into 8 thin slices
1 medium-size onion, peeled and chopped
1 green pepper, cored, seeded and chopped
2 garlic cloves, peeled and crushed
150ml/5fl oz unsweetened pineapple juice
150ml/5fl oz chicken stock (see page 124)
½ teaspoon ground cinnamon
½ teaspoon ground ginger
75ml/3fl oz plain low-fat yogurt
salt and freshly ground black pepper

garnish:
100g/4oz baby sweetcorn, raw or cooked for 4 minutes
4 strawberries, hulled
4 fresh pineapple slices
4 fresh mint leaves
1 green apple, cored and sliced

Heat the oil in a sauté pan and gently fry the turkey slices for 5 minutes, turning them once to cook evenly. Remove and keep hot. In the same oil, stir fry the onion and green pepper for 2 minutes, then add the garlic, pineapple juice, stock and spices. Bring to the boil and boil for 5 minutes. Stir in the yogurt and remove from the heat. Season to taste. Reheat the turkey gently in the sauce for 3 minutes without boiling.

Arrange two turkey slices on each plate with a border of sauce and garnish with the sweetcorn, strawberries, pineapple, mint leaves and apple slices. **Serves 4.**

Suprême de caneton aux pêches • Duck breast with peach purée and peppercorns

Noblemen of the Chinese Han dynasty were breeding ducks for the table 2,000 years ago. Nowadays, ducks are bred by the million in Britain and other western countries, like those at Cherry Valley Farms in Lincolnshire where I was once a creative chef. This output ensures a supply all year round.

If buying a whole duck allow 450g/1lb on the bone per person. To ensure tenderness, see that the bottom half of the beak is soft enough to bend back, the feet pliable and the breast plump. Young ducklings can be cooked in portions but the skin shrinks and is unsightly, so it is best to remove the skin and cut away the fat before cooking to get a lean piece.

4 duck breasts, skinned and boned
1 teaspoon green peppercorns
salt
4 tablespoons sunflower oil
1 small onion, peeled, or 3 spring onions, finely chopped
1 garlic clove, peeled and crushed
3 ripe peaches, skinned, stoned and puréed
300ml/½ pint dry white grape juice
1 tablespoon white vinegar
1 teaspoon pink peppercorns
few mangetout peas

Trim the duck breasts to neat even-sized shapes. Crush the green peppercorns and press into both sides of the duck breasts. Season with a little salt. Heat the oil and sauté the duck breasts over a low heat, covered, for 12 to 15 minutes. Turn them twice during cooking. When cooked, remove from the pan and keep hot. Strain the oil.

Heat a little of the oil in a saucepan and stir fry the onion without colouring for 2 minutes. Add the garlic, peach purée, grape juice and vinegar. Bring to the boil and boil for 5 minutes. Liquidise the sauce.

To serve, pour the sauce on to two plates and arrange the cooked duck breasts on top. Sprinkle a few pink peppercorns over the sauce. Garnish with mangetout peas. **Serves 2.**

L'oie de Noël aux figues fraîches • Goose with fresh figs

At the last function for which I cooked before retirement I featured this dish as a main course – goose with chestnut stuffing, garnished with fresh figs, with a beautifully aromatised fruit sauce. The 200 diners clamoured for more.

When choosing a fresh-plucked goose, a young bird may be recognised by the pliable underbill, supple windpipe and soft legs and feet. Deep yellow fat indicates an old bird, but few of these reach the market. Young goose is rightly regaining popularity as people realise that it is a very pleasant alternative to turkey, and with proper treatment (draining off the fat during roasting, for example) it can fit into a healthy diet, lean goose meat having 300 calories per 100g/4oz portion.

All fruit sauces are suitable for goose: prune, apple and pear, gooseberry, cranberry and other sour types. Here that sharper touch comes from a mix of blackcurrant and cherry, combining with the fresh figs to make a remarkable dish.

1 oven-ready goose, about 4.5kg/10lbs, with giblets
salt and freshly ground black pepper
½ teaspoon each ground ginger, mace and cumin
150ml/5fl oz unsweetened apple juice
1 onion, peeled and sliced
1 carrot, peeled and sliced
sprig of fresh thyme
12 to 16 fresh figs
2 oranges, peeled and segmented

stuffing:
150g/5oz fresh breadcrumbs
150g/5oz cooked or canned chestnuts
1 onion, peeled and chopped
1½ teaspoons chopped fresh sage or wild marjoram
1 tablespoon chopped fresh parsley
3 eggs, beaten

sauce:
225g/8oz stoned black cherries
150ml/5fl oz unsweetened blackcurrant juice
150ml/5fl oz fresh orange juice
1 tablespoon cider vinegar
2 tablespoons soya sauce
1½ teaspoons cornflour dissolved in 5 tablespoons water
chilli powder
ground mace

Cut off the legs and wing tips from the goose; set them aside with the giblets. Mix ½ teaspoon each of salt and pepper with the spices and rub all over the goose, inside and out. Weigh the goose to calculate the cooking time, and place it on a rack in a roasting tin. Roast in a 225°C, 425°F, Mark 7 oven, allowing 15 minutes to each 450g/1lb plus an extra 15 minutes. After 30 minutes' roasting, reduce the heat to 190°C, 375°F, Mark 5. A young goose will take about 2½ hours, a large one up to 3 hours. After the first hour, remove all fat completely from the tin and add 225ml/8fl oz of water. When the goose is cooked, leave it to rest in a warm place.

Meanwhile, make the stock. Remove the meat from the legs and set it aside for the stuffing. Blanch the leg bones, wing tips, neck and giblets (excluding the liver) in boiling water for 15 minutes; drain and return to the pan. Add the apple juice, onion, carrot, thyme and 900ml/1½ pints of water. Bring to the boil and simmer for 1½ hours.

While the stock is simmering, make the stuffing. There should be about 450g/1lb of meat from the goose legs. Mince it twice with the liver and remaining stuffing ingredients. Place in greased, oblong aluminium tins; or, if preferred, shape the stuffing into a loaf and wrap in foil lined with greased parchment paper. Cook the stuffing for 30 minutes with the goose.

When the stock has simmered for 1½ hours, strain it. Boil for about 10 minutes to reduce it further to a concentrated glaze, about one-third the quantity.

For the sauce, liquidise the cherries with the blackcurrant and orange juices. Add with the vinegar and soya sauce to the reduced stock. Bring to the boil and thicken with the cornflour mixture. Simmer for 4 minutes. Season sparingly with chilli powder and mace.

To serve, slice the goose breast thinly and arrange two slices on each plate with a pool of sauce. Decorate with two figs, their tops cut criss-cross and opened up. At the side neatly arrange a slice of stuffing, 2 orange segments and a sprig of watercress. **Serves 6 to 8**.

Pigeonneau à la Nono • Breast of pigeon with mousseline and loquat

Nono was my nickname when I was a young apprentice.

Pigeons, whether they are corn-fed on a farm or wild, have a delicate meat which is well-appreciated by gourmets (the word pigeonneau simply means the young bird). The meat is high in protein and light on digestion.

The loquat, which makes the unusual garnish here, originated in China and South Japan, though it is now imported from other countries. The loquat resembles an apricot, or small plum, with yellow-orange, slightly downy skin. The flesh has a sweet scent. It is eaten raw with the skin or poached in fruit juice, with lime or lemon juice added. With vinegar and honey loquats can be made into a good sauce to go with turkey.

4 oven-ready pigeons, with livers
1 shallot, peeled and chopped
1 garlic clove, peeled
3½ tablespoons sunflower oil
50g/2oz field mushrooms, chopped
50g/2oz walnut kernels
1½ tablespoons toasted breadcrumbs
salt and freshly ground black pepper
2 eggs, beaten
4 loquats, stoned and sliced

sauce:
1 shallot, peeled and chopped
1 garlic clove, peeled
1 teaspoon tomato purée, or 1 large tomato, skinned, seeded and chopped
150ml/5fl oz water
2 loquats, stoned and sliced
juice of 1 lemon
1 teaspoon cornflour mixed with 3 tablespoons water

Remove the breasts from the pigeons and set them aside. Take the meat from the legs of the birds and chop it coarsely with the skin. To make the mousseline (which is a hot pâté), stir fry the shallot and garlic in 2 tablespoons of the oil for 1 minute. Add the chopped leg meat and livers. Cook, stirring, for 2 minutes more. Add the mushrooms, walnuts, crumbs and seasoning and cook for 1 more minute. Liquidise to a paste. Allow to cool, then blend in the beaten eggs.

Grease four small metal dariole moulds and fill with the mousseline. Bake in a tray half-filled with hot water at 200°C, 400°F, Mark 6 for 30 minutes. When cooked, let stand for 5 minutes before turning out.

Meanwhile, cook the pigeon breasts. Cut each breast into three slices and fry in the remaining oil for 5 minutes on each side. Season to taste. Remove the breasts and keep hot. Using the same oil, and adding a little more if needed, stir fry the shallot and garlic for the sauce for 2 minutes. Add the tomato purée and water. Boil a few minutes, then add the loquats and lemon juice. Cook for 2 more minutes. Thicken the sauce with the cornflour mixture, boiling for 4 minutes. Liquidise the sauce to a purée and check the seasoning.

To serve, pour a pool of sauce on each plate and arrange one mousseline and 1 sliced pigeon breast on it. Decorate each portion with 1 sliced loquat, plus a sprig of corn salad or fresh mint. **Serves 4**.

Mignonettes de Jean Lapin aux abricots • Mini rabbit steaks with apricots and tomatoes

One reason why French chefs and gourmets respect rabbit so much is that they know it to be a dainty eater itself, the most fussy of vegetarians. In childhood, I recall feeding rabbits with all my grandmother's finest vegetables – lettuce, clover, carrots and cabbage. They would nibble away with that funny twitch of the nose like highly abstemious connoisseurs. The diet gives them white, tender meat, slightly scented with marjoram.

A rabbit is ready for the market at only ten weeks old. Domesticated rabbit can be had in supermarkets either whole or jointed, fresh or frozen. The flesh should vary from white to pale pink; avoid any with a pronounced reddish look, and the only fat should be a very small amount on the loin. Rabbit has high protein and, because of its leanness, only 124 calories per 100g/4oz.

1 oven-ready domestic rabbit, about 1kg/2lbs, skinned, boned and tough membrane
  skin removed
1 egg, beaten
grated rind and juice of ½ lemon
good pinch of fresh marjoram
salt and freshly ground black pepper
ground mace
2 tablespoons plain flour
4 tablespoons sunflower oil
6 ripe apricots, halved and stoned
6 cherry tomatoes

sauce:
2 large tomatoes, skinned, seeded and chopped
2 fresh basil leaves
1 tablespoon soya sauce
1 shallot, peeled and chopped
1 tablespoon sunflower oil
1 small garlic clove, peeled
1 teaspoon honey
1 teaspoon cornflour mixed with 4 tablespoons water

Remove the meat from the loin and back legs of the rabbit and cut into cubes. (Use the rest of the rabbit for another dish.) Mince the meat coarsely and place in a bowl. Add the egg, lemon rind and juice, and marjoram. Season to taste with salt, pepper and mace. Divide the meat into four equal portions and shape into patties like hamburgers, flouring your hands to assist handling. Dust with flour.

For the sauce, liquidise all the ingredients except the cornflour and pour into a pan. Bring to the boil and boil for 6 minutes. Stir in the cornflour mixture and simmer for 4 minutes to thicken. Keep warm.

Heat the oil in a shallow pan and quickly sauté the rabbit steaks for 3 minutes on each side. Season them.

On each plate pour a little pool of the sauce and arrange two steaks on top, slightly overlapping. Place the apricot halves around the plate border alternating with the cherry tomatoes. Garnish with a sprig of mint or basil and put a twist of lemon on each steak plus a sprinkle of parsley. **Serves 2.**

Caillettes au muscatel • Quails and their eggs in a nest of lettuce

The little game bird, the quail, is now farmed in many parts of Britain, their eggs and meat being in demand by all the best restaurants. They are used in hors d'oeuvre, hot entrées, or in salades tièdes (warm salads) like this one. This is a tasty little frivolity as a starter, a main course on occasions, or a snack. Caillette means a younger bird. It is also an old French term for a flighty woman!

Farmed quail is better-fed than the wild sort and this should be evident from the plumpness of the breast, firm and pinkish colour and fresh scent. The old-fashioned style was to serve a pair of quails on fried bread, the breast only being eaten. This now seems too fastidious. The French just buckled into it, eating the little birds with their fingers. Modern chefs bone the quails, stuff them with a liver filling, and serve on a tartlet crust, a nest of piped potato or celeriac purée. Or they can be barbecued on a kebab skewer.

2 tablespoons plain flour
salt and freshly ground black pepper
grated nutmeg
4 oven-ready quails
1½ tablespoons sunflower oil
150ml/5fl oz water
3 tablespoons white grape juice
1 teaspoon soya sauce
150g/5oz chicken livers, cleaned and cut into small pieces
4 lettuce leaves
4 radicchio leaves
1 orange, peeled and segmented
150g/5oz seeded Muscatel grapes
25g/1oz toasted flaked almonds
8 quail's eggs, hard-boiled and shelled

salad dressing:
1 tablespoon grape juice
1 teaspoon honey
1 tablespoon distilled white vinegar
2 tablespoons buttermilk

Season flour with salt and nutmeg and use to coat the quails lightly. Heat a little of the oil in a pan and brown the quails all over for 6 to 8 minutes, covered with a lid. Remove from the heat and let cool a little, then remove all the breast meat. Cut it into pieces as big as your fingernail, season with black pepper and keep warm.

Discard the oil in the pan and put in the water, grape juice, soya sauce, and the quail carcasses with the legs. Bring to the boil and simmer for 6 minutes.

Meanwhile, toss the pieces of chicken liver in flour to coat. Heat the remaining oil in a pan and sauté the chicken livers for 4 minutes with the lid on, tossing them now and then. Keep them underdone, even slightly pink if you like. Remove from the heat and keep warm.

Drain the quail carcasses, reserving the stock, and remove all the meat from the legs and bones. Cut this meat into fingernail-size pieces and add to the breast meat and the cooked chicken livers. Moisten with the reserved stock. Liquidise the salad dressing ingredients together, and season to taste.

To serve, arrange the lettuce, radicchio and orange segments on four plates with a serving of the drained meat mixture on them. Scatter over a few grapes and flaked almonds and sprinkle with the salad dressing. Lastly add two quail's eggs per portion to this exquisite dish. **Serves 4**.

LES SALADES FRAÎCHES
NATURAL SALADS

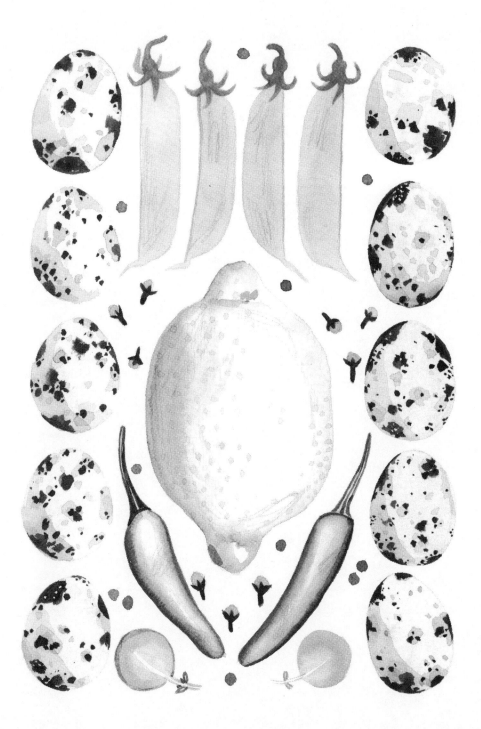

What makes a good salad is a combination of ingredients that have an affinity with each other. So long as this principle is adhered to, as the recipes here will suggest, you can produce a remarkably wide range of salads quite simply. These are dishes that stir the imagination a little, an important aim of Cuisine Fraîcheur.

Another way in which we expand possibilities is by using ingredients that may be somewhat unfamiliar in this context to some home-cooks, though this does not mean that they need to be hard to get. For example, there are all the wild herbs, plants and greenstuff that are familiar in the kitchen as flavourings or aromatisers. Here they can be seen as an ingredient of a salad in their own right. This applies to such things as parsley, which can be added as a complete sprig without being chopped; mint, basil, spinach, sorrel, dandelion and the numerous sea plants can also be employed in this fashion. A variety of seasonal fruits can also intensify the interest of a salad. And, besides that, we also now have available in most good supermarkets a broadening range of new tropical ingredients.

It is important to present any salad in the most attractive manner possible with a restrained amount of dressing. For the purpose of this diet, the amount of oil used in a French dressing can be reduced. A good alternative dressing is to liquidise nuts with water or yogurt. Any dressing should, of course, be added to salad greens only at the last minute, tossing in a large bowl.

Salade chaude de poulet florentine • Hot spinach salad with chicken

Popeye the Sailorman was not the first to sing the praises of spinach. A good many even wiser experts of the table have hailed its virtues ever since it was first introduced to Europe from the Far East by the Dutch in the 16th century. And today it has been having a justified new vogue with our younger chefs, used raw in salads. So long as it is really young and fresh it is an excellent ingredient for this in every way. Its bold green colour catches the eye so it is a first-class 'presentation element'. The iron content gives a positive basic flavour without overdoing it. Even though Popeye's claims that spinach automatically builds the biceps sound spurious, there is no doubt that its high mineral and vitamin content give it a good rating in health terms. As a cooked ingredient, it goes especially well with eggs.

175g/6oz young fresh spinach leaves, washed and drained
6 small spring onion bulbs
2 tablespoons flaked hazelnuts
3 courgettes, sliced very thinly
2 chicken breasts, boned and skinned
4 tablespoons sunflower oil
1 small onion, peeled and finely chopped
1 garlic clove, peeled and finely chopped

2 tablespoons white wine vinegar
1 tablespoon chopped fresh tarragon
salt and freshly ground black pepper
1 small red pepper, cored, seeded and finely chopped

Tear the spinach leaves into pieces and put in a large bowl (if the leaves are small, leave them whole). Add the spring onions, hazelnuts and courgettes.

Cut the chicken into very thin strips. Heat 3 tablespoons sunflower oil in a large shallow pan. Add the chicken, onion and garlic and fry briskly until the chicken is tender. Stir in the remaining sunflower oil, the wine vinegar, tarragon, and salt and pepper to taste. Allow to bubble for 1 minute.

Spoon the hot chicken and dressing over the salad ingredients in the bowl and toss together. Sprinkle with the chopped red pepper and serve immediately. **Serves 4**.

Melon en salade à la Montaigne • Melon and lime salad

Often when the 16th century French writer and philosopher, Montaigne, visited a town in France or Italy, people would shower him with gifts of food or wine, including ripe melons of which he was known to be fond. Among the advice he gave to readers in his essays was: 'I think it is healthier to eat more slowly and less, and to eat more often . . . It is bad manners, besides being harmful to health and even to pleasure, to eat greedily as I do. I often bite my tongue in the process.' This thought makes it fitting to dedicate this recipe to him. It makes a refreshing starter, very low in calories, and might well have had his approval.

1 medium-size Ogen melon
juice of 2 limes
juice of 1 lemon
10 drops of liquid sweetener (optional)
grated rind of 1 lime
1 tablespoon chopped fresh mint

Halve the melon and carefully scoop out the seeds. Using a melon baller, cut the flesh into small balls (or use a small teaspoon to cut neat shapes of melon flesh.) Mix the fruit juices, liquid sweetener, lime rind and chopped mint together; stir in the melon balls. Cover and marinate in the refrigerator for 1 hour.

Serve in small shallow bowls, garnished with mint sprigs and lime wedges. For a special occasion, serve the melon on vine leaves. **Serves 4**.

Salade à la noix de coco • Medley of scallops in a coconut sauce

This is a salad I featured in one of my restaurants in Park Lane in the late Fifties. When I presented it on Eurovision for the first time it made a stir among gourmets and chefs and many letters wondered at my daring in not cooking the scallops. Thirty years later, Japanese raw fish dishes are familiar in the West, with those they have inspired in Nouvelle Cuisine.

I think you will find this an intriguing dish, perhaps suitable for a slightly more exotic lunch with friends, conjuring up a hint of the Pacific Islands, or the Caribbean, or at least somewhere pleasant and spicy.

2 very fresh coconuts
450g/1lb small shelled scallops, well washed
150g/5oz French beans, cut into small pieces
4 large escarole lettuce leaves
large slice of pineapple, peeled and cut into cubes as big as the scallops
1 small papaya, peeled, seeded and cubed similar size

marinade:
2 slices of fresh pineapple, peeled
small piece of fresh ginger (the size of a grape), peeled and chopped
1 green chilli, seeded and sliced
juice of 3 limes
pinch of salt

Make a hole in the coconuts with an ice-pick and drain off the juice or 'milk'. (The juice can be served as an accompanying drink with ice cubes and mint leaves.) Saw the coconuts in half and remove as much of the flesh as you can without damaging the shells.

Add 50g/2oz of the coconut flesh to the marinade ingredients. Liquidise all these together and place in a bowl. Add the scallops and beans and marinate in the refrigerator for 2 to 3 hours.

Meanwhile, coarsely grate some of the remaining coconut flesh for the garnish. For better flavour, toast the grated coconut under the grill. Set aside. (Use the rest of the coconut flesh in another dish.)

Choose four bowls with flat bases that will not wobble, or use four plates with a napkin rolled and knotted underneath to form a base. Place a coconut half on each one. Line the walls of each coconut shell with a lettuce leaf, overlapping it a little.

Drain the scallops and beans and mix in the pineapple and papaya. Spoon into the coconut shells and sprinkle over the grated coconut. **Serves 4**.

Salade norvégienne au calabrese • Calabrese and prawn salad

Supermarket packets of cooked peeled prawns are very convenient, but for this recipe you need to buy them cooked in their shells, from the fishmonger. The shells are needed to make the sauce, giving it the tang of the sea.

750g/1½lb calabrese
450g/1lb cooked prawns in shell
1 tablespoon cider vinegar
1 hard-boiled egg, yolk sieved and white finely chopped

sauce:
1½ tablespoons sunflower oil
1½ tablespoons tomato purée
150ml/5fl oz water
juice of 1 orange
3 tablespoons cider vinegar
2 tablespoons plain low-fat yogurt
salt and freshly ground black pepper

Separate the calabrese stems and florets. Cut into small pieces and blanch in boiling water for 3 minutes. Drain, refresh and set aside.

Peel the prawns and set aside. Lightly crush the shells and heads. For the sauce, heat the oil in a saucepan and stir fry the shells for 4 minutes. Add the tomato purée, water, orange juice and vinegar and boil for 15 minutes. Strain into a bowl and cool, then blend in the yogurt and season to taste. Stir in the prawns.

Place the calabrese on four plates and sprinkle with the vinegar. Arrange the dressed prawns in the centre. Sprinkle the egg over each portion. Serve cold. **Serves 4**.

Salade cerisette à l'orange • Cherry salad with orange and walnut

Sweet dessert cherries fall into two groups, the Geans, which are sweet and soft-fleshed, and the Bigarreaus or hearts, which have firm flesh. The sour culinary kinds are basically Amarelles, the least acid of which have red flesh and colourless juice, and the Morellos. Duke cherries are really a cross between sweet and sour and are suitable both for dessert and cooking.

In Cuisine Fraîcheur cherries are generally used raw, in fruit salad or cold soups for example. They may also be used as an uncooked filling for pies and tarts. All that is required is to pour over them a hot glazing composed of a fruit-flavour jelly. They also make a delicious filling in wholemeal pancakes.

Hardly any dressing is required with this salad because of its high fruit juice content. The peanut dressing suggested makes a nice counterpoint to the sharp juice flavours.

750g/1½lb red cherries
1 small cos lettuce
2 oranges, peeled and thinly sliced
50g/2oz walnut kernels, roughly chopped

dressing:
50g/2oz shelled roasted peanuts
100ml/4fl oz water

To make the dressing, liquidise the peanuts with the water.

Halve and stone the cherries, reserving a few whole ones with stalks for garnish. Line a shallow dish with the lettuce leaves and place the orange slices on them. Toss the cherries in the dressing, add the walnuts and pile up in the centre of the dish. Garnish the edges with the reserved whole cherries. **Serves 4**.

Ruban de volaille • Smoked chicken, melon and avocado salad

This recipe shows perfectly how ingredients in the right combination bring out the best in each other. The Webb's Wonder lettuce makes a good foundation for it. It is a lettuce that has grown in popularity because of its good keeping quality, firm texture and milky taste. It is also economical and available all year round. Lettuce should always be kept cool, preferably in the refrigerator's salad drawer. Make certain to eat the core which can be sliced like a radish.

1 medium-size Webb's Wonder or iceberg lettuce, cut lengthways into thin wedges
1 avocado, peeled, stoned and cut into thin wedges
1 small Ogen or Galia melon, halved, seeded and scooped out into small balls
4 cooked or canned artichoke hearts, quartered
225g/8oz boned smoked chicken, cut into thin strips
2 tablespoons toasted pine nuts
juice of 1 orange
coarsely grated rind of ½ orange
2 tablespoons olive oil or plain low-fat yogurt
1 tablespoon chopped fresh mint
salt and freshly ground black pepper

Arrange the wedges of lettuce in a shallow salad bowl. Add the slices of avocado, melon balls and artichoke hearts. Arrange the strips of chicken on top and sprinkle with the pine nuts.

Mix the orange juice with the grated rind, olive oil (or yogurt), mint and seasoning to taste. Spoon the dressing evenly over the salad and garnish with sprigs of fresh mint. **Serves 4**.

Salade bruxelloise aux carottes ◆ Raw Brussels sprout and carrot salad

Brussels sprouts developed from wild cabbage and were introduced from Belgium. They were in the markets there and in the north of France as long ago as the 13th century, but they did not get on to British tables until the 18th century.

In shopping, choose sprouts that are small, green and firm. The larger size have a stronger flavour. For short term keeping, they can be stored in the refrigerator in a polythene bag.

Because of their small size, sprouts can easily be boiled to disaster. Cuisine Fraîcheur gets the best out of them by serving them raw, whether in a salad or with dips. If cooking them, do it at the last moment before the meal. Just a quick blanching is all that is required, then refreshing with ice water. A sprinkling of toasted sesame seeds over them is a good idea.

450g/1lb Brussels sprouts, trimmed and washed
1 tablespoon finely chopped onion
2 medium-size carrots, peeled and grated
2 tablespoons sultanas

dressing:
1 tablespoon sunflower oil
1 tablespoon cider vinegar
¼ teaspoon made mustard
salt and freshly ground black pepper

Remove a slice from the base of each sprout, then shred them coarsely. Mix with the onion, grated carrot and sultanas.

Blend the dressing ingredients well together. Toss enough of the dressing with the salad just to moisten it. **Serves 4**.

Salade de pissenlit amienoise • Dandelion and smoked salmon salad

My grandmother used to make us a lovely salad of dandelion leaves with smoked ham or bacon. If you are lucky enough to have a country-person's palate that is well worth trying. This smoked salmon version with some refreshing lime juice is even better in my opinion and I have presented it in some high-class restaurants, invariably to favourable comment. If you want to get used to the dandelion flavour, collect a few leaves on your next country walk, wash them well and add them, chopped, to an ordinary salad.

The French name *pissenlit* is merely meant as a tribute to the diuretic properties of dandelion, but there is no need to be unduly alarmed. You will mainly experience the lively tonic flavour of a plant that has even more iron than spinach.

450g/1lb dandelion leaves, trimmed and washed
225g/8oz new potatoes, cooked and diced
100g/4oz smoked salmon, diced
1 teaspoon capers

dressing:
50g/2oz walnut kernels
50ml/2fl oz plain low-fat yogurt
juice of 2 limes
1 teaspoon chopped fresh dill
salt and freshly ground black pepper

Arrange the dandelion leaves on four plates with a portion of potato on top. Sprinkle over the diced smoked salmon and the capers.

Liquidise the dressing ingredients and pour over each serving, or serve separately. **Serves 4.**

Trévisse au bouquet de mer • Radicchio salad with prawns, salmon and pears

Radicchio is a wild red-coloured chicory orignally from the Venetian area of Italy. Now it is widely cultivated in Italy, France and Holland for its artistic uses in salad. In flavour it is not quite as good as curly lettuce, but together they make a good pairing. Radicchio is well supplied with vitamins and minerals and is a good blood tonic.

Radicchio comes in three types: Red Verona which has short leaves and a roundish heart; Treviso with long tapering leaves and heart; and Castelfranco with red spots and streaks and a round heart.

While good on its own in a raw salad, radicchio is even better when mixed with green lettuce for colour contrast and flavour. To prepare, twist or slice off the tiny root which is attached to the head. Discard any wilted leaves, wash and rinse immediately. The bright colour and bitter astringent taste will add a new dimension to your salad bowl. When blanched for 15 seconds and pat-dried it can be used as a substitute for spinach, as in lining a dish for a terrine.

4 raw king prawns
100g/4oz smoked salmon (4 slices)
1 large radicchio, leaves separated
4 green lettuce leaves
1 ripe pear, cored, peeled, sliced and soaked in lemon juice

dressing:
1 hard-boiled egg, shelled
juice of ½ lemon or lime
1 teaspoon made mustard
1 garlic clove, peeled and crushed
3 fresh basil leaves
1 tablespoon raspberry vinegar
2 or 3 tablespoons sunflower or walnut oil or plain low-fat yogurt

First, liquidise the dressing and put aside in a bowl.

Cook the prawns for 5 minutes in boiling salted water. Cool and remove the shells. Wrap each prawn in a thin slice of smoked salmon.

Arrange the radicchio and lettuce leaves in a nest in pretty contrast on two plates. Place two prawns in the middle of each with pear slices. Sprinkle on a little of the dressing and serve the remainder in a jug. **Serves 4.**

Brochette de fruits tropicaux en verdure ◆ *Smoked chicken and tropical fruit kebab*

Corn salad or lamb's lettuce is known as mâche in France and very tasty it is too when blended with celery and a julienne of beetroot. This was a speciality of my father's restaurant in Paris, often served with kebabs combining chicken and fruits. I use smoked chicken in this recipe as it has an exotic flavour and no cooking of the brochette is needed. All good supermarkets and delicatessens can supply smoked chicken.

Corn salad is available all year round, but more especially during the winter months when other such greenstuff can be scarce. Its soft texture and slightly astringent flavour make it a handy alternative to lettuce. It needs careful washing as grit can get between the leaves. To freshen, dip in a bowl of cold water. In this diet we use corn salad raw, but lightly cooked it can be treated as spinach.

2 smoked chicken breasts, boned and cut into 4cm/1½ inch cubes
150g/5oz fresh pineapple, peeled and cut into cubes
1 papaya, peeled, seeded and cut into cubes
1 banana, cut into chunks
1 green and 1 red pepper, cored, seeded and cut into 4cm/1½ inch squares
8 large spinach leaves
1 large carambola, about 100g/4oz, sliced crossways
bunch of corn salad

marinade:
juice of 2 limes
1 teaspoon cider vinegar
1 tablespoon sunflower oil
salt and freshly ground black pepper

Whisk the marinade ingredients together and soak the chicken pieces in it for 2 hours.

Thread the pineapple, papaya, banana, peppers and chicken pieces on to four kebab skewers in alternate colour and variety. Arrange two spinach leaves on each of four plates and place the kebabs on top. Sprinkle some marinade on the kebabs and serve the remainder separately. Garnish with the carambola and the corn salad in neat sprigs all around. **Serves 4**.

Truite fumée cressonière aux pâtés • *Smoked trout pasta salad*

Smoked trout is one of the most exquisite of fish, a fine component of salad dishes. In this recipe we add an interesting touch of contrast by serving the trout cold, aromatised with herbs, with hot shell pasta on a bed of watercress. With the fish providing the protein, this makes an intriguing and nourishing dish.

Smoked fish can vary in flavour depending on the kind of wood used to smoke it. The best is a fresh-sawn unseasoned hardwood. Oak, juniper, apple and cherry wood are among those used. The fish is immersed in brine for an hour before smoking for 3 to 6 hours; in a hot smoking process the temperature is raised for the last 20 minutes. If you get the fish from a reliable smoker you will detect the delicate flavour of natural sawdust — and, incidentally, avoid those impostors created with artificial smoke essence, as is often done with kippers and haddock.

2 smoked trout, 100g/4oz each, skinned, boned and filleted
150g/5oz coloured shell pasta
bunch of watercress, stalks removed
2 kumquats, sliced
50g/2oz walnut kernels

dressing:
75ml/3fl oz plain low-fat yogurt
75ml/3fl oz mayonnaise
6 sprigs of watercress
1 teaspoon prepared horseradish cream
salt and freshly ground black pepper

Cut the trout fillets into 4cm/1½ inch long pieces. Set aside.

Cook the pasta in boiling water for 6 minutes. Drain.

On two plates arrange the watercress leaves in a nest form, leaving the centre clear. Spoon the pasta into the centre. Arrange the pieces of trout and slices of kumquat in alternating rows on the watercress.

Liquidise the dressing. Put half on the pasta; serve the remainder separately. Garnish with the walnuts. Serve immediately so that the pasta is warm while the other ingredients are cool and fresh. **Serves 2.**

Mousse de truite garnie ◆ Trout and cheese mousse with tamarillo

You may have noticed that I occasionally slip a surprise ingredient into one of my recipes. It seems to me in the spirit of Cuisine Fraîcheur to keep a sense of adventure about new materials as well as new methods, the best way to stay out of the rut in the kitchen. In this delicate mousse I have combined two fruits imported from New Zealand, the tamarillo and the more familiar kiwi.

Tamarilloes are sometimes known as tree-tomatoes and do in fact belong to the tomato family. They are egg-shaped, about 4cm/1½ inch long, with a hard red or yellow skin. The yellow types tend to be sweeter than the red and are thought to resemble Cape gooseberries in flavour. Although the skin is tough it can be easily peeled away leaving firm flesh. It can be grilled like a tomato, cooked in a compote, or made into a purée for fools, sorbets or a coulis sauce.

1 trout, 225 to 250g/8 to 9oz
salt and freshly ground black pepper
1 tablespoon cider vinegar
2 eggs, separated
150g/5oz fromage frais (see page 179)

pinch of chilli powder
1 tablespoon powdered gelatine
4 tablespoons apple juice

garnish:
curly lettuce leaves
radicchio leaves
2 medium-size ripe kiwi fruit, peeled and sliced
2 tamarilloes, skinned and sliced

Poach the trout in simmering salted water, acidulated with the vinegar, for 8 minutes. Drain. Discard skin and bones and flake the fish into a bowl.

Beat the egg yolks into the cheese and season with chilli powder and pepper. Dissolve the gelatine in the heated apple juice and add to the cheese mixture. Blend in the flaked trout. Beat the egg whites until stiff and fold gently into the mixture.

Turn into four 150ml/5fl oz capacity moulds, either crown-shaped, oval or round. Allow to set in the refrigerator for 2 hours, then turn out into the centre of each of four plates. Surround with curly lettuce, radicchio, sliced kiwi and tamarillo in alternate rows or overlapping, according to taste. **Serves 4.**

Mélange de salade naturelle ◆ Medley salad with celeriac

This is the kind of salad that would make a Marilyn Monroe or a Joan Collins send for the chef. It is ideal for a light luncheon snack, and has a beautifully light, lemony flavour.

Lemon is in fact the best acidulant of Cuisine Fraîcheur. It gives a good fresh tangy flavour to a salad dressing and, of course, has a variety of other uses besides being famously rich in vitamin C. The best varieties are the Genoa lemon, oval in shape with a thick rind; the Lustrato thin-skinned type with a fragrant rind; and the citron lemon with a thick rugged skin used to make essences and candied peels.

1 medium-size head of celeriac
juice of 1 lemon
2 heads of chicory
100g/4oz small mangetouts
100g/4oz bean sprouts

dressing:
2 hard-boiled eggs, shelled and separated
2 tablespoons olive oil
2 tablespoons plain low-fat yogurt

juice of ½ lemon
1 teaspoon honey
1 garlic clove, peeled and crushed
1 tablespoon chopped fresh parsley
salt and freshly ground black pepper

Peel the celeriac and grate or shred it coarsely. Mix it with the lemon juice immediately to prevent discolouring. Shred the chicory or cut into rings. Mix the celeriac, chicory, mangetouts and bean sprouts together in a salad bowl.

For the dressing, crumble or sieve the hard-boiled egg yolks. Mix with the olive oil, yogurt, lemon juice, honey, garlic, parsley and seasoning to taste. Chop the egg whites finely and stir into the dressing. Spoon the dressing over the salad ingredients and toss together. **Serves 4.**

Terrine de lentilles volaillère • Lentil and chicken loaf

I should like to have been present when Esau sold his birthright to his brother Abel for a dish of cooked lentils – the celebrated 'mess of pottage'. It must have been quite a dish, but perhaps not as good as this delicious chicken and lentil terrine which is as nourishing as any beef steak.

Lentils are a very ancient food, a strong feature of Middle Eastern cookery and that of India, as dhal. Split red lentils, available everywhere, can be cooked very quickly. They are especially valuable in this cuisine for their high protein content.

225g/8oz split red lentils
sprig of fresh sage or wild marjoram
1 small onion, peeled and stuck with 4 cloves
1 garlic clove, peeled
1 medium-size onion, peeled and finely chopped
75g/3oz Cheddar cheese, grated
150ml/5fl oz plain low-fat yogurt
2 eggs, beaten
1 tablespoon chopped fresh mint
175g/6oz cooked chicken meat, finely chopped
salt and freshly ground black pepper
1 small Webb's Wonder lettuce, shredded

tomato dressing:
2 large tomatoes, skinned, seeded and chopped
1 tablespoon wine vinegar

2 tablespoons sunflower oil
¼ red pepper, seeded and chopped
1 shallot, peeled and halved
2 garlic cloves, peeled
2 sprigs of fresh basil
1 teaspoon honey
1 small red chilli, seeded

Put the lentils into a pan. Add sufficient water to cover, together with the sage, the onion with its cloves and the garlic. Bring to the boil, cover and cook the lentils until they are tender – about 20 to 25 minutes. Drain the lentils, and discard the onion with its cloves and the sage.

Liquidise the cooked lentils and garlic with the chopped onion, grated cheese, yogurt, beaten eggs, mint, chopped chicken and seasoning to taste, to a smooth purée.

Grease a medium-size loaf tin and line the bottom with greased foil or greaseproof paper. Fill with the lentil mixture, smoothing the surface level. Bake at 180°C, 350°F, Mark 4 for 1 hour. Allow to cool slightly in the tin before turning out.

Meanwhile, liquidise all the tomato dressing ingredients together.

Serve the terrine cut into slices with the dressing. Garnish with the shredded lettuce. This loaf is equally delicious served cold. **Serves 6.**

Charentaise au flétan ◆ Marinated halibut and melon salad

Halibut is the largest member of the flounder or flat fish family. It can grow to great size, perhaps 50kg/110lbs or more. At your fishmongers it will probably be no larger than a turbot or brill; though not as delicate as those two it is cheaper. The best halibut should be clear white on the underside. The flesh is clear and firm though it can be dry. The fins and flaps are tender and used in Chinese cookery or in modern fish soups. The fish is also smoked, salted or dried to keep for longer periods.

Halibut lends itself well to a variety of uses. It may be grilled or poached, or baked in a court bouillon and served with an egg sauce. In this recipe the Charentais melon adds a subtle aromatic flavour to the fish. Other firm white fish may be prepared in the same way.

700g/1½lbs halibut, filleted and skinned
juice of 3 limes
juice of 3 lemons
1 garlic clove, peeled and crushed
1 tablespoon chopped fresh tarragon
salt and freshly ground black pepper
2 small Charentais melons

Cut the fish into 2.5cm (1 inch) cubes and put into a shallow dish. Add the lime and lemon juices, garlic, chopped tarragon, and seasoning. Stir the fish so that it is evenly coated with the marinade. Cover and chill for 4 hours.

Halve the melons and scoop out the seeds. With a parisenne cutter or melon baller, cut the melon flesh into small balls. Stir the melon balls into the fish pieces.

To serve, spoon onto plates lined with spinach, sorrel or corn salad leaves. Sprinkle grated lime or lemon rind over each portion and garnish with fresh tarragon sprigs. Serve with hot French bread. **Serves 4.**

Tangelo saumoné ◆ *Salmon trout mousse with ugli fruit*

Hybrids of fruits and plants are now so common that a whole range of new ingredients has appeared in the markets. The ugli fruit is one of the many 'tangelos' – that is a cross between a tangerine, an orange and a grapefruit. It is an unshapely fruit with a thick knobbly skin coloured orange and green, roughly the size of a grapefruit, though sweeter in flavour. Do not be put off by its appearance: it makes delicious eating.

It can be prepared in the same way as orange or grapefruit. It can be used in salads, as in this recipe, eaten on its own as a starter, used as a garnish with poultry, or combined in a fruit salad with other fruits. Its sweetness makes it useful in Cuisine Fraîcheur, in helping us to avoid artificial sweetening.

2 teaspoons finely grated ugli fruit rind
150ml/5fl oz mayonnaise, preferably home-made
1 ripe avocado, peeled, stoned and cut fanwise
4 oak-leaf lettuce leaves
2 curly lettuce leaves
1 ugli fruit, peeled and segmented
4 fresh mussels, boiled for 3 minutes in water with 1 teaspoon vinegar, top shell removed
2 strawberries, hulled and halved

mousse:
1 small salmon trout, 700g/1½lbs, gutted, filleted and skinned
150ml/5fl oz water
juice of ugli fruit
few black peppercorns, crushed
salt
sprig of fresh mint
1 small shallot, peeled and sliced
2 teaspoons powdered gelatine

First, prepare the mousse. Place the fish fillets in a shallow pan with the water and the ugli fruit juice (reserving 1 tablespoon of it for the dressing). Season with the peppercorns and a little salt. Add the mint and shallot. Bring to a simmer and poach for 3 minutes. Cool the fish in the liquor, then remove and set aside.

Strain the liquor and return 75ml/3fl oz to the pan. Sprinkle over the gelatine and heat gently, stirring until completely dissolved. Cool until the mixture is thick, then liquidise with the fish.

Lightly whisk the ugli fruit rind and reserved juice into the mayonnaise. Mix 50ml/2fl oz of the mayonnaise into the fish mixture.

To serve, arrange the sliced avocado on two plates. Pipe the salmon mousse in a little scroll around the base of the avocado. Arrange a few leaves of lettuce, contrasted by colour, red and green on the plates. Arrange the ugli fruit segments to form part of the pattern; add the mussels and strawberry halves. Serve the remaining mayonnaise separately. **Serves 2**.

Fritots de chèvre en verdure • Goat cheese fritters with curly leaves

All cheeses, whether soft or hard, can be fried to produce a very flavoursome effect, and goat cheese lends itself to this treatment particularly well. It acquires a savoury pungency that complements the freshness of the salad. Camembert and Brie can also be prepared in this way, allowing 75g/3oz cheese per portion.

1 egg, beaten
2 tablespoons plain low-fat yogurt or soured cream
plain flour
salt and freshly ground black pepper
garlic salt (optional)

celery salt (optional)
1 small tubular-type goat cheese, cut into 12 slices
50g/2oz mixed nibbed almonds and cornflakes, finely crushed
sunflower oil
4 leaves each of curly lettuce, radicchio and dandelion or corn salad

dressing:
2 tablespoons walnut oil
1 tablespoon wine vinegar
1 spring onion
¼ teaspoon made English mustard

Mix the beaten egg with the yogurt in a shallow dish. Season some flour with salt, pepper and garlic and celery salts. Coat the goat cheese slices all over with the seasoned flour. Dip them in the egg and yogurt mixture, then coat in the mixture of almonds and cornflakes.

Heat oil in a shallow pan and fry the cheese slices for 30 seconds on each side until just coloured golden brown. Drain well on paper towels.

To serve, arrange the salad leaves on four plates in a neat pattern and place the cheese on them or at the side. Liquidise the dressing ingredients, with seasoning to taste, and drizzle a little over the salad; serve the remainder separately. **Serves 4.**

Coupe martiniquaise au riz d'amérique • Sweet and sour rice salad with fruit

Rice makes a very good basic ingredient for salad. While highly palatable in itself, it also seems to 'hold the dish together' very nicely, as you will find in this and other rice salads.

Any sort of rice that has had the husk removed but not the bran is called brown or wholegrain rice. If bought loose, brown rice takes 30 to 40 minutes to cook. I prefer the brand-named Uncle Ben's wholegrain rice which takes just 20 minutes to cook and is also a larger and plumper grain than you would usually find.

100g/4oz wholegrain rice
½ each red and green pepper, seeded and chopped
1 onion, peeled and chopped
1 mango, peeled, stoned and sliced
2 slices of fresh pineapple, peeled and cut into small pieces
100g/4oz strawberries, hulled and sliced
small bunch each of black and white grapes, halved and seeded

dressing:
50ml/2fl oz cider vinegar
100ml/4fl oz vegetable stock
3 tablespoons sunflower oil
1 tablespoon soya sauce
pinch of ground ginger
salt and freshly ground black pepper

Simmer the rice in salted water, covered, over low heat for 20 minutes. Drain, then leave to cool.

Add the red and green peppers, onion, mango, pineapple, strawberries and grapes to the rice, reserving a few of each fruit for the garnish.

Whisk the dressing ingredients together and add to the salad. Toss well to mix. Serve in individual glasses, garnished with the reserved fruits and a sprig of mint. **Serves 4**.

Champignonnade de truite arc en ciel • Rainbow trout and mushroom salad

The girolles can be quickly stir fried in a little oil if preferred, but the white button mushrooms are best raw.

2 tablespoons cider vinegar
juice of 1 lemon
sprig of fresh dill
1 teaspoon Dijon mustard
salt and freshly ground black pepper
700g/1½lbs rainbow trout, filleted, skinned and sliced
3 tablespoons olive oil
8 asparagus tips, cooked for 30 seconds only
4 girolle mushrooms, raw (optional)
4 button mushrooms, sliced
radicchio leaves
frisée or endive leaves

Combine the vinegar, lemon juice, dill and mustard with seasoning to taste. Add the fish and stir to coat. Leave to marinate for at least 6 hours. Drain the marinade from the fish and whisk the oil into it to make a dressing.

Arrange the asparagus, mushrooms, radicchio and frisée on individual plates and add the slices of fish. Garnish with fresh coriander leaves. Serve the dressing separately. **Serves 4**.

Salade florale • Green salad with flowers

2 radishes
1 spring onion
1 leaf each of corn salad, frisée (endive), fresh coriander, mint and escarole
2 each nasturtium and chive flowers
2 cherry tomatoes, preferably red and yellow
50g/2oz bean sprouts
few cashew nuts
few walnuts
sprig of fresh dill

vinaigrette:
2 tablespoons cider vinegar
1 tablespoon lemon juice
1 tablespoon sunflower oil or plain low-fat yogurt
½ teaspoon made mustard
pinch of chopped fresh parsley
1 garlic clove, peeled and finely chopped (optional)
salt and freshly ground black pepper

Cut the radishes into roses: trim the ends, then make cuts downwards around the sides. Make fine cuts lengthways into the green part of the spring onion. Put the radishes and spring onion into a bowl of iced water and soak for 1 hour until the radish 'petals' open and the spring onion curls. Drain.

Arrange all the salad ingredients decoratively on a flat glass plate. Whisk together the vinaigrette ingredients and serve with the salad. **Serves 1**.

Salade manomin • Wild rice and lentil salad

The wild rice used here is, in fact, not really a rice. It comes from a tall North American aquatic plant, Zizania aquatica. *It can be bought loose and takes 55 minutes cooking time. Uncle Ben's does a packeted product that mixes long grain and wild rice; this takes only 20 minutes to cook. It is also cheaper than the plain wild rice, which in Indian cookery goes by the name of* manomin.

225g/8oz long grain and wild rice, cooked as directed on the packet
150g/5oz cooked lentils
bunch of spring onions, chopped
bunch of radishes, sliced
4 tomatoes, skinned, seeded and quartered
2 apples (not too sweet), cored and sliced
2 bunches of watercress

dressing:
100ml/4fl oz chicken stock (optional)
4 tablespoons sunflower oil
4 to 6 tablespoons tarragon vinegar
juice of 1 lemon
dash of Worcestershire sauce
salt and freshly ground black pepper

Put the cooked rice and lentils in a bowl. Add the spring onions, radishes, tomatoes and apples and mix well.

Whisk together the dressing ingredients. Dress the salad, then leave to marinate in the refrigerator for 30 minutes. Serve garnished with watercress. **Serves 4.**

Salade à l'orange sanguine • Blood orange salad

1 yellow curly lettuce, leaves separated
bunch of watercress leaves
100g/4oz shelled hazelnuts
2 blood oranges, peeled and segmented
1 avocado, peeled, stoned and sliced

dressing:
juice of 1 lemon
3 tablespoons walnut oil
salt and freshly ground black pepper

Arrange the curly lettuce on a plate with the watercress leaves. Scatter over the nuts. Place the segments of blood orange and avocado slices on top.

Whisk the dressing ingredients together and sprinkle over the salad. If preferred, the oil may be omitted and the salad dressed with lemon juice only. **Serves 4.**

Les pouces de légumineux printaniers • Chicken salad with mung bean and lentil sprouts

All kinds of grains and seeds can be sprouted and used in salads. Besides being very crisp and tasty, such sprouts are a good source of vitamins B and C, and are more nourishing than a lettuce. Several varieties of sprouts can now be purchased in supermarkets, or you could try your hand at sprouting them yourself in jam jars. In addition to the mung bean and lentil sprouts used here, other good sources of sprouts are adzuki beans, alfalfa, barley, blackeye beans, chick peas, fenugreek, sunflower seeds and soya beans.

1 small tender chicken, cooked
1 tablespoon chopped fresh mint
juice of 1 grapefruit
salt and freshly ground black pepper
75g/3oz mung bean sprouts
75g/3oz lentil sprouts
100g/4oz tiny broccoli florets
2 large courgettes, coarsely grated or shredded
1 grapefruit, peeled and segmented

Skin the cooked chicken and remove the meat in strips. Put these into a shallow dish. Mix the chopped mint with the grapefruit juice and salt and pepper to taste. Pour over the chicken and chill, covered, for 30 minutes.

Toss the chicken lightly with the mung bean and lentil sprouts, broccoli, courgettes and grapefruit segments. Garnish with sprigs of fresh mint and serve. **Serves 4**.

Pouces chinoises au fromage de soya • Mixed sprouts with tofu

100g/4oz lentil sprouts
100g/4oz alfalfa sprouts
100g/4oz mung bean sprouts
2 tablespoons radish sprouts
2 tablespoons sunflower sprouts
2 tablespoons sunflower oil
225g/8oz tofu, cubed
2 shallots, peeled and chopped
2 garlic cloves, peeled and chopped
1 teaspoon sesame seeds
juice of 1 orange
salt and freshly ground black pepper

Combine all the sprouts in a large bowl, then arrange a portion on four individual plates or salad dishes.

Heat the oil in a frying pan and toss the tofu cubes with the shallots for 1 minute. Add the garlic and sesame seeds and cook for 30 seconds. Garnish each salad with this mixture. Sprinkle the orange juice over and season to taste. **Serves 4.**

Salade hivernale • Winter vitamin salad

75g/3oz each of peeled and grated swede, carrot, parsnip and beetroot
1 onion, peeled and cut into thin strips
salt and freshly ground black pepper
75g/3oz bean sprouts

dressing:
50g/2oz toasted almonds or peanuts
juice of 1 grapefruit
2 tablespoons water

In a bowl combine all the grated vegetables and onion strips, and mix them well. Season to taste. Divide the mixture into individual bowls and top with the bean sprouts.

Liquidise the dressing ingredients and add a little to each salad. **Serves 4.**

Les Feuilles Sauvages en Salade ◆ Wild Plants for Salads

There is a wide variety of wild plants that can be used in the composition of healthy dishes. If you are a country-dweller you may already know many of them; if an urbanite, it is worth learning to recognise the more common of these plants to lend interest (and sustenance) to your rural outings.

Such plants and herbs have a number of uses. Even in small quantity they can give a difference to a conventional green salad. Or, as the several recipes included here suggest, they can add a little extra dimension to combinations of fish, vegetables or fruit. Because most wild plants contain iron as one of their minerals, they tend towards bitterness and astringency. They are often mildly aperient and diuretic, and perhaps for that reason often have a reputation as a remedy among country people. Here is a list of some of the more familiar plants:

Alexanders *Smyrnium olusatrum*
The stem of this plant can be used like asparagus, especially the shoots of early spring. They can be eaten raw with vinaigrette or, if preferred, blanched for 5 minutes. The leaves are also edible in salad. One French herbalist, Dr Losch, in his *Les Plantes Médicinales*, suggests its use in a gourmet dish served as a fritter.

Comfrey *Symphytum officinale*
Found in damp and marshy places, comfrey comes in several varieties, some with white flowers, some with red. Much used in Nouvelle Cuisine for salad presentation, it is very mucilaginous and its jelly makes it an interesting plant to cook with fish. When raw, it goes well with nuts or cheese; it also makes a good tisane.

Laver *Porphyra umbilicus*
A rock plant with a sea flavour, this is recommended for fish and potato salads. Laver bread (the purée) is a Welsh speciality; it can also be served raw if marinated in a good dressing. Rich in minerals, especially iodine, it is extremely nutritious.

Bistort *Polygonum bistorta*
Rich in tannin, the leaves of bistort can be used in salads though highly astringent. The plant is an old herbal remedy for kidney and stomach ailments. The roots can be boiled like small turnips.

Sorrel *Rumex acetosa*
The French use this very useful herb in egg dishes, omelettes and their 'health soup'. In herbal lore it gets high marks as a good laxative. The garden sorrel *R. scutanus* is milder and less sour. The juice of the leaves will curdle milk and is often used as rennet by vegetarians. When cooking sorrel use a stainless steel pan as its chemicals react with iron. Sorrel makes an excellent sauce to go with rainbow trout, salmon or mackerel.

Sweet Cicely *Myrrhis odorata*
This very pleasant aromatic herb should be used more frequently in salads, soups and sauces. The root can be boiled like a turnip or eaten in salads with a vinegar dressing. The stem can be boiled as asparagus. The flower is good for dish decoration. This herb is found mainly in northern England and the Scottish borders.

Hawthorn *Crataegus monogyma*
The very young leaves of the hawthorn, known as 'Bread and Cheese', are often eaten by children on the way to school. A wine is made with the flowers and the berries are edible and therapeutic.

Marsh Samphire *Salicornia europaea*
This plant, *salicorne* in French, has made a hit with younger cooks as a perfect garnish with fish. It has a slight lemony acid taste and if young can be used raw. Older plants can be cooked and served like asparagus. Rock samphire (*Crithmum maritimum*), although similarly named, is no relation to marsh samphire. It should be cooked before eating or, like marsh samphire, can be pickled.

Burnet *Poterium sanguisorba*
This is a blood tonic plant, taken by the Pilgrim Fathers to the New World in the belief that it was good for health and sanity. The leaves are best used to flavour beverages and fruit cups although a few leaves in a salad have the same effect as the dandelion.

Sea Lettuce *Ulva lactuca*
This sea algae, coloured translucent green, is common all round the coast of Britain and northern France and is an attractive ingredient for salad. It can be eaten raw, marinated in a dressing or itself made into a dressing the Japanese way.

Horseradish *Armoracia rusticana*
Both root and leaves are used medicinally for their antiseptic properties. The leaves can be used in salads.

Burdock *Arctium minus*
Flowers from July to September all over Britain. It is well known in herbal medicine as a blood purifier. Both leaves and roots can be eaten raw in salads.

Red Clover *Trifolium pratense*
'Eat clover and bowl me over', is an ancient French saying which hints at the magical power attributed to this high-protein plant beloved of cattle, sheep and rabbits. An attractive salad can be made from the uncooked leaves and flowers combined with dandelion and apple and a garlicky dressing.

Seakale *Crambe maritima*
Found on sandy areas of the coast, this plant was known to the Romans and eaten raw

with apples. If eaten cooked it should not be boiled for more than 4 minutes. Excellent with peanut butter or avocado dip.

Tansy *Tanacetum vulgare*
The name derives from the Greek *athanasia*, meaning immortality. It is a flavouring ingredient similar to nutmeg and cinnamon, often used with fruit cups.

Dulse *Rhodymenia palmata*
This plant, with its dark red fronds rich in iodine, is found in rocky coastal places. It is tasty served raw with cucumber, apples and walnuts in a lemon and cider vinegar dressing.

Dandelion *Taraxacum officinale*
One of the best and easiest wild ingredients for a salad. Rich in iron and well-known for its diuretic properties, a handful of chopped dandelion leaves gives an astringent and tonic effect to salads. Especially good when counterbalanced with fruits such as citrus and apple.

FRAÎCHEUR VÉGÉTARIENNE
VEGETARIAN FRAÎCHEUR

A good many purely vegetarian dishes have already been included in previous chapters. A number of others containing white meat or fish could also be adapted by the imaginative cook by substituting a suitable form of vegetable protein. But here we concentrate more directly on the needs of vegetarians. Many will already include a proportion of raw food in their diet. In this chapter we add more recipes to show how pleasurable and healthy it can be to raise this to the level recommended by Cuisine Fraîcheur, while also including a proper balance of protein. The underlying theme of the chapter is to extend the vegetarian range which can, at certain seasons anyway, get stuck within a too narrow range of foods. Here we introduce some *soupçons* of adventure with new ingredients and new methods, believing that these are very stimulating for the stomach as well as the spirit.

The chapter is divided into five sections: cereals, cheeses, tropical vegetarian dishes, oriental stir fried vegetable dishes, and wild mushroom dishes. The cereals section will show how these taken-for-granted grains and flours can be turned into interesting dishes. The second section suggests the delectable range of recipes possible with various cheeses. The third brings in the widening variety of tropical fruits and vegetables now becoming familiar in the supermarkets, in the hope that the recipes will embolden vegetarians and others to try these interesting products of the hot countries. In the fourth section we get into the world of oriental stir fry, which is quick, wholesome and capable of taking in the widest variety of vegetarian ingredients. Lastly come the mushroom family, offering new opportunities for delicious combinations but much under-used in British kitchens.

Various seaweeds and sea vegetables are also becoming available in health food shops and some supermarkets. Though still unfamiliar to most of us, they have been used for many centuries in the Far East. Cuisine Fraîcheur recommends them, believing them to be an important ingredient of the future with much health value.

Cereals

Wheat, millet, oats, barley, buckwheat, maize, rice, semolina, rye and spelt (also known as German wheat) are all cereals now used in vegetarian cookery. The part used is the grain or seed, an important source of secondary protein.

Like eggs, cereals are made up of three parts: a) a protective outer layer or husk, which may be compared to an egg shell, b) a nutrient store, mainly starch and protein, and c) the germ, rich in vitamins, which will grow into a new plant.

One of the attractions of cereals for the cuisine is that they can be served in such a great variety of form, either as a main ingredient or as the friendly partner to a great range of other foods. Here, in a short selection, we begin with a couple of pasta dishes, then move on to some dumplings, a cereal terrine, savoury cakes, a casserole, pancakes and some unusual rice dishes.

Rice is the most popular vegetarian plant in use apart from bread. It makes an excellent basis for many dishes. Its only minor drawback in dietary terms is that it has 87 per cent carbohydrate (compared to 70 per cent for wheat) and the rather high calorie rating of 354 calories per 100g/4oz portion of cooked rice. So it makes sense to add only protein-rich vegetables to rice dishes. Some examples would be peas, beans and lentils, while onion, celery, garlic, tomato, and a variety of herbs and spices contribute nicely to the flavour.

A surprising number of people complain of not being able to cook perfect rice. Rather than expand on that interesting topic, I would only suggest the short cut I take myself, which is to use Uncle Ben's rice, available in long grain and whole grain, both processed to cook in 20 minutes.

Coquillettes Tante Bette • *Shell pasta with celeriac and chicory*

As you will find, this dish has pleasant contrasts of hot and cold, cooked and raw – a good example of a Fraîcheur recipe.

> 225g/8oz wholemeal pasta shells
> salt and freshly ground black pepper
> 50g/2oz polyunsaturated margarine
> 50g/2oz Gruyère cheese, grated
> 225g/8oz chicory, sliced across into strips
> 1 celeriac, peeled and cut into strips or grated
> 150ml/5fl oz plain low-fat yogurt
> 4 large tomatoes, skinned, seeded and coarsely chopped
> 6 fresh tarragon leaves

Cook the pasta for 12 minutes in boiling salted water. Drain and place in a bowl. Season to taste and toss in the margarine and grated cheese. Add the chicory, celeriac and yogurt and toss the salad once more while the pasta is still hot.

Arrange the salad in four soup plates and decorate with the chopped tomatoes and tarragon leaves. **Serves 4.**

Vermicelle japonaise • *Vermicelli with seaweed and mushrooms*

> 12cm/5 inch strip of dried kombu seaweed, soaked for 1 hour
> 225g/8oz very fine rice vermicelli
> 150g/5oz mushrooms, sliced
> 1 stick of celery, thinly sliced
> 8 lychees, peeled, halved and stoned
> small piece of fresh root ginger (the size of a grape), peeled and chopped

dressing:
slice of fresh pineapple, peeled
50g/2oz soft tofu, cubed
1 garlic clove, peeled
2 tablespoons soya sauce
salt and freshly ground black pepper

Drain the kombu and cook for 20 minutes in boiling salted water. Drain again and cut into small pieces. Cook the vermicelli in boiling salted water for 1 to 2 minutes and drain. Combine the vermicelli and kombu in a bowl. Add the mushrooms and celery.

Liquidise the dressing ingredients, add to the salad and toss.

To serve, arrange the salad in four bowls and garnish with lychees. Sprinkle over the ginger. **Serves 4**.

Boulettes de semoule algérienne • Semolina dumplings

Semolina is made from durum wheat and is rich in protein. These dumplings (called gnocchi *in Italian) served in a rich tomato sauce make an ideal vegetarian dish which I think is better than ravioli.*

50g/2oz polyunsaturated margarine
1 large egg, beaten
150g/5oz medium grain semolina (couscous)
225g/8oz cherry tomatoes
freshly grated Parmesan cheese

sauce:
3 tablespoons sunflower oil
1 red onion, peeled and chopped
2 garlic cloves, peeled and chopped
2 tablespoons tomato purée
300ml/½ pint water
1 vegetable stock cube
1 teaspoon honey
1 teaspoon vinegar
1 stick of celery, chopped
1 slice of fennel, chopped
1 teaspoon cornflour dissolved in 5 tablespoons tomato juice
salt and freshly ground black pepper

For the sauce, heat the oil in a saucepan and stir fry the onion and garlic for 1 minute without browning. Add the tomato purée and cook 1 minute more. Pour in the water and add the crumbled stock cube, honey and vinegar. Bring to the boil, then add the celery and fennel. Simmer for 15 minutes.

Meanwhile, in a bowl combine the margarine, beaten egg and semolina to make a soft dough. Divide into 12 equal pieces and shape into balls. Drop the dumplings into a pan of boiling salted water and poach gently for 5 minutes.

Add the cornflour mixture to the sauce and simmer for a further 4 minutes, stirring frequently. Season to taste. Drain the dumplings.

Pour the tomato sauce on to four plates and place three dumplings in each. Add cherry tomatoes at the side and garnish with a few fresh coriander leaves in the sauce. Sprinkle with grated Parmesan cheese and serve. **Serves 4**.

Gâteau d'orge perlé aux cacahouettes • Peanut and barley loaf

Barley is a light and refreshing cereal with a reputation for easing tummy upsets in children and adults. The malted sprouts of barley can be used in salads while malt syrup plays its part in making delicious brown bread. The barley flakes now available in health food shops are usually made into porridge in combination with oats and served with milk or yogurt. Barley water is a refreshing drink which can be easily made by boiling 50g/2oz of barley in 1 litre/1¾ pints of water for about 1 hour.

150g/5oz pot barley
500ml/16fl oz water
2 eggs, beaten
50g/2oz mushrooms, chopped
225g/8oz shelled roasted peanuts, crushed
1 small onion, peeled and chopped
1 tablespoon mixed chopped fresh parsley, coriander and young garlic sprouts
50g/2oz polyunsaturated margarine
salt and freshly ground black pepper

Cook the barley in the gently simmering water for 1 hour or until tender. Drain. In a bowl combine the cooked barley, beaten eggs, mushrooms, nuts, onion, herbs and margarine. Season to taste.

Grease an oblong baking dish or loaf tin and fill with the mixture. Bake for 20 minutes at 200°C, 400°F, Mark 6. When ready, the loaf can be used as a stuffing for cooked marrow halves or, if preferred, simply served with Chinese leaves. **Serves 4**.

Pain de maïs • Indian corn cakes

Maize has a sweeter taste than any other cereal. Its protein is not so complete as that of wheat, so eggs or cheese can usefully supplement it. It is always attractive in its familiar form of corn-on-the-cob when young. Simply boil for 5 to 6 minutes and serve with a little plain yogurt. In this recipe we use cornmeal which is a kind of maize semolina.

600ml/1 pint water
salt and freshly ground black pepper
150g/5oz cornmeal
2 eggs, beaten
4 large tomatoes, sliced
2 green peppers, sliced across and seeded
½ cucumber or 2 courgettes, sliced slantways

Bring the water to the boil in a pan with a little salt added. Sprinkle in the cornmeal gradually, stirring, and simmer for 15 minutes until thick. Remove from the heat and blend in the eggs. Season. Cook gently for a further 5 minutes.

Oil a 700g/1½lb capacity oblong tin that is 2.5cm/1 inch deep. Pour the cooked cornmeal mixture into it and leave to cool. When cold turn out on to a clean board and cut into regular squares or slices.

To serve, arrange the corn cakes on four plates and garnish with tomato, pepper and cucumber or courgette. A little vinaigrette may be used with the raw garnish if wished. **Serves 4**.

Timbale de millet Moulin Rouge • Millet casserole with red vegetables

Millet is the African cereal most closely resembling wheat. In Arab countries the semolina made of millet is the staple food. Millet semolina, which sometimes goes by the name couscous, can be bought from supermarkets in 500g/1lb packets. It can be cooked in 6 minutes.

Millet is noted for its high proportion of silicic acid which promotes healthy skin, hair, teeth and nails, and for its magnesium and lecithin content. The latter is essential to the development of the brain – though in our modern world millet is considered an excellent food for our pet budgerigars! It can be purchased in grain or flakes or semolina granules.

125g/4½ oz millet
350ml/12fl oz water
¼ teaspoon salt
150g/5oz pumpkin flesh, cut into cubes

4 tablespoons sunflower oil
1 red onion, peeled and chopped
1 red pepper, cored, seeded and chopped
2 large tomatoes, skinned, seeded and chopped
2 carrots, peeled and chopped
1 red chilli, seeded and chopped
1 small radicchio, leaves separated
6 red radishes, sliced

dressing:
2 tablespoons sunflower oil
1 tablespoon raspberry vinegar
1 tablespoon tomato ketchup
2 tablespoons plain low-fat yogurt

Wash the millet in several waters and drain well. Simmer in the measured salted water for 25 minutes. Meanwhile, cook the pumpkin in boiling salted water for 8 minutes; drain. Drain the millet.

In a pan, heat the oil and stir fry the onion for 2 minutes. Add the millet, pumpkin, red pepper, tomatoes, carrots and chilli. Simmer for 10 minutes. Liquidise the dressing ingredients.

Serve the millet mixture hot, on the radicchio leaves, garnished with sliced radishes. Serve the dressing separately. **Serves 4**.

Crêpes au sarrasin • Buckwheat pancakes

Bretons have adopted buckwheat as their staple food for centuries, especially for making their famous crêpes, or pancakes. Buckwheat has a good, dry flavour, able to be a partner to almost anything. Known as kasha *in Russia, it is used there in soups and stews and their famous fish pie,* coulibiac.

100g/4oz buckwheat flour
1 tablespoon plain flour
2 eggs, beaten
150ml/5fl oz water
75ml/3fl oz soured cream, plain low-fat yogurt, buttermilk or whey
good pinch of salt
sunflower oil, for frying
4 eggs, poached
bunch of spring onions, chopped

In a bowl, combine the buckwheat flour and plain flour with the eggs, water and soured cream to obtain a thin batter. Add the salt. Heat a little oil in a 20cm/8 inch pancake or frying pan and pour in about one-quarter of the batter. Cook for about 2 minutes, turning the pancake over half-way through, then tip out of the pan. Repeat to make three more pancakes.

Place a hot pancake on a plate and put a poached egg in the middle. Fold over and serve sprinkled with the spring onions. **Serves 4**.

Le plat de l'empereur • The imperial platter

Sometimes in composing a new dish one has the feeling that all the complex flavours and textures suddenly come right and 'hit it off' together in some especially apt way. It is rather like a music composer – if it is not too grand to say so – finding that all the little tunes in a symphony work together to make a rounded whole. I felt enthusiastic enough about this dish to give it an exalted and noble title.

> 4 tablespoons sunflower oil
> 225g/8oz spring onions, sliced across
> 1 red, 1 yellow, 1 green and 1 purple pepper, cored, seeded and cut into matchstick julienne, 4cm/1½ inches long
> 1 small green chilli, seeded and sliced
> 225g/8oz mushrooms, sliced
> 4 okra, sliced across
> 150ml/5fl oz orange juice
> 150ml/5fl oz tomato juice
> 150ml/5fl oz vegetable stock or water
> 2 tablespoons soya sauce
> 2 tablespoons sherry vinegar
> 1 tablespoon honey
> 100g/4oz cooked brown rice
> salt and freshly ground black pepper
> 4 quail's eggs, hard-boiled and shelled
> bunch of fresh chives, snipped with scissors

In a sauté pan or wok, heat the oil and stir fry the spring onions for 30 seconds. Add the peppers, chilli, mushrooms and okra and stir fry for 1 minute.

Pour in the orange and tomato juices, stock, soya sauce, vinegar and honey and stir in the cooked rice. Cook for 10 minutes. Season to taste.

Serve in attractive individual bowls with one egg each (halved if liked), sprinkled with chives. **Serves 4**.

Riz isiki • Rice with isiki seaweed

The Japanese use iziki seaweed as a rejuvenating treatment, and it is claimed, for example, that they owe their remarkably healthy hair to its consumption. They rarely go bald or grey. While there may be some ethnic factor in it I suspect that their healthy diet of raw fish and vegetables does play a part. Iziki can be purchased in health food shops.

> 1 tablespoon sunflower oil
> 25g/1oz iziki seaweed, soaked in water 1 hour, drained and chopped
> 125g/4oz long grain rice
> 750ml/1¼ pints boiling water
> 1 medium-size onion, peeled and chopped
> 2 mooli, peeled and sliced or diced
> 8 large plums (Victoria type), stoned and sliced

> dressing:
> 2 tablespoons soya sauce
> 2 tablespoons cider vinegar
> 2 teaspoons honey
> salt and freshly ground black pepper

Heat the oil and stir fry the chopped seaweed for a few minutes (you will begin to smell the sea). Just cover with water and simmer for 25 to 35 minutes until tender. Meanwhile, cook the rice in the water for 20 minutes; drain if necessary.

Whisk together the dressing ingredients in a bowl. Add the hot cooked rice and onion and toss to mix. Arrange the rice on four plates. Garnish with the raw mooli and plums, and the long ribbons of seaweed spread around. **Serves 4**.

Say Cheese . . .

France produces 375 different kinds of cheese out of the 600 known in the world. New or little-known types of British cheese are nowadays constantly coming to the market from smaller producers and can be found in the more specialist cheese shops. So the vegetarian is presented with a good choice of textures and flavours. Ideally, of course, one should opt for a low-fat cheese in a healthy diet, for example cottage cheese and Nicotta with only 4 per cent fat. Occasionally a creamier result is desired, though, when curd cheese at 12 per cent fat is called for.

In Fraîcheur, while warmly approving such occasional treats from the shop, we recommend home-made cheese as the steady basis of your cheese consumption, for reasons of both economy and pleasure. It should be fresh, low in fat and not too salty. Such fromage frais not only lends a rustic simplicity to a meal; it enables the creative cook to give it great variety by flavouring with such herbs as thyme, mint and parsley or spicy ingredients such as paprika, curry powder, chillies, garlic and onion.

There are two ways to produce fromage frais at home. The easy method is to curdle heated milk with lemon juice, making a quark-style cheese. I prefer yogurt cheese in which the curdling is done with lactic acid provided by using yogurt as the culture. The method reduces the sugar content to the bare minimum, and if you use skimmed milk to make it you have the finest cheese for a healthy diet, just the thing to bring out the best in a range of raw fruit and crudité accompaniments.

Fromage au yaourt • Yogurt cheese

You can make yogurt quite successfully in a thermos flask, leaving it in a warm place such as the airing cupboard overnight. But if you make yogurt regularly, an electric yogurt-maker, in which the temperature is controlled, is an excellent addition to your kitchen appliances. The one I use at home is a Bell brand which has six glass containers each holding 100ml/4fl oz. It is quite a cheap contraption, well worth the investment. It enables you to make your own yogurt every day, or once a week if you are not using so much, very easily indeed. Once made, the yogurt will keep at least a week in the refrigerator. After every five or six batches of yogurt, start off the next one using bought live yogurt: the bacterial culture in your home-made yogurt will have lost its potency by then.

600ml/1 pint milk
100g/4oz plain low-fat yogurt
50g/2oz skimmed milk powder

Scald the milk, then allow it to cool (UHT or long-life milk does not need scalding). Beat the yogurt (bought live yogurt to start with) and milk in a jug with a whisk, gradually adding the skimmed milk powder. Fill each glass container in the yogurt-maker with the mixture. Fit the caps, switch on the power, and allow the mixture to incubate for 8 hours. Cool it for 1 hour, then refrigerate, and your thick yogurt is made.

Next, the cheese-making process. You simply remove the liquid whey by tying up the yogurt in a muslin bag and leaving it to drain for up to 2 hours in a colander. Finally add 1 per cent salt – that is for 500g/1lb of yogurt cheese you season with 1 teaspoon of salt, or less if you prefer. The cheese can be served plain, or with whatever flavouring takes your fancy. **Serves 6.**

Fromage aux herbes • Cheese with herbs

This herby cheese can be used in many ways: with toast, French bread or crispbread; on canapés for a party; or as a dip with crudités such as sticks of celery or fennel.

4 fresh mint leaves
sprig of fresh thyme or marjoram
50g/2oz blanched almonds or walnuts
1 garlic clove, peeled
½ teaspoon salt
good pinch of freshly ground black pepper
500g/1lb thick yogurt cheese

Liquidise the herbs, nuts, garlic and seasoning with a little of the yogurt cheese until ground finely. Combine this purée with the remaining cheese. Check the seasoning, place in small jars with lids, and keep refrigerated. **Serves 6**.

Phyllo pastry

This pastry is suitable for ravioli, strudel and the Greek nut dessert Baklava.

1kg/2lbs strong bread flour
1 teaspoon salt
400ml/14fl oz water
4 tablespoons olive or sunflower oil

Sift the flour and salt into a mixing bowl and gradually work in the water and oil. Work to a soft dough, then knead well for 10 minutes: the dough is sticky at first but becomes more resilient after kneading. Gather the dough into a ball, wrap up and leave to rest at room temperature for 1 hour.

Divide the dough into 12 equal pieces and form each into a ball. Dust the work surface with flour and use a rolling pin to roll out one piece into a 15cm/6 inch square.

Dust the board again. Using a dowel pin no less than 60cm/2 feet long and 2cm/¾ inch diameter, roll thinner until the pastry sheet is 25 × 30cm/10 × 12 inches in size. (An ordinary rolling pin can be used, but the dowel pin makes the job much easier.) Use the back of the hand under the sheet of pastry to stroke and stretch it further until it is almost transparent, without breaking. Its final measurement should be 35 × 45cm/14 × 18 inches.

Place the sheet between greaseproof paper. Continue rolling and stretching the balls of pastry, one at a time, stacking them up in a neat pile. **Makes 12 sheets**.

Fromage frais • Quark-style cheese

This fromage frais can be used in sandwiches with cress or lettuce or, for children, with banana, strawberries or other soft fruit; or it can be eaten with an apple, pear or tomato. It makes an inexpensive snack or meal, with good protein and mineral content. The fat content of the cheese will vary according to the type of milk used – skimmed, semi-skimmed, homogenised or Channel Island and South Devon.

1 litre/2 pints milk
juice of 1 lemon

Bring the milk just to the boil and remove from the heat. Add the lemon juice and reheat until the milk just comes to the boil again without churning movement. Remove from the heat, and the milk will clot. Tie the mixture into a muslin bag and leave to drain in a colander for 2 to 3 hours, pressing the bag occasionally to extract as much whey as possible. When dry enough, remove from the bag and place in a bowl. Season with a little salt and flavour as desired. **Serves 6 to 8.**

Gâteau au fromage tiropita • Cheese pie

For those who prefer a more highly-flavoured cheese, home-made fromage frais can be mixed with a combination of the harder cheeses – Cheddar, Gruyère or Parmesan – to produce my version of this well-known Greek dish.

600ml/1 pint milk
100g/4oz coarse wheat semolina
100g/4oz fromage frais (see page 179)
100g/4oz Cheddar or Gruyère cheese, grated
25g/1oz Parmesan cheese, grated
3 eggs, beaten
75g/3oz fresh spinach or green cabbage, shredded
2 garlic cloves, peeled and crushed or chopped
2 tablespoons mixed chopped fresh coriander and parsley
grated nutmeg or mace
salt and freshly ground black pepper
75ml/3fl oz sunflower oil
12 sheets of phyllo pastry, bought or home-made

In a large saucepan, heavy-bottomed if possible, bring the milk to the boil and sprinkle in the semolina. Cook, stirring, until it has the thickness of porridge, approximately 5 minutes. Away from the heat, blend in the cheeses. Let cool a little, then blend in the eggs. Add the chopped spinach, garlic, herbs and nutmeg, salt and pepper to taste.

Oil a shallow 25 × 30cm/10 × 12 inch baking dish and line with six sheets of pastry, cut to fit, brushing each sheet with oil. Spread the filling over and top with six more sheets of pastry, cutting and oiling them as before. With the tip of a knife, mark the top with crossing parallel lines to form a diamond or lozenge pattern.

Bake for 30 minutes at 200°C, 400°F, Mark 6. Cool for 10 minutes, then cut along the marked lines. **Serves 6.**

Roulade de fromage au citron • Lemon cheese strudel

225g/½lb home-made phyllo pastry dough
melted polyunsaturated margarine

filling:
225g/8oz fromage frais without salt (see page 179)
75g/3oz honey
50g/2oz sultanas, soaked in water for 30 minutes and drained
grated rind and juice of 2 lemons
good pinch of ground cinnamon
50g/2oz fresh brown breadcrumbs
2 egg whites

Cover the kitchen table or a large work surface with a clean tablecloth. Roll out the pastry on this very thinly as described in the phyllo pastry method, and finally stretch to a 43cm/17 inch square.

In a bowl, combine the filling ingredients, except the egg whites, and blend well. Whisk the egg whites until stiff and fold into the mixture. Spread the filling evenly over two-thirds of the pastry area, then roll up like a Swiss roll, rolling the filling up first. Start rolling with your hands; once a rounded tube shape has formed lift the tablecloth and the strudel will roll itself up. Use the cloth and your hands to get an even shape all along the strudel.

Cut the roll into two or three sections to fit a greased baking tray. Brush the top of each strudel with melted margarine. Bake at 200°C, 400°F, Mark 6 for 30 minutes or until golden. Allow to cool, then cut slantways into portions. Serve with berries, or sliced bananas and cranberries on the side of the plate. **Serves 6.**

Poire et pomme divine • Pear and apple with cheese

It is strange but true that contrasting temperatures in a dish can seem to enhance the flavour of the food. Take, for example, banana with hot chocolate sauce, or hot mackerel and cold gooseberry purée. In this delicious light starter I have made a double strength contrast of raw pear and cooked apple with hot and cold stuffings. The effect – to quote a ravishing actress who complimented me on this creation – 'stupendous'!

2 large cooking apples, halved and cored
2 red and 2 green lettuce leaves
2 large ripe Comice pears, halved lengways at last minute and cored
few cranberries
few shelled walnuts

stuffing for the apples:
50g/2oz fromage frais (see page 179)
40g/1½ oz polyunsaturated margarine
25g/1oz walnut kernels, chopped
25g/1oz seedless raisins, soaked in hot water for 10 minutes and drained

stuffing for the pears:
50g/2oz polyunsaturated margarine
2 eggs, beaten
3 tablespoons soured cream
1 tablespoon chopped fresh parsley
salt and freshly ground black pepper

Place the apples in a greased baking dish and bake at 200°C, 400°F, Mark 6 for 15 minutes until soft. Cool. Meanwhile, combine the ingredients for the apple stuffing.

For the pear stuffing, heat the margarine in a pan and scramble the eggs. Mix in the soured cream, parsley and seasoning to taste.

On four plates arrange a nest of lettuce in alternate colours with a little watercress or corn salad. Place one apple half and one pear half on top. Spoon the respective stuffings on to the fruit. Garnish with cranberries and walnuts and serve promptly. **Serves 4.**

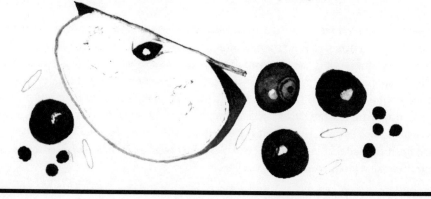

Tropical Vegetarian Dishes

It is exhilarating for good cooks to see such an abundance of unusual vegetables and fruits appearing in our shops and markets. At first these tropical ingredients came in as a trickle to meet the nostalgic appetites of the immigrant population. Then a wider public began to try them, at home or in restaurants, and found how good they were, and the trickle has become a steady volume of supply. Some supermarkets even give special attention to presenting them.

It is now a little strange to think how many good ingredients such as okra, ackee, mango, breadfruit, mooli, chayote and so on remained purely local and largely peasant ingredients throughout the days of the British Empire. Only in recent years, with the Empire disappeared, does the home country get a taste for its diversity of produce. Better refrigerated transport has much to do with this improved supply, of course. Whatever the reasons, I find the development an exciting one, as I try to express in the following recipes, which so neatly adapt to the principles of Cuisine Fraîcheur.

A vital part of tropical cookery is the herbs and spices used. Such ingredients are valuable in our diet because they reduce the need for salt and sugar and stimulate aroma and interest. Many such spices have been used in the home country for centuries. In these days of convenience foods they tend to find their place on the shelf in packaged, ready-to-use form.

This may be the opportune moment for an old chef to pass on an important piece of advice – grind your own spices. Yes, get your pestle and mortar tomorrow. It will transform your dishes and even your attitude to cooking. 'Can't be bothered' has no place in the kitchen. Not surprisingly it is those who automatically reach for the packet and the easy short cut who feel cooking is rather a chore. Only freshly ground spices possess the subtle fragrance of their aromatic oils. Once you have taken the simple steps to organise it, grinding your own becomes the easy task of a few extra minutes. You will feel more professional, pleased and proud of yourself, knowing that the dish is going to be as good as you can make it. And that's real cookery.

Now, after that little lecture, let us return to our saucepans . . .

Casserole guadeloupaise • Breadfruit with spicy sauce

Breadfruit resembles a melon in size and appearance, round or oval in shape with a tough green skin and a corky centre which is removed after cooking. Despite its fruity name – and it does have that sort of sweetness – it is used more in the style of a root vegetable such as potatoes or yams.

It can be simply cut into pieces and boiled, made into casseroles and puddings, or cut into thin slices and fried like chips. In the South Pacific the cooked fruit is eaten with sauces, mostly made from coconut. Mashed breadfruit with coconut cream or yogurt makes a pleasant meal when served with a salad of cold cooked lentils and lettuce with a lime dressing.

Breadfruit is available most of the year in Asian shops or in supermarkets that take a special interest in tropical products.

½ medium-size breadfruit, quartered lengthways and cored
75g/3oz rice, cooked and kept hot
50g/2oz hot cooked peas
50g/2oz hot cooked green beans
50g/2oz shelled roasted peanuts, toasted

sauce:
2 tablespoons sunflower oil
1 medium-size onion, peeled and chopped
1 tablespoon curry powder
2 tablespoons tomato purée
2 garlic cloves, peeled and crushed
50g/2oz desiccated coconut
1 small green chilli, seeded and sliced
600ml/1 pint water
salt

Cook the breadfruit for 40 minutes in just enough boiling water to cover.

Meanwhile, for the sauce, heat the oil and stir fry the onion until translucent. Add the curry powder and cook for 20 seconds to develop flavour. Stir in the tomato purée, garlic, coconut, chilli and water. Simmer for 20 minutes. Season.

To serve, drain the breadfruit and place on four plates. Cover with the sauce and garnish with the rice, peas and beans, neatly presented. Sprinkle over the peanuts, crushed, left whole or split as preferred. **Serves 4.**

Grosse banane des Antilles • Plantain pie

Plantains resemble ordinary bananas in shape but are larger and always eaten when the skin is green. They are usually cooked in the same way as potatoes or used in stews, and are also the basis of some very tasty and popular Jamaican dishes. Plantain can be bought at Asian shops or supermarkets. The protein content is low, but it makes a good energy food.

1kg/2lb plantains, peeled
juice of 1 lime
50g/2oz polyunsaturated margarine
1 green chilli, sliced and seeded
1 teaspoon made mustard
300ml/½ pint milk
2 eggs, beaten
50g/2oz cashews or shelled roasted peanuts, chopped
225g/8oz Cheddar cheese, grated

Cook the plantains in boiling water, with the lime juice added, for 30 minutes until soft. Drain. Slice the plantains and place in a pudding basin greased with the margarine. Blend the chilli, mustard and milk with the beaten eggs and add to the basin. Sprinkle the nuts and grated cheese all over the surface.

Bake at 200°C, 400°F, Mark 6 for 20 minutes until golden brown. **Serves 4.**

Karella asiatique • Karella with mustard sauce

Karella is a pod-like fruit-vegetable also called a bitter gourd. It is green in colour, pointed at the ends with a peculiar rough skin, and hollow. When treated as in the method below to remove the bitterness, it can make a delicious cold dish. It has aperient qualities.

> 6 karella, peeled
> salt and freshly ground black pepper
> juice of 1 orange
> 2 tablespoons cider vinegar
> 1 teaspoon made mustard

Cut the karella into thick slices, removing seeds. Sprinkle salt over the slices to draw out the bitter juice as one does with aubergines and courgettes. Leave to drain for 30 minutes, then rinse in plenty of water to remove traces of salt. Dry in a clean cloth and place in individual bowls. Combine the remaining ingredients and sprinkle this dressing over the karella slices. Leave to marinate for 12 minutes before serving. **Serves 4 to 6.**

Quenelles de manioc à l'anis • Cassava dumplings

Cassava is the West Indian name for the shrubs and rootstock of the Manihot family (also known elsewhere as manioc or yucca) largely used in the production of tapioca. The root has the appearance of a rough sort of parsnip. It is very popular in Caribbean cuisine.

Cassava is usually peeled, cut into fairly small slices and boiled for 25 minutes, with a dash of lime juice in the water to keep the vegetable white. It consists mainly of starch and glucose so it is more an energy food than an all-round nutrient.

> 100g/4oz wholemeal flour
> 2 tablespoons desiccated coconut
> 1½ teaspoons baking powder
> 150g/5oz peeled and grated cassava
> 1 teaspoon aniseed
> good pinch of salt

25g/1oz polyunsaturated margarine, melted
1 teaspoon honey
125 to 175ml/4 to 6fl oz water

Combine the flour, coconut, baking powder, grated cassava, aniseed and salt. Add the melted margarine, honey and enough water to make a dough. Divide the dough into 16 equal pieces and shape into balls with your hands.

Bring a wide shallow pan of salted water to the boil, add the dumplings and simmer for 20 minutes. Remove with a slotted spoon, and serve in a vegetable stew, in a rich curry sauce, or in soups such as tomato or pea. **Serves 4.**

Chaudron de légumes exotiques • Hot pot of exotic vegetables

The French word chaudron means cauldron and hints at a really robust stew. Here it is given tropical undertones of flavour, and served on a chilly winter's day, it may bring you a whiff of the sun and the palm trees.

The chayote is a solid, pear-shaped, green-skinned vegetable, ridged along its length. Its character is drawn out best when cooked with other vegetables as in this dish I devised long ago in Jamaica. It has a buttery taste and pleasant marrow-like flavour.

2 large chayotes (christophines)
4 tablespoons sunflower oil
1 large onion, peeled and chopped
¼ cabbage, shredded
½ small cauliflower, in florets
2 carrots, peeled and chopped
2 red peppers, cored, seeded and chopped
2 sticks of celery, chopped
1 green chilli, sliced and seeded
2 tablespoons soya sauce
juice of 1 lime
salt

Cut the chayotes in quarters lengthways and remove the stones. Peel if you wish and slice thinly lengthways.

Heat the oil in a flameproof casserole and stir fry all the vegetables for 1 minute. Cover with a lid and sweat gently for 5 minutes to extract maximum flavour, then add the soya sauce, lime juice and just enough water almost to cover the vegetables. Season to taste. Bring to the boil and simmer for 20 minutes. **Serves 4.**

Gombos à la purée de poivrons rouges • Okra with hot pepper sauce

Okra, also known as ladies' fingers, are small and tapering green pods, containing tiny edible seeds. They originated in Africa but ample supplies now reach Britain from a number of hot countries and this means they can often be found at ordinary greengrocers. They are rich in a gelatinous substance which helps them to improve the consistency of stews, curries and so on, while being a tender mouthful in themselves. They also go well with pepper and tomato as in this recipe. Buy them firm and slightly under-ripe, picking out small and bright green samples of quality.

To prepare, wash and dry the okra. Snip off the stem without damaging the pod. Place the pods in a solution of 600ml/1 pint water and 75ml/3fl oz distilled vinegar and soak them for 30 minutes. Drain and boil for 5 minutes in salted water. Refresh in icy water to retain the bright green colour, and drain again. They are now ready to serve or to be added to any stew or casserole, for a maximum of 12 minutes simmering time.

450g/1lb okra, prepared as above
sauce:
1 red chilli, seeded and chopped
1 red pepper, cored, seeded and chopped
1 large tomato, skinned, seeded and chopped
1 avocado, peeled, stoned and sliced
juice of 2 limes
1 teaspoon honey
2 fresh basil leaves
salt and freshly ground black pepper

Liquidise the sauce ingredients and check the seasoning.

To serve, pour a pool of sauce on to four plates. Arrange the okra on top like a necklace Serve with rice. **Serves 4.**

Stir Fried Vegetables

You may not want stir fried dishes every day, but this method of cooking is an excellent way o bringing a fresh and wholesome variety into your cuisine on occasions. The oriental chefs wh devised the technique centuries ago saw that ingredients cooked quickly retain their nutrients an texture. At the same time the high heat and constant stirring helps to develop the fragrance of th vegetables and the herbs and spices used for flavouring, while the speed of the operation leaves th crispness and semi-raw taste of the uncooked ingredient. So the method fits in with the aims o Cuisine Fraîcheur very well.

One basic principle to observe in stir fry cooking is that all ingredients must be cut into equal shapes, either as strips, shreds or small cubes. This ensures that all get equal cooking. Every item needed should be prepared in advance and immediately to hand beside the stove as the ingredients need constant stirring and tossing over a very short period. The Chinese wok is much the best cooking vessel to use because of its rounded shape. In Cuisine Fraîcheur we suggest using the minimum amount of fat for cooking, with sunflower, walnut, groundnut, peanut or olive oil as the best choices.

The usual accompaniment for stir fried dishes is a sweet-sour sauce – what the French call aigre-doux and the Italians agro-dolce. Such a sauce, usually made from fruit juice, vinegar and a little honey, is now very fashionable, having replaced the creamy sauces of classic cuisine. Fraîcheur advocates freshly squeezed rather than packet juices in the sauce – you will distinctly taste the difference. Different flavours can be introduced by using the juices of lemons, oranges, grapefruit, pineapple, raspberries, apples and pears. Sometimes a stock is needed to build up a stir fry sauce. This is easily made by boiling 500g/1lb of mixed diced vegetables such as carrot, leek, cabbage, onion and parsnip, with celery and thyme as the dominant flavourings, in 1 litre/2 pints of water. When the vegetables are soft, strain the stock.

Verdure tonkinoise • Chinese greens in a wok

4 tablespoons sunflower oil
175g/6oz Chinese leaves, shredded
175g/6oz Brussels sprouts, shredded
175g/6oz leeks, shredded
175g/6oz tiny cauliflower florets
2 tablespoons soya sauce
salt and freshly ground black pepper

Heat the oil in a wok or deep frying pan. Add the prepared vegetables and stir fry for 4 to 5 minutes; the vegetables should still be slightly crunchy. Sprinkle with the soya sauce and salt and pepper to taste. Serve immediately. **Serves 4.**

Chinoiserie charismatique • Chinese magic medley

100g/4oz each carrots, turnips, parsnips, beetroot, leeks, celery, fennel and red
    pepper, peeled as necessary
6 tablespoons sunflower oil
150g/5oz Brussels sprouts, sliced
150g/5oz cauliflower florets
150g/5oz canned water chestnuts

pinch of ground cumin
pinch of paprika
2 tablespoons soya sauce or home-made vegetable stock
salt and freshly ground black pepper

Cut the carrots, turnips, parsnips, beetroot, leeks, celery, fennel and red pepper into strips 5cm/2 inches long and 3mm/⅛ inch thick. Heat the oil in a large wok and stir fry the leeks, fennel and celery for 2 minutes to develop flavour. Add all the remaining vegetables and cook for 5 minutes, tossing and stirring evenly. Near the end of the cooking time season with the spices, soya sauce, salt and pepper. Remember that at the finish, the mixture should be only half-cooked and still crisp. **Serves 4.**

Pouces d'haricots aux carottes • Stir fried carrots and mung bean sprouts

4 tablespoons sunflower oil
225g/8oz each carrots and turnips, peeled and cut into julienne strips 2.5cm/1 inch
   long
½ red chilli, sliced and seeded
small piece of preserved ginger, cut into strips
150g/5oz mung bean sprouts
salt and freshly ground black pepper

Heat the oil in a wok and stir fry the carrots, turnips, chilli and ginger for 3 minutes. Add the sprouts and stir fry for a final minute. Season and serve with boiled rice. **Serves 4.**

Chiffonade de légumes à l'Indochine • Chinese-style stir fried vegetables

175g/6oz each Chinese leaves, Brussels sprouts, leeks, cauliflower florets, carrc
   celery, green pepper, mung bean sprouts
1 fresh green chilli, seeded and thinly sliced, or Chinese chilli sauce
6 tablespoons sunflower oil
3 tablespoons soya sauce
salt

Prepare the vegetables for cooking, peeling and seeding where necessary. Shred or thinly

Brochette de fruits tropicaux en verdure · Smoked chicken and tropical fruit kebab (page 150)

Above: La poire d'avocat aux fraises poivrées · Avocado with strawberry sauce (page 202)

Below: Salade à l'orange sanguine · Liotro orange salad (page 161)

Poire et pomme divine · Pear and apple with cheese (page 181)

Above: Poire Mathilde · Pear with tropical
medley (page 203)

Below: Briquette de pomme et poire Conil · Apple, pear
and orange jelly (page 208)

slice the Chinese leaves, Brussels sprouts, leeks, carrots, celery and green pepper into pieces of approximately the same size. Mix together all the vegetables in a large bowl. Add the chilli, if using.

Heat 2 tablespoons of the oil in a wok or frying pan and add one-third of the vegetables. Stir fry for 5 minutes or until the vegetables are tender but still crisp. Season with 1 tablespoon soya sauce, salt to taste, and 1 or 2 dashes of chilli sauce if using. Turn into a warm serving dish and serve, or keep hot while you cook and season the remaining vegetables, in two batches, as before. **Serves 6.**

Champignons Sauvages ◆ Wild Mushrooms

If you have only sampled field or cultivated mushrooms, then you have a treat in store trying other fine specimens of the mushroom family. Wild mushrooms can add subtly different flavours to dishes and lend a fine dash of extra interest to their appearance. Always used extensively in French cooking, wild mushrooms are becoming more available in good British supermarkets and delicatessens, both fresh – which we recommend – canned or dried, needing only a soak in water to reconstitute.

Omelette aux chanterelles ◆ Chanterelle or girolle omelette

Chanterelles or girolles (Cantharellus cibarius) are found in woodlands, from July to October. They have an egg yolk colour and a faint smell of apricot. They are identified by the way the gills run down the stem.

225g/8oz fresh chanterelles or girolles
¼ Webb's Wonder lettuce, shredded
50ml/2fl oz sunflower oil
1 small onion, peeled and chopped
4 eggs, beaten
salt and freshly ground black pepper
2 tablespoons flaked almonds
1 tablespoon coarsely chopped fresh parsley
75ml/3fl oz fresh pineapple juice

Separate the mushroom stalks from the caps. Trim the ends of the stalks, then chop finely. Slice the caps and reserve for the garnish. Divide the shredded lettuce between two plates. Set aside.

Heat half the oil in a shallow omelette pan and stir fry the onion and chopped mushroom stalks for 2 minutes. Add the seasoned eggs, scramble a little and cook until the bottom of the omelette is set. Place under the grill and cook for 1 minute to set the uncooked top of the omelette. Slip it on to a plate and cut in half.

Put the omelette halves on top of the shredded lettuce. Sprinkle over the sliced mushroom caps, almonds and parsley. Season and flavour with the pineapple juice. **Serves 2**.

Méli-mélo de champignons aux haricots • Mushroom medley with beans

The saffron milk cap mushroom (Lactarius deliciosus) *is a great favourite on French tables. I use it here to create a* salade tiède, *now so fashionable in restaurants.*

225g/8oz fine French beans, trimmed
2 tablespoons sunflower oil
1 medium-size onion, peeled and cut into rings
225g/8oz fresh saffron milk cap, quartered or sliced
2 garlic cloves, peeled and finely chopped
1 tablespoon fresh coriander leaves, not chopped but picked into pieces

dressing:
juice of 1 orange
juice of 1 lemon
50ml/2fl oz plain low-fat yogurt
salt and freshly ground black pepper

Liquidise the dressing ingredients and place in a bowl. Add the French beans and marinate in the refrigerator for 1 hour, turning occasionally. (If preferred, the beans may be blanched in boiling water for 30 seconds, drained and refreshed before being added to the dressing.)

When ready, heat the oil in a sauté pan and stir fry the onion to soften without browning. Add the mushrooms and garlic and cook for 4 minutes only.

To serve, divide the beans with the marinade on to two plates. Pour over the mushroom mixture. Garnish with the coriander. **Serves 2**.

Cèpes en papillote • Cep in foil

Cep (Boletus edulis) is the most sought-after wild mushroom in Europe. It flourishes from mid-summer to early November, and is one of the Bordeaux region's main specialities. It has no gills. The under pores should be white; if yellowish the mushrooms are best left alone. The pronounced flavour does not appeal to everyone.

225g/8oz fresh cèpes
2 large lettuce leaves
2 garlic cloves, peeled and chopped
1 small onion, peeled and thinly sliced
1 tablespoon fresh chervil or coriander leaves
50g/2oz shelled walnuts, finely chopped
4 anchovy fillets, desalted and finely chopped
1 tablespoon capers
4 black olives, stoned and sliced
handful of bean sprouts
1 tablespoon wheat bran
salt and freshly ground black pepper

Use the cep stalks as well as the caps, but discard the end bit which may be earthy. Cut into quarters.

On the table spread two 25 × 10cm/10 × 4 inch pieces of foil. On each one place a lettuce leaf. Blend together all the other ingredients in a bowl and place half the mixture on each leaf. Wrap the foil over like an envelope four times to form a parcel. Bake at 230°C, 450°F, Mark 8, or cook under the grill, for 12 minutes, turning the parcels after 6 minutes. Serve immediately. **Serves 2**.

Morilles au jus de pomme • Morels in apple juice

This is one of the great spongy mushrooms of Haute Cuisine. Rarely served on its own, it is often used as a fine garnish for many entrées.

225g/8oz fresh morels, well washed

sauce:
3 tablespoons plain low-fat yogurt or soured cream
1 teaspoon cornflour, arrowroot or potato starch
1 tablespoon mixed chopped fresh tarragon and parsley
2 tablespoons sunflower oil

2 shallots, peeled and chopped
150ml/5fl oz unsweetened apple juice
juice of 1 lemon
salt and freshly ground black pepper

Cut the morels in half if large. Blanch for 2 minutes in boiling water, then drain.

For the sauce, mix the yogurt with the cornflour. Add the tarragon and parsley. Heat the oil in a pan and stir fry the shallots for 3 minutes without browning. Add the apple juice and boil for 4 minutes. Add the morels and cook gently for a further 4 minutes. Remove the morels with a slotted spoon and keep warm.

Bring the liquid back to the boil and thicken with the yogurt mixture. Simmer for 4 minutes, then add the morels and lemon juice. Season to taste.

Spoon on to two plates and garnish with shredded lettuce. **Serves 2**.

LES DESSERTS DE SANTÉ
HEALTHY FRUIT DESSERTS

There is little need to emphasise the importance of fruit in Cuisine Fraîcheur or any healthy diet. Fruit provides good fibre, essential vitamins and minerals and, not least, adds to the enjoyment of mealtimes. Moreover, its natural sweetness has the great merit of helping us to dispense with the sugar bowl.

Previous chapters have shown how all kinds of fruit can be used as an ingredient or garnish to enhance a wide range of dishes, whether soups, salads, hors d'oeuvre or main courses. Here we come to fruit as the main component of a dish, and a glance at the illustrations shows what appetising results can be achieved. A little trouble taken in presenting fruit dishes attractively will significantly increase your pleasure and that of your guests.

While some dishes use fruit entirely in its raw state, though blended with other things, a number continue the Cuisine Fraîcheur principle of combining raw and cooked. The raw garnish ensures that the right level of vitamins and minerals is maintained and broadens the variety of the dessert menu. Since another fruit can often be substituted for the one called for in a recipe, depending on season, you can enjoy these dishes the whole year round.

I have further widened the scope of the dessert recipes by including some new exotic fruits which are now becoming available in better greengrocers and supermarkets or Asian shops. I urge you to try such tropical delights as carambola, babaco and guava, besides the lychees and mango you may already know.

If you have a 'sweet tooth' it is important to accustom yourself to using less refined sugar to satisfy it. Sugar is not at all good for health for a number of reasons, just one of them being that it has the very high calorie rating of 448 per 100g/4oz. Where a little extra sweetness seems desirable in these recipes we use a little honey, or a low-calorie liquid or powdered sweetener.

For similar reasons of sugar-avoidance we have omitted sorbets and ice-cream from the desserts because to make them the right texture 35 to 40 per cent sugar is needed. An attempt to make a sorbet out of unsweetened fruit juice can produce a pretty child's lollipop of hardened crystals, but not an edible dessert. However, you will find a method I have devised in these recipes of making a delicious, lightly frosted dessert which can replace the sorbet type of sweet.

The chapter is divided into four sections: Breakfasts of fruit and cereal; Fruit desserts, including fruit salads and cocktails; Sweets in jellied or moulded form, and mousses; and Sweets in a bread case or set in a custard, including gratins and pizzas.

◆ FRUIT AND CEREAL BREAKFASTS ◆

Breakfast has established itself as the meal where many people give some attention to health food, whatever the merits of their diet during the rest of the day. But the range of choice they give themselves is too often a narrow one. Using ripe fruit and a range of cereals that most health-food shops will stock plus a little imagination, we can extend our horizons well beyond the limited half-grapefruit or bowl of bran cereal.

Undoubtedly the best start to this meal is a glass of freshly squeezed fruit juice, so much more refreshing on the palate than the packaged kind. For variety I also recommend the fruit drinks in Chapter 1. Then comes a choice of muesli or another cereal dish. Fruit can be mixed with most of these. Or there is fruit on its own, or with a garnish, and some delicious and easily prepared compotes.

Fresh fruits for breakfast

When I directed the restaurant and cuisine of a superb luxury hotel in Jamaica in the 1960s (The Frenchman's Cove at Port Antonio), we always had a variety of fruit on the menu at breakfast. The guests often commented on the inviting appearance of a generous slice of fresh melon, papaya or pineapple as a starter to the day. Now that all kinds of fruits from hot countries are so plentifully imported, you can get the same luxury-hotel experience quite easily at home.

Papaya with lime: cut the papaya in half or quarters, depending on size, remove the seeds, and serve with a wedge of lime.

Grapefruit cocktail: peel the grapefruit, removing all white pith, and segment it. Mix the segments with a little honey and sprinkle with toasted desiccated coconut or chopped cashew nuts or peanuts.

Watermelon fraîcheur: serve a large slice of watermelon on its own. It is eaten with the seeds (rich in protein). If you have time (or guests) it can look more elegant to cut the melon into chunks – with a first cut along close to the rind – but leaving the wedge intact on the skin.

Pineapple fraîcheur: this also looks more attractive if presented in a similar way to the melon. Cut the fruit vertically in wedge-shaped quarters, leaving each section of leaves intact as ornament. Then cut into chunks as above, but serve on the skin in a complete wedge.

Charentais melon fraîcheur: this combination of the juicy flesh of the melon and the slight refreshing acidity of the tangerine makes a delicious breakfast dish. Halve the melon and remove the seeds; peel and segment the tangerines. Fill the cavities of the melon halves with tangerine segments. Serve garnished with fresh mint leaves.

Normandy fraîcheur: core one apple and one pear and cut into thin slices with the skin. Serve in a bowl with a little single cream or plain low-fat yogurt.

Basic muesli

Portions given here are for one serving; larger quantities of the dry ingredients can be made up and stored in an air-tight jar or container. Muesli variations:
Use toasted sunflower seeds, pumpkin seeds or watermelon seeds instead of cereals.
Use goat's milk or cow's milk instead of yogurt.
Use any fruit juice instead of yogurt, or papaya liquidised to a purée.
Vary with the addition of different fruits such as summer berries or, in winter, mandarins, bananas, pears, pomegranates, dates, prunes, apricots, peaches or any of the many dried fruits.
Vary by using different seeds and nuts, desiccated coconut, roasted peanuts, etc.

> 1 tablespoon oat flakes or grains, rye flakes, wheatgerm, seedless raisins and chopped mixed nuts (almonds, hazelnuts, cashews, walnuts), about 50g/2oz maximum in total
> 5 tablespoons plain low-fat yogurt
> 1 apple, grated with skin
> juice of ½ orange
> juice of ½ lemon
> pinch of ground cinnamon
> 1 tablespoon honey

Soak the oat flakes and rye in hot water overnight. Soak the raisins for 10 minutes. Drain the oats, rye and raisins.

Put the soaked cereals and raisins in a bowl with the yogurt, nuts, apple, and orange and lemon juices. Mix well together. Flavour with cinnamon and honey to taste, and sprinkle wheatgerm on the top. **Serves 1**.

Special fruit muesli

> 100g/4oz mixed grains (wheat, rye, barley, oats)
> 1 dessert apple, cored and sliced with skin
> 1 pear, cored and sliced with skin
> 100g/4oz each strawberries and redcurrants

4 tablespoons seedless raisins
50g/2oz hazelnuts, chopped
few drops of vanilla essence
1 tablespoon honey
100ml/4fl oz plain low-fat yogurt
50ml/2fl oz soured cream or Greek-style strained yogurt

Roughly grind the grains in a food processor, then stir with enough hot water to make a thick porridge. Leave to soak overnight.

Next morning, add the apple, pear, strawberries and redcurrants to the grains. Stir in the raisins and hazelnuts. Combine the vanilla essence, honey, yogurt and soured cream and spoon over the cereal. **Serves 4**.

Crêpes aux fruits • Pancakes with fruit

This recipe makes a nice spongy pancake, softer than the traditional French crêpe, which makes a lovely light breakfast with its filling of mashed banana and nuts. Perhaps try it as your Sunday morning treat. The batter could be made the night before. If serving it to children be advised they will ask for it again and again. Other fruit can be used to vary it and toasted nuts of various kinds are always a good addition.

25g/1oz plain flour
25g/1oz oat flakes
¼ teaspoon baking powder
pinch of salt
1 egg, beaten
225ml/8fl oz soured cream
sunflower oil, for frying

filling:
2 ripe bananas, peeled and mashed
1 tablespoon flaked toasted almonds

Whisk all the pancake ingredients into a thin batter. Grease a 20cm/8 inch pancake or frying pan with a little oil. When it is hot pour in about half of the batter and tilt the pan to spread it out evenly. Cook for 2 minutes, tossing or turning over once. Place half the mashed banana-and-nut filling on the pancake and fold over. Serve hot. Make another pancake in the same way. **Serves 2**.

Fruit Compotes

The French are very fond of compotes and serve them in wide variety. The wine often used across the Channel is, of course, omitted here, but spices and citrus rinds are used to produce good flavours. Made in a few minutes, a compote can add a further dimension to your breakfast menu, served alone or with a cereal such as cornflakes. It is an easy way of satisfying children's appetites for sweet things in a healthy way, and is a godsend to anyone having trouble with regularity, though this should never be a problem for anyone following the principles of Cuisine Fraîcheur. Both in winter and summer there are ample fruits available which can all be adapted to the basic methods of very light poaching or overnight soaking described here.

Compote de figues • Fig compote

150ml/5fl oz liquid honey
150ml/5fl oz water
450g/1lb fresh green figs
grated rind of ½ lemon

Boil the honey and water together for 5 minutes. Add the figs and poach them over a low heat for 6 to 8 minutes. Stir in the lemon rind and leave to cool in the liquid. **Serves 4**.

Pruneaux au jus de pomme • Prunes with apple juice

225g/8oz prunes
300ml/½ pint apple juice, freshly extracted if possible

Soak the prunes in the apple juice overnight and serve without cooking. This is more flavoursome than with the usual hot water soak. **Serves 2**.

Compote de rhubarbe • Rhubarb compote

225g/8oz young rhubarb, scraped and cut into pieces 3cm/1½ inches long
50g/2oz honey

Place the rhubarb and honey in a saucepan without water and cook gently for about 6 minutes until tender. Allow to cool. **Serves 2**.

Compote de poire au cassis • Pear and blackcurrant compote

  2 ripe pears, peeled, halved and cored
  3 tablespoons unsweetened blackcurrant juice

Place the pear halves in glass bowls and pour over the blackcurrant juice and lemon juice. (This can be done the previous evening to let the flavours meld.) Serve chilled. **Serves 2**.

Compote hivernale • Winter compote

  50g/2oz dried apricots
  50g/2oz Californian prunes
  camomile tisane (see page 28)
  100g/4oz cooking apple, peeled, cored and sliced
  6 fresh mint leaves or ½ tablespoon dried mint
  150ml/5fl oz water
  ½ teaspoon mixed ground ginger and cinnamon
  50g/2oz honey, or less
  2 tangerines, peeled and segmented

Soak the apricots and prunes overnight in camomile tisane to cover. Drain if necessary. Stone the prunes.

Put the soaked fruit and apple in a pan with the mint and water. Bring to the boil and simmer for 15 minutes, then liquidise to a purée. Add the spices, and sweeten to taste with the honey. Serve cool or chilled in individual bowls with the tangerine segments. **Serves 2**.

◆ FRUIT SALADS AND COLD DESSERTS ◆

Fruits à la normande ◆ *Normandy dessert*

2 ripe peaches, peeled, stoned and sliced
3 pears, peeled, stoned and sliced
12 greengages, stoned and sliced
150g/5oz raspberries
150ml/5fl oz soured cream or Greek-style strained yogurt

Mix together the peaches, pears and greengages. Liquidise the raspberries and soured cream and add to the fruits. Fold together gently. Serve chilled in individual glasses. **Serves 4**.

Salade exotique au babaco ◆ *Exotic fruit salad*

Originally from South America but now imported from New Zealand, the babaco is a large five-sided fruit, related to the papaya family. Very digestible itself, it also helps in digesting fats and proteins in foods that accompany it, besides having a high vitamin C content. It is mainly available in Britain over the Christmas period.

Babaco is green when unripe and ready to eat when yellow all over. To prepare, it should be washed and cut widthways in 2.5cm/1 inch slices. These can be eaten as they are, including the skin, just sprinkled with lime juice. Babaco can be put in a juice extractor or liquidiser to make a drink or sauce, or used as a garnish for salad, egg, fish or poultry dishes, or it can be made into chutney or pickle. Cut up in a dish with orange juice or cereals it makes a tasty breakfast dish.

1 small pineapple
1 babaco
2 kiwi fruit
2 carambolas
1 mango
juice of 1 orange
juice of ½ lemon
few drops of rosewater essence

Cut the pineapple in half lengthways, leaving the crown of leaves intact on each half. Carefully scoop out the pineapple flesh to leave a 'shell' about 1cm/½ inch thick. Cut the pineapple flesh into small cubes.

Peel and slice the babaco and kiwi fruit. Slice the carambolas. Peel the mango, remove the stone and thinly slice the flesh. Toss all the prepared fruits in the fruit juices with the rosewater essence added. Cover and chill for 1 hour.

Pile the fruit mixture and its juices into the two pineapple shells. To serve, scoop the fruit from the shells into small dessert bowls. **Serves 6 to 8.**

Étoile du paradis en brochette • *Kebab of tropical fruits*

Carambolas are another of the interesting new tropical fruits now being imported, in this case from the Caribbean and Brazil. They are bright yellow in colour, waxy-looking and up to 10cm/4 inches long. They are sometimes known as 'star fruit' because of their resemblance to five-sided stars.

With their delicious sweet-sour taste, carambolas lend themselves to various dessert uses, most simply added to a fruit salad. In India they are made into chutneys and pickles to go with curries. In this recipe they make a handsome fruit kebab with lychees.

The lychee, familiar to many people now from Chinese restaurants, is a small plum-sized fruit cased in a thin pinkish-brown shell. This is easily peeled off leaving the pearly-white translucent flesh. The stone is bitter and should be discarded. Lychees are delicious eaten raw.

1 carambola, sliced
24 lychees, about 450g/1lb total weight, peeled and stoned
6 large strawberries, hulled
12 cherries, stoned
slice of pineapple, peeled and cubed
12 grapes, white and black, halved and seeded

Thread the fruits alternately, to vary colour and shape, on to eight 12cm/5 inch wooden skewers. Serve on plates, two kebabs per portion, decorated with sprigs of mint and slices of lime. **Serves 4**.

La poire d'avocat aux fraises poivrées • *Avocado with strawberry sauce*

Avocado has become one of the most popular and familiar tropical fruits in recent years, and not without reason when it serves so deliciously as a starter, either alone or with a vinaigrette or filling, or sliced in salads, or made into a chilled soup. It can also readily be liquidised into dips and sauces with low-fat yogurt, adding a dash of lime or lemon juice.

In this recipe I present the avocado with strawberries as a dessert, but one made slightly peppery with a turn or two of the pepper mill. The pepper is optional but worth trying for piquancy. In Latin American countries people use chilli powder or a Tabasco type of condiment to flavour avocados and strawberries.

1 ripe avocado, peeled, halved and stoned
juice of 1 lime
good pinch of freshly ground black pepper

sauce:
100g/4oz strawberries, hulled
juice of ¼ orange
juice of ½ lime

Cut several slices lengthways in each avocado half, but without cutting right through at the end. This is left as a sort of hinge.

Liquidise the sauce ingredients to a purée and pour a pool of it in the middle of two plates. Spread out each avocado half fanwise and place on the sauce. Squeeze the lime juice on the avocado to keep it from discolouring. Finally grind some black pepper over the fruit, quantity according to taste. **Serves 2**.

Poire Mathilde • *Pear with tropical medley*

The Comice pear, large and luscious, is one of the most opulent of fruits – golden in colour, with a wonderful texture and brimming with juice. On that account, it is perhaps best eaten in the genteel way with a knife and fork or even scooped with a spoon rather than in the hand if consumed on its own. Though it is rather an aristocrat among fruits, and the one most chosen for pear desserts, it is a good mixer with other ingredients. Here it helps to show off a number of principles of Cuisine Fraîcheur desserts: how you can make original dishes by combining temperate and tropical fruits; how some fruits can rejuvenate others in a tasty partnership; and what nuts can do.

4 large, ripe Comice pears
1 small carambola, sliced
1 small papaya, peeled, sliced, seeded and sliced into half rings
100g/4oz strawberries, sliced
50g/2oz raspberries
50g/2oz toasted almonds or hazelnuts, chopped

sauce:
50g/2oz each strawberries, raspberries and peeled banana
juice of ½ lemon
slice of red chilli (optional)

Peel the pears, leaving the lower half of the skin intact for decorative effect. Cut a thin slice from the bottom of each pear to produce a flat surface on which the pear can stand up. Core the pears from the bottom.

Liquidise the sauce ingredients.

To serve, pour a little of the sauce on to four plates, reserving some for pouring over the top of the pear at the last moment. Stand the pear in the middle of the sauce and decorate all around with grapes, papaya, strawberries and raspberries, and a few fresh mint leaves. Pour the remaining sauce over the pears and finish with a sprinkling of nuts. **Serves 4**.

Jardin du paradis ◆ *Fruit platter with mousse*

This fruit platter comes to table looking truly splendid, in the very top league of fruit desserts for flavour and appearance. It should be composed with as wide a variety of fruits as you can reasonably get hold of, including some unusual or tropical fruits to make it more intriguing. The raw fruit accompanies one or, for preference, several mousses made from the pulp of whichever fruit you fancy.

The mousse consists basically of fruit pulp, egg white and gelatine, and is very quick and easy to make. The recipe given here is for mango and lime mousse, but virtually any other fruit could be substituted for the mango, such as guava, papaya, blackcurrants, raspberries, strawberries, oranges, pineapple, bananas or passion fruit. Each mousse should include the given quantity of lemon or lime juice in order to acidulate the fruit used. The mousse can be moulded individually.

1 lime, halved
4 mangoes, peeled and stoned
150ml/5fl oz water
2 tablespoons honey
2 teaspoons powdered gelatine
50g/2oz fromage frais (see page 179)
50ml/2fl oz low-fat plain yogurt
2 egg whites

Squeeze the juice from the lime halves into a blender or food processor. Scoop the pulp from one half, discard any seeds, and add to the juice with the mangoes and water. Liquidise to a purée, then pour into a saucepan. Add the honey. Bring to the boil and boil for 4 minutes (this is always necessary when using fresh fruit juice with gelatine; it is to inactivate the enzymes which would otherwise prevent setting). Sprinkle in the gelatine gradually, stirring. When dissolved, remove from the heat and cool quickly by placing the mixture in a metal bowl on a tray of ice cubes or in the freezer for 10 minutes.

When cold, blend in the cheese and yogurt. Whisk the egg whites until stiff and fold into the mixture. Allow to set in a bowl or individual moulds.

To serve, use an oval spoon to give the helping of mousse a nice shape. If you have several mousses, put a small spoonful of each kind in the centre of each plate and decorate with a sprig of lemon balm or mint.

Circle the mousse with the fruit selection, for example a small sprig each of black and white grapes, slices of mango, nectarine, peach, pear, apple or kiwi, a few cherries on stalks, red and yellow melon balls, a bunch of redcurrants, sliced fresh figs and dates, raspberries or sliced strawberries, and halves of passion fruit and lychees. **Serves 4.**

Mélange de fruits aux noix • Nutty fruit salad

2 kiwi fruit, peeled and diced
1 mango, peeled, stoned and diced
100g/4oz each strawberries and blackberries
1 small cantaloupe melon, peeled, seeded and cubed
50g/2oz each of shelled pistachios, walnuts and pine nuts, chopped
100ml/4fl oz yogurt
100ml/4fl oz single cream
few drops of vanilla essence
2 tablespoons honey

Combine all the fruits and nuts in a bowl and carefully mix together. Divide between six individual bowls. Blend together the yogurt, cream, vanilla and honey, and spoon this over the fruit. **Serves 6.**

Fruit and Yogurt Desserts

Banane au yaourt • Banana yogurt ice

2 ripe bananas
50g/2oz carob bar, grated
50g/2oz honey
50ml/2fl oz plain low-fat yogurt

Mash the peeled bananas and mix with the carob, honey and yogurt into a smooth mixture. Place in shallow freezer trays, cover with foil and freeze for 3 hours. Serve in glasses with a garnish of banana slices and a few toasted nuts. **Serves 2**.

Pomme au yaourt • Apple and yogurt Eskimo

150g/5oz cooked apple purée
50g/2oz quince preserve, preferably reduced-sugar
100ml/4fl oz plain low-fat yogurt

Combine all the ingredients and freeze for 2 hours in foil-covered freezer trays. Serve in glasses with mint leaf decoration. **Serves 2**.

◆ FRUIT JELLIES AND MOULDS ◆

These dishes allow and encourage a little showing off. And why not, indeed? To be a good cook and presenter of dishes it is essential to feel something of an impresario, however modest the routines of peeling an apple, and so on. With a few minutes' work and usually some refrigeration your delightful jellies and mousses, suggesting hours of planning, are beautifully presented at table. In this case do as all the master-chefs do: accept the admiration and keep your secrets.

Chartreuse écarlate ◆ Red fruit jelly

A chartreuse is the name given in French cuisine to a number of moulded dishes and need not contain the famous liqueur. I especially recommend this dish as a way of using imported strawberries. Nowadays strawberries are imported all year round. It is cheering to see them, but the flavour of fruit from an English strawberry farm is not quite there. Ripened gradually in a British garden, picked fresh in June and July, home-grown strawberries must be among the world's finest fruits, easily matching anything from the tropics. Simply served with cream or Greek-style strained yogurt they are mouth-watering. At the same season, the French prefer them with red wine or lemon juice. Far worse, I can reveal that Escoffier, one of the greatest French chefs of all time, advised me to serve wild strawberries with the chocolate liqueur, Crème de Cacao. This recipe will give imported fruit a bit of a natural lift, like a lady who has put on a new dress.

150g/5oz young rhubarb, scraped and cut into chunks
1 cooking apple, peeled, cored and sliced
75g/3oz honey
75g/3oz strawberries, hulled
2 teaspoons powdered gelatine, soaked in 5 tablespoons water

decoration:
150g/5oz strawberries, hulled and halved
75g/3oz raspberries
fresh mint leaves

Place the rhubarb, apple, honey and strawberries in a saucepan. Simmer for 5 to 8 minutes until soft. Liquidise and reheat. Add the soaked gelatine and heat gently without boiling until the gelatine dissolves, stirring constantly.

Cool, then pour into four 150ml/5fl oz capacity individual jelly moulds. Put them in the refrigerator to set until firm.

Turn out the jellies on to four plates and decorate with a circle of halved strawberries, raspberries and mint leaves. Arrange a half-strawberry on top of each jelly. This dessert goes well with Greek-style strained yogurt, if you wish. **Serves 4**.

Briquette de pomme et poire Conil ◆ Apple, pear and orange jelly

5 blood oranges
50ml/2fl oz lime juice cordial
150ml/5fl oz water
600ml/1 pint unsweetened apple juice
25g/1oz powdered gelatine
2 tablespoons orange blossom essence
2 bunches of fresh mint or lemon balm
2 green apples, peeled, cored, sliced and blanched for 3 minutes
3 ripe pears, quartered, cored and sliced
navel or Jaffa oranges, peeled and segmented

sauce:
225g/8oz cranberries
50g/2oz honey
5 tablespoons water
juice of ½ lemon
½ teaspoon cornflour dissolved in 3 tablespoons water (optional)

Using a zester, thinly pare the rind from two of the blood oranges. Candy the rind by boiling in the lime juice cordial and water for 8 minutes. Drain if necessary. Set aside.

Squeeze the juice from one of the pared oranges and mix it with the apple juice. Dissolve the gelatine in a little of this juice mixture, simmering it in a small pan, then add to the remaining juice. Allow to cool, then flavour the syrup with the orange blossom essence.

Grease a 900ml/1½ pint oblong mould with sunflower oil. Pour about 50ml/2fl oz of the syrup into the mould and chill until set. Meanwhile, peel and segment the remaining blood oranges.

Arrange a few mint leaves in the mould to cover the base of the set jelly completely. Brush the sides of the mould with the syrup and stick more mint leaves all round the sides. Arrange a layer of apple, pear and orange segments in the mould and cover with a layer of syrup. Chill again until firm, in the refrigerator or freezer.

Repeat the layers of fruit and jelly, making sure each layer is set before the next is added. Then leave the briquette to set in the refrigerator for 3 hours.

For the sauce, boil the cranberries with the honey and water for 5 minutes. Liquidise, then add the lemon juice to revive the red colour. Thicken with the cornflour mixture and boil for 4 more minutes. The thickening is optional, but it improves the texture.

To serve, turn out the briquette and slice it thickly. Place a slice of briquette in the centre of each plate, in a pool of sauce. Decorate with the orange rind julienne and a few mint leaves. **Serves 8**.

Pomme d'Adam à la citronelle • Frozen apple mousse

A purée of apple reinforced with concentrated apple juice can be the basis for a variety of light and healthy desserts because it can easily be flavoured with aromatic fruits, such as orange, lemon, raspberries or blackcurrants, according to your taste and what is in season. In this recipe the juice and rind of the lime add a pleasant touch of sharpness while the meringue element lends a nice texture. This refreshing dessert can be frozen until needed.

450g/1lb apples, such as Granny Smith or Golden Delicious, or a mixture of dessert
    and cooking apples, peeled, cored and sliced
150ml/5fl oz concentrated apple juice
100g/4oz honey
grated rind and juice of 1 lime
25g/1oz powdered gelatine
3 eggs, separated
75ml/3fl oz low-fat orange or lime yogurt
pinch of salt
1 red and 1 green apple, cored and sliced, to decorate

Poach the apples in the apple juice with the honey and lime juice until soft. Liquidise to a purée, then reheat. Dissolve the gelatine in the purée and simmer for 5 minutes.

Combine the egg yolks and yogurt and add to the purée. Cook very gently for 4 more minutes, stirring constantly; do not boil. Cool completely.

Beat the egg whites with the salt until stiff. Fold into the cold purée. Place in a bowl and chill until set.

Using an ice-cream scoop, put three scoops of mousse on each of four plates. Freeze for 30 minutes to 1 hour.

To serve, sprinkle the lime rind over the mousse and top each portion with a mint leaf. Arrange the red and green apple slices around the plate in groups of three. **Serves 4**.

Mousse limousine ◆ Nectarine mousse

The nectarine is a hybrid fruit produced by crossing a peach with a plum. Its flesh is as juicy as that of the real peach, though firmer, but less juicy than a plum. Its flavour combination of sweetness with a refreshing and slightly acid tang makes it a good fruit for this mousse. All fruits can be made into a mousse similarly.

6 large ripe nectarines, stoned
450ml/¾ pint concentrated apple juice
25g/1oz powdered gelatine
150g/5oz honey
4 drops of lemon or orange blossom essence
2 egg whites
300ml/½ pint plain low-fat yogurt
3 ripe nectarines, sliced, to decorate

Liquidise the stoned nectarines with the apple juice. Bring to the boil, then stir in the gelatine until completely dissolved. Add the honey and cool. Stir in the lemon or orange blossom essence.

Beat the egg whites until slightly stiff and fold into the mixture alternately with the yogurt. Place in individual dishes and chill for 2 hours until set. Serve with a decoration of nectarine slices arranged on top of each mousse. **Serves 6.**

Gloutonnerie de goyave ◆ Layered guava cream

Guavas, a very versatile and tasty apple-like fruit, were first brought to Europe by the Spaniards and are now widely grown in tropical countries. Rich in vitamin C, they are highly scented with an aromatic sweet-acid taste.

The skin is thin and green in colour, turning pale yellow when ripe, while the flesh varies from white to deep pink and usually contains hard seeds which have to be removed. The fruit can be eaten raw – simply halved and the pulp scooped out with a spoon. The half-shells can be filled with fromage frais, scrambled eggs or fish, with the pulp being used as part of the filling. Guavas can be puréed for mousses and sorbets or made into an excellent jelly as they are rich in pectin. Blended with other fruit purées like apple, pear, strawberries or apricots, as in this recipe, guava improves the dessert with its delicate perfume and gells the mixture too. This dish is also delicious for breakfast.

pulp of 2 guavas, about 225g/8oz
50ml/2fl oz water
4 tablespoons honey
1 cardamom pod, crushed
finely grated rind and juice of 1 lemon
1 tablespoon powdered gelatine soaked in 50ml/2fl oz water
300ml/½ pint) soured cream or Greek-style strained yogurt
4 apricots, about 100g/4oz, stoned and sliced

Place the guava pulp, water, honey and cardamom in a saucepan and simmer for 5 minutes. Add the lemon rind and juice. Liquidise the ingredients and return to the boil. Stir in the gelatine until dissolved, then remove from the heat and cool.

Blend three-quarters of the soured cream or yogurt into the purée. Put a spoonful of the mixture in the bottom of four fluted dessert glasses. Top with a little of the remaining soured cream, then add more guava mixture and so on to fill the glasses. Decorate the top with slices of apricot. Chill until set. **Serves 4.**

Raisinade au gratin ◆ *Glazed grape custard*

This dessert is based on the principle of combining fruit with a custard topping and is very popular. It presents itself attractively at table and tastes as good as it looks, with an original and memorable flavour. Other fruit such as peaches and nectarines may also be used in this way. If large muscat grapes are used, they should be halved and seeded; there is no need to skin them. Black grapes, with tougher skins, should be blanched in boiling water for 20 seconds; the skins will then peel off easily.

> 225g/8oz black grapes, skinned and seeded
> 4 egg yolks
> 100g/4oz honey
> 300ml/½ pint soured cream
> 2 tablespoons unsweetened apple juice
> 25g/1oz flaked almonds

Divide the grapes between 6 lightly greased cocotte dishes or ramekins.

Put the egg yolks and honey into a bowl and whisk until thick and light. Stand the bowl over a pan of gently simmering water and slowly whisk in the soured cream and apple juice. Whisk the mixture over the heat until it is thick and creamy and greatly increased in volume.

Pour this custard over the grapes, leaving a shallow rim showing in each dish. Glaze the tops quickly under a hot grill. Scatter the surface generously with the flaked almonds.

Stand each dish on a plate lined with a doily and serve immediately, with small *langues de chat* biscuits. **Serves 6.**

Pudding hivernal • Fruited winter pudding

thin slices of wholemeal bread, crusts removed
5 tablespoons water
5 tablespoons unsweetened apple juice
2 tablespoons honey
juice of ½ lemon
good pinch of ground cinnamon
15g/½oz powdered gelatine
2 dessert apples, peeled, cored and sliced
1 Comice or Doyenne pear, peeled, cored and sliced across
75g/3oz blackberries or blueberries

sauce:
225g/8oz blackberries or blackcurrants
75g/3fl oz cooked apple purée
100g/4oz honey
juice of ½ lemon

decoration:
1 red apple, cored and sliced with skin
16 blueberries
4 fresh mint leaves
1 ripe pear, cored and sliced with skin

Grease four 150ml/5fl oz pudding basins with polyunsaturated margarine. Line each basin with some of the bread cut into fingers, using a circular piece of bread for the bottom.

Place the water, apple juice, honey, lemon juice and cinnamon in a saucepan and bring to the boil. Dissolve the gelatine in this, then add the apple and pear slices and poach for 5 minutes. Stir in the berries and leave to cool. When cold, fill the basins to the top with the fruit mixture and cover with a circle of bread the same diameter as the basin. Leave to set in the refrigerator for at least 4 hours.

Liquidise together the sauce ingredients. Heat the sauce for 1 to 2 minutes. Turn out the puddings on to four plates and cover with the sauce. Decorate the top with apple slices, a few berries and a mint leaf. Garnish the side of the plate with pear slices. **Serves 4**.

Flognarde fanfaronne • Country flan with pears and plums

The flognarde is a country-style flan, similar to a clafoutis, composed of an oven-baked egg batter with fruit. In this recipe I have left the plum garnish raw to put more sparkle into the presentation and for the flavour contrast. If preferred, the plums can be cooked with the pears, and flaked almonds dusted on top just before serving.

225g/8oz wholemeal flour
pinch of salt
300ml/½ pint milk
4 large eggs, beaten
50g/2oz polyunsaturated margarine
2 ripe Comice pears, peeled, cored and sliced
1 tablespoon icing sugar, sifted (optional)
225g/8oz large, ripe red plums, halved and stoned
50g/2oz blanched almonds

Place the flour and salt in a large bowl. Gradually blend in the milk and beaten eggs to obtain a smooth batter.

Use all the margarine to grease the bottom and sides of a 16cm/6½ inch diameter flan tin. Arrange the sliced pears neatly in the bottom and cover with the batter. Bake for 45 minutes at 200°C, 400°F, Mark 6.

Dust the top with icing sugar and cut into six portions. Serve with two plum halves each; in the hollow of each plum half place an almond. **Serves 6.**

Pain galette aux fruits • Fruit pizza

dough:
1 teaspoon dried yeast
400g/14oz wholemeal flour
225ml/9fl oz lukewarm water
few drops of vanilla essence
1 tablespoon grated orange rind
pinch of salt
2 tablespoons sunflower oil

topping:
4 bananas
4 kiwi fruit
2 peaches
4 slices of fresh pineapple
100g/4oz black cherries, stoned (fresh or canned)
200g/7oz fromage frais (see page 179)
300ml/½ pint single cream
4 eggs, beaten
few drops of vanilla essence

Mix the yeast and 1 teaspoon flour with 4 tablespoons of the lukewarm water. Leave for 10 minutes until frothy. Then combine with the remaining flour, the vanilla, orange rind and salt. Add the oil and remaining water and knead to a smooth dough. Cover with a moist tea towel and leave to rise in a warm place for at least 30 minutes.

Divide the dough into four equal portions. Roll out each thinly into a 12.5cm/5 inch round and place on greased baking sheets. Alternatively, roll out the dough and use to line four 12.5cm/5 inch flan dishes.

Prepare the fruit, removing skin, stones and seeds as necessary, then cut it into small pieces. Spread on the pizza bases.

Combine the cheese with the cream, eggs and vanilla. Spread this mixture equally on the four pizzas. Bake at 200°C, 400°F, Mark 6 for 20 to 25 minutes. Serve hot. **Serves 4.**

◆ THE LOVE APPLE DIET ◆

Early morning juices

Take a glass of juice such as Citronnade au miel (p. 9), Pamplemoussette (p. 9)
or Mandarinette (p. 10).

Breakfast

1 egg, poached, boiled or coddled, with wholemeal toast and polyunsaturated margarine
or porridge with milk and honey
or Special fruit muesli (p. 197)
plus
A cup of tisane (pp. 26–28) without sugar.

Midmorning snack

Choose from the following: 1 apple, 1 apricot, 1 banana, 75g/3oz berries, 75g/3oz plums
or damsons, 75g/3oz fresh figs, 75g/3oz grapefruit or orange segments, 75g/3oz grapes,
75g/3oz fresh fruit salad, 100g/4oz melon, 75g/3oz peach, 75g/3oz soaked prunes, 75g/3oz
peeled tangerine, 50g/2oz walnut kernels
or 100ml/4fl oz low-fat yogurt, plain or with fruit
or 1 slice of wholemeal bread or crispbread with fromage frais (see p. 179)
or A fibrous juice such as Elixir de pomme à la menthe (p. 11), Pomme citronelle (p. 12),
Mûres et pomme (p. 11).

Luncheon

A bowl of soup such as Avocadine (p. 50), La soupe de figue de barbarie (p. 51), La soupe
de potiron aux abricots (p. 57) or Crème gauloise rabelaisienne (p. 58), served with
wholemeal bread or crispbread
or 50g/2oz of a dip (pp. 31–46) with 225g/8oz crudités, and wholemeal bread or crispbread
or An hors d'œuvre such as La pomme d'Adam au fromage blanc (p. 67), La salade
ortanique (p. 69), Primeur de maïs aux pouces de soya océanique (p. 70), Roulade de
truite saumonée florentine (p. 72), served with wholemeal bread or crispbread
plus
A light entrée such as Tangelo saumoné (p. 156), Filet d'anguille fumée aux deux choux
(p. 80), Pascaline de kiwi au fromage (p. 77), Royal Crécy aux fèves des Marais (p. 84)

or A fresh salad such as Salade à la noix de coco (p. 145), Ruban de volaille (p. 147), Salade bruxelloise aux carottes (p. 148), Trévisse au bouquet de mer (p. 149), Brochette de fruits tropicaux en verdure (p. 150), Les pouces de légumineux printaniers (p. 162), Mélange de salade naturelle (p. 153).

Afternoon snack

Choose from the following: 1 apple, 1 pear, 75g/3oz peach, 75g/3oz papaya, 1 banana, 1 orange, 1 tangerine, 75g/3oz tomatoes
and/or
A drink such as La papayade au citron vert (p. 14), Framboises au jus d'ananas (p. 15), Nectar de Saleux à la rhubarbe (p. 16), Cocktail de carottes aux abricots (p. 21), Fraîcheur mousseuse (p. 17), Charentaise (p. 22), Lait de soya aux mandarines (p. 24), Lait de noisettes (p. 29).

Dinner or supper

A seafood dish such as Soupe de truite provençale Paul Cézanne (p. 103), Truite marinée à la moutarde (p. 105), Les coquilles St Jacques Côte d'Opale (p. 104), Filet de sole charentaise Conil (p. 108), Blanc de turbot aux nectarines (p. 113), Loup de mer à la vapeur aux rameaux de salicornes (p. 116), Romance de la mer (p. 114)
or A poultry dish such as Suprême de volaille au vinaigre en brochette (p. 125), Poulet en gelée (p. 124), Terrine de poulet verdure (p. 127), Poulet à la marocaine (p. 128), Escalopine de dindonneau aux fruits citronés (p. 126), Suprême de caneton aux pêches (p. 134), Pigeonneau à la Nono (p. 136), Tranche de pintade aux deux sauces fruitées (p. 131), L'oie de Noël aux figues fraîches (p. 135), Mignonettes de Jean Lapin aux abricots (p. 138)
or A vegetarian dish such as Boulette de semoule algérienne (p. 171), Chaudron de légumes exotiques (p. 185), Gombos à la purée de poivrons rouges (p. 186), Pain de maïs (p. 173)
plus
A salad (pp. 141–163) or raw vegetables such as tomatoes and cucumber
and
A dessert such as Poire Mathilde (p. 203), Pain galette aux fruits (p. 214), Salade exotique au babaco (p. 201), Etoile du paradis en brochette (p. 202), Raisinade au gratin (p. 212).

Bedtime

A warming drink such as Lait de poule (p. 29), Lait à l'orge fermentée (p. 29), La verveine sabayonnée (p. 30)
or A tisane such as Tisane camomile (p. 28).

Protein requirements

Protein requirements vary according to height, weight, age, sex and state of health. An intake of between 50 and 70 grams per day covers the average adult's requirements.

The following chart gives an idea of the amount of protein in everyday foods:

	Protein
4oz/112g Meat, poultry, fish	24 grams
½pt/285ml Milk	9 grams
4oz/112g Low fat cheese	15 grams
2 Eggs	12 grams
4 slices/112g Wholemeal bread	10 grams
6oz/170g Pulses (lentils, etc.), cooked	12 grams
4oz/112g Nuts – e.g. brazil nuts	13 grams
peanuts	27 grams

Ovo-lacto vegetarians omit all flesh foods – meat, poultry and fish – but still consume milk, milk products and eggs. These animal products provide complete protein, i.e. all eight essential amino acids which the body is unable to manufacture for its protein requirements. Equally valuable protein can be derived from the combination of plant foods such as pulses (peas, beans, peanuts, etc.), nuts and seeds together with grain foods (rice, wheat, barley, oats, etc.). It is important that the groups are combined and eaten together at the same meal so that the essential amino acid pattern is complete; if one is eaten in the absence of the other the protein is deficient, cannot be used by the body for protein growth and turnover, and will end up as a source of energy only.

The Love Apple Diet can easily be adapted to ensure correct protein intake for vegetarians. Provided they choose a balanced and varied diet, vegetarians are at no disadvantage compared to flesh eaters.

◆ INDEX ◆